Testing Death

TESTING DEATH

Hughes Aircraft Test Pilots and Cold War Weaponry

George J. Marrett

Foreword by D. Kenneth Richardson

NAVAL INSTITUTE PRESS
Annapolis, Maryland

Naval Institute Press
291 Wood Road
Annapolis, MD 21402

First Naval Institute Press paperback edition published in 2008.

Library of Congress Cataloging-in-Publication Data
Marrett, George J.
    Testing death : Hughes Aircraft test pilots and Cold War weaponry / George J. Marrett; foreword by D. Kenneth Richardson.
        p. cm.
    Includes bibliographical references and index.
    ISBN 978-1-59114-512-7 (pbk. : alk. paper)   1. Marrett, George J.   2. Test pilots—United States—Biography.   3. Airplanes, Military—United States—Armament—Testing. 4. Hughes Aircraft Company—History. I. Title.
    TL540.M3485 2008
    629.13092—dc22
    [B]
                            2008005117

Printed in the United States of America on acid-free paper

14   13   12   11   10   09   08   9   8   7   6   5   4   3   2
First printing

To my wife, Jan, who stood by me through the Vietnam War, flight tests in the U.S. Air Force and Hughes Aircraft Company, and finally many days with my head in the clouds.

Contents

A photo essay follows page 68.

Foreword

We at Hughes Aircraft Company were an inspired bunch. By the late 1980s our staff had reached 85,000 employees; 22,000 were engineers and scientists, 4,000 with PhDs. The engineers were a creative lot, driven by technology pressures to deter the U.S.S.R. in the Cold War, with an undying motivation to leap forward with inventions in previously uncharted waters. We all felt the technical advancement of our weaponry was a chief spur on our world rival to try to reach our performance levels. The Soviet Union seldom matched our technical prowess, resulting in an economic collapse that forced them to end the Cold War.

Hughes Aircraft Company's origins enjoyed the creative genius and "do it differently" techniques of its founder, Howard R. Hughes. In the late 1940s its business of aircraft design, construction, and a supplier of aircraft subassemblies transitioned to first-line electronics. We could well have been renamed "Hughes—Everything Electronics—Company." Our inventions enabled combat aircraft to find air and ground targets, compute and analyze the best intercept approach, prepare and launch guided weapons, as well as to keep the aircrew visually and audibly informed. These electronic products were called integrated weapon control systems. They included radars, computers, displays and controls, guidance devices for missiles, and the aerodynamic flight controls and propulsion of the weapons.

As the years progressed, Hughes Aircraft Company engineers designed and manufactured all types of radars, infrared detection and tracking systems, six different types of guided missiles, very sophisticated computers, torpedo guidance systems, diverse display devices for weapon operators, flight simulators, and a wide range of electronic support equipment to diagnose and repair broken hardware. From these roots evolved an extremely diverse spacecraft design and manufacturing segment. Our satellites ranged from scientific exploration and overhead surveillance and countermeasures for the military, to the most prolific communication and television relays for the worldwide public.

Most of us felt that working in this environment was more fun than playing. Lofty technical challenges, a high sense of integrity, and the feeling that what we did could make a difference in world politics kept us working long hours. Daily association with oceans of creative talent was exhilarating, and the opportunity to provide essential weaponry to our military was highly motivating and energizing.

The private ownership of Hughes Aircraft Company (by Howard Hughes and, in 1953, given to the Howard Hughes Medical Institute) rather than public stockholders generated a great deal of comfort in conducting our mission. Research and development budgets were large and malleable, there was little pressure to assure profits for demanding shareholders, and operational goals were long term rather than short term. Most executives and employees had a strong sense of dedication and integrity. The "big picture" was what counted. What a perfect environment for active and dynamic creativity!

This corporate philosophy permitted policies of understanding and responding to customer needs, driving for technical excellence, and placing equipment performance in the field far ahead of the profit motive. One might list our management psyche and priority as: world leadership in research and development, employee happiness and security, product excellence and with continuous improvement, long-term decision making, integrity and business ethics, economic flexibility, and reasonable profit levels. We did want to stay in business, so profit levels could not be completely ignored. Peak annual sales, with numerous product lines, reached over $7 billion by 1985.

Many good things resulted from senior managers understanding the technology, interacting with the users, operating the devices, and participating in flight test evaluation. These activities allowed us to transfer to the rest of our staff the real conditions, emotions, and expectations, which enabled meaningful leadership. There was little substitute for the effectiveness of "hands-on" experience.

The following is an awesome problem that the company signed up to solve. As a manager, place yourself in this technical and business situation. The problem is to ensure virtually flawless air defense for a Navy Carrier Task Force faced with a large number of attacking aircraft equipped with long-range, anti-ship cruise missiles.

As an engineer you must find a way to detect and track many hostile aircraft at very long range, compute the optimum positioning of your fighter, prepare as many as six guided missiles for simultaneous launch at targets widely separated by 50 miles, and ensure that each missile destroys its assigned target. Those targets would use electronic countermeasures and physically evasive maneuvers. There might be decoys, background clutter obscuring radar images, and bad weather. Remember that all your equipment must fit into a fighter aircraft; meet limitations on weight, power, and cooling usage; and be of high reliability, easily maintained aboard ship, and consistently manufactured at relatively low cost. Do this in a short time, because the U.S. Navy may soon need it. All that is quite a challenge!

To do that job correctly, we needed to understand the Air Navy's operational conditions. As senior manager of the Hughes Aircraft Company's AWG-9 system and AIM-54 Phoenix Missile Program, to be installed on the Grumman F-14A Tomcat, I flew many times in various Navy fighters. I experienced catapult launches and traps on several aircraft carriers, conducted discussions with Top Gun instructors and students at Miramar Naval Air Station, visited electronics maintenance areas, and did a week-long cruise to observe Vietnam combat operations in the Gulf of Tonkin aboard the USS *Kittyhawk*. All the lessons I learned were presented to the entire engineering and manufacturing staff, who were assigned to design, develop, and produce the new weapon system and its missiles. This was to ensure that our equipment would match the conditions aboard ship.

As the design proceeded in its evaluation phase, I felt the need to fully comprehend the operation of the system we were creating. There was an opportunity to participate in an F-14A test flight from Naval Air Station at Point Mugu, California. I would be the back seat radar operator (termed Naval Flight Officer—NFO—in the Navy) with our company test pilot, George Marrett (this book's author), in command. Our flight test plan called for a 6G maneuver, air combat with an LTV F-8 Crusader opponent, and two simulated launches of AIM-54 Phoenix missiles. This intercept was a real data-gathering mission, not just a joy ride. Previous trial runs of these two intercept missions had not been successful.

To be comfortable with the operation of the Hughes AWG-9 system, I first acquired and tracked commercial airliners, some at a range of 230 miles. For the first simulated missile shot, I acquired the F-8 target at about 30 miles on a head-on pass. When we reached 10 miles I punched the fire button to simulate a launch while the F-14 was turning at 3Gs. The missile was retained on its launcher but fully operating as if it were to hit the target; instrumentation measured the behavior. Any problems would be remedied in the laboratory before the actual launch mission.

Immediately after this first intercept, we crossed right beneath the F-8 target, made a 6G turn to its rear, and commenced a tail attack. I re-engaged the target using a more difficult radar mode and then simulated the launch of the second missile at a range of only one mile. Both attack missions were flawless (the novice back seater was much aided by the wisdom and calm of test pilot Marrett). The next day two instrumented AIM-54 Phoenix missiles were fired at drones in the Navy outer sea test range, resulting in two direct hits—a huge success for our aircrew and the test program.

The complexity and sophistication of these weapon systems required extensive testing in our laboratories and in flight. We had to know whether aircrews could successfully understand and operate the equipment in combat. Many unknown integration and computer software problems were discovered and remedied in flight test. Confirmation of those fixes required more rigorous in-flight evaluation. Meeting the contract-specified performance by these flight tests was monitored and accepted by the Department of Defense customers.

As senior executives, we truly appreciated the efforts of our dedicated flight test professionals, exemplified by George Marrett, who often risked their lives to ensure success of our products. This book by George will give you a feel on how those difficulties and challenges were met for many front-line weapon systems developed by Hughes Aircraft Company. And those did help the United States bring an end to the Cold War.

D. KENNETH RICHARDSON—
former President and Chief Operating Officer
Hughes Aircraft Company

Preface

Air Force Colonel John P. Stapp became the fastest person on earth in 1954 when the medical doctor rode Sonic Wind 1, a rocket-propelled sled, to 632 miles per hour at the Holloman Air Force Base, New Mexico, high-speed test track. The sled reached its top speed in 5 seconds and then slammed to a stop in 1.4 seconds, sustaining a deceleration force of 43Gs—equivalent to hitting a brick wall at 60 miles per hour. The high-speed run tested the limits of the human body for windblast and impact, simulating the effects of a supersonic ejection from a jet aircraft. Simultaneously, Stapp's sled experiments demonstrated the effectiveness of safety harnesses and seat belts for increasing chances of surviving an airplane crash.

As a jet pilot I had flown twice as fast as Colonel Stapp in the air—but never that fast on earth. I met Stapp over 10 years ago, after both of us had retired from aerospace. I found him to be witty, brilliant, and especially gifted in understanding the historical significance of our past aviation efforts. He told me that few people knew that a famous precept began with Air Force engineer Captain Ed Murphy. In 1949, Murphy was working at the Aero Medical Research Laboratory at Wright-Patterson

Air Force Base, Ohio, in support of Colonel Stapp's experimental crash research testing at Edwards Air Force Base. Frustrated with a malfunctioning piece of equipment, Murphy remarked to Stapp concerning a technician who had wired it, "If there is any way to do it wrong, he will." The term "Murphy's Law" soon was assigned to the statement.

On December 12, 2004, a re-enactment of Stapp's 1954 rocket sled ride was conducted on the 50th anniversary of the historic event. Wilford Stapp had tears in his eyes as he joined ceremonies commemorating his late brother's historic rocket sled ride a half-century earlier that had proved humans could survive the strain of many times the force of gravity.

Wilford Stapp, 86, of San Antonio, Texas, hit a switch that set off another rocket-propelled sled at the high-speed test track to re-enact the historic ride—this time with a mannequin. Flames shot from behind the sled, which rocketed down the track faster than the speed of sound in a trip that ended in about nine seconds.

"I could see my older brother; I could see him in my mind," remarked Wilford Stapp. "He would be very proud today of what he achieved, finding ways to preserve life."

He added, "My brother told me this was very careful research he was doing. It wasn't about speed, it was about safety."

Colonel Stapp, who retired from the Air Force in 1970, took 29 of the grueling rocket sled rides in the 1950s, proving human beings could withstand more than 40 times the force of gravity. Those experiments provided criteria for crash protection designs for aircraft, space cabins, and ground vehicles, as well as for tolerance limits for pilots in aircraft ejection seats.

Major James Colebank, Operations Officer for the 846th Test Squadron at Holloman that conducted the re-enactment, said Stapp was responsible for saving more than 250,000 lives through his research on seat belts.

Wilford Stapp said that his brother told him about his experiments and that he often wondered if John was overdoing it. "I remember him coming to visit one time, and he asked me to get his bags out of the trunk for him. I found out later that he had broken both of his arms on a sled ride."

Before his death in 1999, Colonel Stapp told me, "The Cold War was won by aerospace companies that stayed well ahead of the Soviet

Union in aircraft and weapon design and the civilian and military test pilots who risked their lives daily in the skies above Southern California to test the equipment. These test pilots often ended as unheralded casualties, the testing deaths of the war."

I agreed. It was a phone call from him on this subject that gave birth to this book.

Acknowledgments

Special thanks and recognition go to my wife, Jan, for her support of my writing and for her editing of this book. She has been my copilot for 48 years and, as she did with my other two books, has provided love, encouragement, and helpful suggestions.

To my older son Randy, Professor of Geology at the University of Texas, Austin, thanks for encouraging me to write about my aviation experiences and to record my history for our family.

To my younger son, Scott, marketing manager, thanks for reading and reviewing these words. Scott is also a storyteller who greatly enjoys a well-told tale.

I am deeply grateful to my father, George Rice Marrett, who taught me the value of hard work and encouraged me to be honest and faithful to Hughes Aircraft Company, where I was employed for 20 years. He worked for just one firm, National Cash Register Company, for all his 49 years of employment.

Love to my mother, Julia Etta (Rachuy) Marrett, who at age 95 still has a wonderful memory and sense of humor. Thanks, Mom, for encouraging me to write and having faith in me.

A special thanks goes to D. Kenneth Richardson for writing the Foreword to this book. Ken retired in 1991 as President and Chief Operating Officer of Hughes Aircraft Company. Richardson reminded me of movie idol Jimmy Stewart, with his tall, slim build and soft-spoken humor. He was always optimistic about the future of our company and defense of the United States. Born in Honolulu, Hawaii, Ken graduated from Punahou School and received his BS degree in mechanical engineering, magna cum laude, from Tufts University in Massachusetts. He earned an MSME, cum laude, from the University of Southern California (USC) and an MBA from the University of California, Los Angeles (UCLA), and he completed the UCLA Executive Program. Ken is also an instrument-rated pilot who took time out of his executive chores to fly a test mission with me in the F-14A Tomcat. The great success of Hughes Aircraft Company came about because of the superior management by Richardson and his staff.

To Elizabeth Demers, Acquisition Editor for Praeger Security International of the Greenwood Publishing Group, go my thanks for selecting this manuscript about my 20 years as a test pilot for Hughes Aircraft Company developing electronic weapons designed for the Cold War.

I am particularly indebted to John P. Stapp, Colonel, USAF (Medical Corps), who contributed to the Preface of this book. He was one of the distinguished pioneers of flight test at Edwards Air Force Base, California, and his name will always be linked to aircrew biomedical safety. It was a phone call from him about the Cold War and flight testing that gave birth to the idea of this book.

Appreciation goes to Evelyn Ludeman, sister of Hughes test pilot Chris M. Smith, who put me in contact with his daughter, Carolyn (Smith) Beatson. Carolyn Beatson typed her father's handwritten manuscript, about his experiences at Hughes Aircraft Company, and gave me permission to use his stories.

A special recognition goes to Obbie Atkinson and Al Schade, two of the founders of the Estrella Warbird Museum in Paso Robles, California. Both are dedicated aviators and military veterans who have encouraged me to write and support my present flying.

I especially want to thank the following individuals, of whom some provided photographs, some connected me with other people who had information on Hughes Aircraft Company, some kindly agreed to be interviewed for this publication, and some have supported my writing:

Nick Allen, Neil Austin, Carolyn Beatson, Dick Belmont, Joe Benson, Walter J. Boyne, Pat H. Broeske, Bruce Bromme Jr., John Bryant, Bruce Burk, Richard Chikami, Dave Congalton, Margaret Cook, Marshall Cook, Diane Dryden, Harry Dugan, James Eastham, James Easton, Jack Fahey, Hal Farley, Mike Glenn, Dr. Richard P. Hallion, Bob Hedin, Katherine Huit, John Jamar, Penny Jessup, Paul H. Kennard, Meade Livesay, George Larson, Don S. Lopez, David Ludwick, William R. Lummis, Mike Machat, Eugene "Oops" Martin, Steve Millikin, Gale J. Moore, George Parsons, Roger Post, Pete Purvis, Jack Real, Don Roudenbush, Heather Staines, Barrett Tillman, and Jim Young.

Last, I would like to recognize my four grandchildren: Cali Marrett, seventeen; Casey Marrett, fifteen; Tyler Marrett, thirteen; and Zachary Marrett, eleven. Our grandchildren are our hope and dream for the future; they fill us with joy every single day. I pray that my writing will encourage them to someday put their life experiences in print.

CHAPTER 1

Sore Feet

Once when Howard Hughes was in a plane crash, someone pulled him out and thus saved his life. Hughes called a friend and said, "What would you tip for help like that?"

The Encyclopedia of Howard Hughes Jokes, compiled and edited by Frances Spatz Leighton and Jim Gordon Atkins. Published by Acropolis Books, Washington, DC (1972)

Everything came together to make Bill Bush and I feel relaxed about our flight test mission on October 6, 1969. The flying weather was perfect: a bright blue sky with only a few benign white clouds. A Santa Ana weather condition covered Southern California with strong surface winds from the Mojave Desert blowing hot air into the Los Angeles basin. The flight visibility was unlimited—you could see forever.

Life was finally peaceful for me. It was just six months since I had returned from flying combat over Vietnam as an Air Force pilot. The United States continued to be engaged in a Cold War with the Soviet Union to prevent the spread of communism across the globe.

Now I was a civilian test pilot employed by Hughes Aircraft Company, working from the Hughes private airfield at Culver City, just a few miles north of Los Angeles International Airport. Our mission was to fly an 85,000-pound Navy experimental fighter aircraft: the Grumman Aircraft Company F-111B Sea Pig, as many called it, though the aircraft had no official nickname. We were to fly over the Santa Barbara Channel northwest of Los Angeles, testing the Hughes AIM-54A Phoenix missile and AWG-9 air-to-air system.

When Bush and I walked out to the F-111B parked on the Hughes flight line, we went over it like doctors giving a quick physical examination to a healthy patient, looking only for obvious trouble like hydraulic fluid leaks or loose aircraft panels. We climbed inside the cockpit to go through a long checklist to make sure the internal organs of our patient were also working satisfactorily.

I sat in the pilot's seat, on the left side of the cockpit. Forty-six-year-old Bill Bush, a retired Marine who had flown in World War II as a rear gunner in a Douglas SBD-2 Dauntless dive bomber, acted as the Naval Flight Officer (NFO) and settled into the right seat.

Our checks completed, I started the twin jet engines on the F-111B and taxied to Hughes Runway 23, an 8,200-foot asphalt strip. The aircraft, held by foot brakes, strained to break free as I pushed the throttles to the firewall. After a final check of all aircraft instruments, I released the brakes and selected afterburners. Each engine was burning 50,000 pounds of fuel per hour as the plane thundered down the runway, creating a tremendous noise that made academic life difficult for the students above the Westchester bluff in nearby Loyola University.

We felt the familiar *thump-thump* as the wheels retracted into the fuselage, followed by sudden quiet as the plane smoothly accelerated. I turned slightly right, flying near Marina Del Rey and over the Santa Monica Bay. It was mid-afternoon, but no sailboats could be seen in the bay due to the strong surface winds. Lovely ocean white caps were evident from 2,000 feet altitude as we leveled off and passed the coastline parallel to the deluxe movie star homes in Malibu.

"How's the radar look today?" I asked Bush, using a microphone inside my oxygen mask connected to an interphone system.

Concentrating, he stared down into the black hood over the radar screen and studied the green lines that shaped the Malibu coastline and inland features. We needed to know exactly how well the radar was performing, as it was critical to the upcoming test.

"Looks good," he remarked.

We were carrying the AIM-54A Phoenix, a 1,000-pound advanced air-to-air missile, on the left wing. Hughes Aircraft Company had built the missile as a long-range weapon designed to shoot down enemy aircraft up to 100 miles away. Each missile would cost about $1 million when produced in quantity. Our missile, called the T-20, was a specially instrumented model with strain gauges to record missile fin deflection while the pilot maneuvered the aircraft. The Navy and Hughes had invested about $4 million in this particular missile, a one-of-a-kind test prototype.

The F-111B wings were designed to sweep from 16 to 72 degrees in flight. The Phoenix missile, attached to a pylon under the left wing, rotated on its launcher rail to always remain parallel to the airstream regardless of wing sweep angle. It was a highly complex engineering design but successful in our tests up to that point.

Approaching a military warning area about 20 miles off the California coast, I contacted Plead Control, the Navy ground radar operators who controlled all military aircraft flying in restricted airspace. Our mission had been scheduled the previous day, so we were quickly identified by ground control and allowed to enter. We also kept in radio contact with Hughes engineers in Culver City, who would listen to the progress of our flight and be available if problems should develop with the missile.

A year earlier the Navy had canceled production of the F-111B aircraft. The AWG-9 system and Phoenix missile, both produced by Hughes for the F-111B, would be installed in the future replacement aircraft also made by Grumman Aircraft—specifically, the sleek F-14A Tomcat. Only seven F-111Bs were made before the program was canceled. We were flying the third plane, Bureau Number 151972, a hand-built prototype. It made sense for the Navy and Hughes to continue testing the radar and missile on the F-111B; that way, the development of the weapons would be further along before the first F-14A was to fly by the end of 1970.

Our mission consisted of flying the aircraft at 600 knots and a 10,000-foot altitude and then, at a variety of wing sweep angles, recording the missile fin deflection as I pulsed the control stick fore and aft, pushed the rudders left and right to fishtail the aircraft, and banked the aircraft steeply to pull 3Gs. Even though we had 32,000 pounds of fuel at takeoff, vast amounts would be consumed at this altitude and high speed.

When I was ready to begin a test sequence, I would tell Bush to activate the instrumentation. Then he would read and record the data counters, and I would fly the maneuvers. It was crucial to fly exactly on the preplanned airspeed, altitude, wing-sweep angle, and maneuvering G. The data recorded would be analyzed for days by a team of Hughes engineers to determine whether the missile was performing to design standards.

We completed several of these tests with a 26-degree wing sweep. The next test point was at 5,000 feet above the ocean, 50-degree wing-sweep angle, and 600 knots, just slightly subsonic and very fast for that low altitude.

The F-111B aircraft had a history of engine compressor stall problems, and I could expect them anytime during these tests. Just two years earlier, the pilot of the number four F-111B prototype experienced engine compressor stalls on both engines after takeoff from Calverton, New York, due to the translating engine cowls closing by mistake. The aircraft crashed and killed Grumman test pilots Ralph H. Donnell and Charles E. Wangeman.

Engine compressor stalls occurred at high angle of attack, on takeoff, landing, or high-G maneuvering. A stall sounded to the pilot like an explosion inside the aircraft. Engine stalls could be resolved if the pilot had sufficient altitude: He simply pulled the throttles back to idle and pushed forward on the control stick to pick up more airspeed and reduce the angle of attack. I was ready and knew how to quickly recover if I experienced an engine stall.

The Gs came on the plane as I banked into the turn. Approaching 3Gs, there was a single loud bang in the plane that sounded like a metal rod breaking. The flight controls felt as though I had pulled on the doorknob of a jammed door that suddenly opened and hit me in the face.

In this case, the control stick slammed back into my lap and the Gs on the aircraft increased. I immediately pushed the stick full forward against the instrument panel. Several warning lights illuminated on the instrument panel, signaling trouble. Engine instruments were reading normal—no engine stall. The aircraft was still in a left-hand turn, bank angle of 60 degrees pulling 2G's, with the control stick full forward against the instrument panel. I had been a pilot long enough to know that airplanes don't fly that way. Something was terribly wrong.

Both throttles were pulled back, and airspeed started to decrease. I couldn't roll the wings to level flight, because the nose would start to rise. If we climbed with the nose high in the air, we would stall the wings and the aircraft would go out of control. We were in deep trouble.

Bill Bush could tell that I was fighting hard to control the aircraft. He shut down the radar and instrumentation. The warning lights on the instrument panel signaled a flight control problem. The prototype F-111Bs had several rotary electronic switches that could be used to excite or calm the aircraft response to pilot control input. Even in the full-calm position, this beast was giving me the ride of my life.

Around and around we went in a left bank with the control stick full forward against the instrument panel. We were at least stabilized in that flight condition and were in no immediate danger. There was plenty of fuel onboard, so we had time to troubleshoot and even get advice from people on the ground. However, the aircraft could not be landed in its present condition. We needed to solve this emergency.

"Plead Control, Bloodhound 103 declaring an emergency!" I stated over the UHF radio.

"Bloodhound 103, Plead Control state condition of emergency, pounds of fuel and number of souls aboard?" they replied.

I explained our flight control difficulties as best I could to the ground controller. It was standard procedure for them to ask, "What are your intentions?" The only answer I could give was to continue to circle to the left until we could figure out what else to do. Hughes engineers called on the radio to say they would try to contact one of the other Hughes test pilots that had flown the F-111B to give me assistance.

My mind raced back to a period just 13 months earlier, when Hughes test pilot Bart Warren and his NFO Tony Byland were killed in the number two prototype F-111B, a sister ship to the number three I was flying. Warren and Byland crashed at sea about 40 miles from my present position in shark-infested waters just west of San Miguel Island, the westernmost island in the Channel Islands chain. Some type of flight control problem had caused Warren to lose control of the aircraft, and it went into a spin. Since it was a hazy day over the Pacific, some pilots felt that both Warren and Byland could not tell the difference between the "hazy blue sky" and the "hazy blue ocean" as they tumbled in the plane. They must have become disoriented because they even failed to eject from the aircraft. A seat cushion was all that was found floating in the ocean.

On the ground in Culver City test pilot Chris Smith spoke to me on the UHF radio. Smith had flown North American P-51 Mustangs in Europe during World War II and had been a personal pilot for Howard Hughes back in the 1950s. I replaced Smith by flying the F-111B when I initially came to work for the company.

"What seems to be the problem, George?" he asked.

I gave a long, detailed description of my difficulties with the aircraft. Smith felt I might have the same problem that Warren and Byland had experienced.

"You might consider ejecting over the Pacific," Smith recommended.

Ejection was certainly an option, and it would be best for the aircraft to crash at sea and not over the populated coastline of Southern California some 10 miles away. But Bush and I would then also parachute into rough, cold water. I could swim, but I didn't look forward to getting wet that day.

Many years earlier, my Navy test pilot friend Floyd Nugent had had a close call over the Pacific. As Nugent was launched from an aircraft carrier in a Vought F7U Cutlass, one of the landing gears fell off the aircraft and sunk to the bottom of the ocean. Landing a Cutlass back on the carrier missing one gear was definitely not possible. Even landing on a hard surface runway back on land at North Island Naval Air Station in San Diego was not recommended. Nugent flew about 30 miles out to sea, pointed the Cutlass west, and ejected. The aircraft continued to fly as Nugent floated down in his parachute. A rescue helicopter picked him up and transported him back to North Island. Standing on the helicopter pad at North Island, Nugent was surprised to see a Cutlass fly over without a canopy. It was his aircraft! After circling Point Loma several times, the aircraft crashed just off the beach— not hurting anyone but giving the local surfers a thrill.

Planning to eject in such a way that the aircraft crashed at sea and the pilot landed on ground was a great idea. But Nugent was out to sea and could even head the aircraft away from populated areas, and it didn't work for him. I was going around in tight circles only a few miles from shore. If I ejected, the plane could crash anywhere.

Sitting quietly in the right seat, Bush could sense we were in an extremely dangerous situation and our lives were on the line. He told me his choice was to eject. As we circled in the left bank, his sitting position on the right side of the cockpit placed him a foot or so above me. Even a foot of higher altitude seemed slightly safer. We each had individual ejection seats, wore Navy life vests, and were sitting on a green plastic survival kit that contained a one-man raft, standard Navy survival equipment for the time.

Surface winds over the ocean were still very strong, even greater than the Malibu area I had flown over on takeoff. The Malibu area had wind protection from the Santa Monica Mountains directly north of the bay. Coming down in a parachute with wind gusts on the ocean up to 25 knots seemed like suicide.

About 10 years earlier, Lieutenant Ken Mason, a pilot friend of mine, had successfully ejected from a Lockheed F-104A Starfighter and landed in only a couple of feet of water. Because he could not get released from the parachute canopy, the wind pulled him under the water and he drowned. So ejecting from our disabled aircraft would still not guarantee survival.

When I came to work for Hughes Aircraft, I had already flown the Air Force version of the F-111. The aircraft was designed for use by both the Air Force and the Navy. However, it was manufactured in different models: F-111A Aardvark for the Air Force and F-111B for the Navy. Two years earlier, I had been qualified to fly the Air Force version as a fighter test pilot at the Air Force Flight Test Center located at Edwards Air Force Base, California. At the time I was also flying the F-104A Starfighter, F-4C Phantom II and F-5A Freedom Fighter. All were top-notch military fighters used in combat in Vietnam at that time.

The F-111 fighter was the result of a contractual battle between the Boeing Aircraft Company and General Dynamics. The aircraft was dubbed the TFX—Tactical Fighter, Experimental. There was a lot of political jockeying and playing of procurement games by both of these giants and among the selection committees. The military board selected the Boeing version, but then-Secretary of Defense Robert S. McNamara overrode that decision and selected General Dynamics.

Flying the Air Force F-111A was a real disappointment to me. All new aircraft have some birthing problems, but not like the F-111A. It was severely overweight, was grossly underpowered, and had poor cockpit visibility for a fighter. It was also a maintenance nightmare. Test flight after test flight was canceled, with the pilot still sitting in the cockpit on the ramp with the engines running because some system had failed. Likewise, half of our airborne test flights were terminated early due to component failures. I recalled a military Teletype message we received from McNamara that ordered the test pilots "to be optimistic about the F-111."

"What a joke," I exclaimed. "The F-111A was the worst aircraft I had ever flown!"

Captain Herb Brightwell was an Air Force test pilot that checked out in the F-111A at Edwards Air Force Base during the same time that I started flying the plane. Brightwell had been a fighter pilot flying the North American F-100 Super Sabre, assigned to Tactical Air Command (TAC), before he came to Edwards. He did some flight testing at Edwards, but his primary duty was to act as an instructor pilot in the F-111A and to train TAC pilots to fly this particular model. The F-111A, unlike the F-111B, was dual-controlled: a flight control stick and engine throttles available to both pilots. In early 1967, Herb was instructing in one of the F-111A early prototypes. Brightwell sat in the right seat, with his student, an Air Force colonel, in the left seat.

The F-111A was the first operational sweep-wing aircraft—its wing position could be varied from a position of 16 degrees forward to 72 degrees aft. This allowed the aircraft to be flown slowly and still have plenty of lift at the 16-degree position for takeoff and landing. The 72-degree wing sweep position was used for high-speed flight.

Logically, the cockpit selector handle for moving the wing position would be moved in the direction of wing motion, but a strange philosophy of cockpit design intruded. The first batch of F-111As had the wing moving in an opposite direction from the movement of the selector handle. Only one wing sweep selector handle was installed in the cockpit. It could only be operated from the left seat.

To make the wing go forward, the pilot moved the handle back. To make the wing go back, he moved the handle forward. The logic for this scheme was that the wing selector handle should be considered as a throttle—to go fast, push the handle forward and the wing would go back, and to go slow, pull the handle back and the wing would go forward, slowing the aircraft. One can imagine how confusing its use was in actual operation. Nevertheless, the idea was incorporated—and on the first of these aircraft some enterprising test pilot doctored a decal near the wing position indicator to display: *fore is aft and aft is fore.*

When I needed to sweep the wing, I simply moved the handle in either direction while watching the wing sweep indicator. If the wing moved the wrong direction on the gauge, I would reverse the motion.

Brightwell's student was flying the F-111A from the left seat, practicing landings on the Edwards's 15,000-foot runway. About 5 miles from the end of the runway and around 1,000 feet in the air, the student's airspeed slowed and an excessive rate of descent built up. In a moment of stress, the student pilot selected the wrong wing position. He wanted the wings forward to give him more lift and slow his sink rate, but he pushed the selector handle forward, causing the wing to sweep back. The resulting loss of lift increased the rate of sink, and the aircraft crashed a mile short of intended landing.

Both pilots survived the impact with the ground. Brightwell opened his canopy on the right side of the aircraft and exited to the desert. He went around the nose of the aircraft to help his student get out of his cockpit. The F-111A's fuselage had broken apart from ground impact and unburned jet fuel had spilled on the ground. Brightwell got the student pilot's canopy open; however, a flash fire erupted and he was killed from severe burns. The student pilot survived the crash but received third-degree burns and never flew again. The F-111s had taken a terrible toll on test pilots.

None of these memories was encouraging as I continued to circle over the Pacific. It would be far too hazardous to consider flying back to the Culver City airport. The San Diego Freeway ran a half-mile east of the end of our Hughes runway, and Los Angeles International Airport was only 3 miles south—definitely not an area to lose control of a disabled aircraft and crash in a densely populated area.

Years earlier Howard Hughes had lost control of his twin-engine, experimental aircraft and crashed in the exclusive town of Beverly Hills. He had taken off from the Culver City airport on the first flight of the XF-11 reconnaissance aircraft. About an hour after takeoff the right engine developed an internal oil leak causing the rear propeller to go into reverse. Like me, Hughes did not have any cockpit instruments to help him determine the precise failure. By mistake he thought he had a landing gear malfunction. Because of the drag from the propeller in reverse, Hughes lost airspeed and altitude in the XF-11. Also like me, Hughes was unable to control the heading of the plane. Eventually he crashed into two homes in Beverly Hills and was severely injured. Similar to Hughes, I was flying a twin-engine fighter with some unknown and undetermined flight control failure and was unable to maintain the heading of the plane. Staying over the Pacific Ocean seemed to be the best plan to follow until I could resolve my problem.

I had been flying the F-111B in a left-hand turn for about 20 minutes with the control stick firmly pushed against the instrument panel. The aircraft speed was down to about 250 knots, a speed less likely to cause us injury if we ejected. By then I had found that gradual application of nose-down electrical pitch trim could be used to reduce some of the forward pressure on the control stick. I even started to shallow out the steep bank angle.

Ground radar controllers vectored the pilot of a Navy F-4B Phantom to my position to lend assistance. When he had me in sight, he asked permission to join in formation.

"Don't get too close," I cautioned him. "I might lose control at any moment and have to eject."

Naval Air Station Point Mugu, California, was the closest military field and had a runway that edged right up to the sea. Our best chance of survival, it seemed, was to fly a straight-in approach from the sea, aimed directly at Point Mugu. I contacted Mugu tower, informed them of our emergency, and asked for fire trucks to be on standby.

My reasoning led me to believe our only hope was to extend the tail hook on the F-111B and make an arrested landing (called a "trap" in the Navy), similar to the procedure used on aircraft carriers. But I was an Air Force–trained pilot; I had never made a trap before!

Bush and I then turned our attention to getting the aircraft configured for landing. The first thing I needed to do was jettison the Phoenix missile over the Pacific. As I pressed the jettison button, I watched the missile drop cleanly off the pylon and fall away. Bush made a note of our position from Point Mugu to assist during missile recovery operations. I hated to see a $4 million missile fall from the aircraft, but we had no choice. If we crashed, I didn't want a tumbling missile added to our misery.

The next problem to solve was extension of the landing gear and tail hook. By this time, I was flying the aircraft entirely on electrical pitch trim. Any attempt to move the control stick either forward or aft resulted in a wild up-and-down porpoising motion. I would then find myself back in a left-hand bank with the control stick forward against the instrument panel.

With the F-4B Phantom a safe distance on my right side, I extended the landing gear. The Phantom pilot reported that the gear appeared to be down and locked, and we heard the same *thump-thump* we had experienced more than 40 minutes earlier. Getting the gear down was the first good news that Bush and I had experienced that far during this entire episode. It would take a lot of luck and flying skill to ever get this plane safely on deck; we still had a long way to go.

Next came the extension of the arresting hook. I was beginning to feel the effects of all the physical exertion and mental stress. How much energy should I save for a swim back to the shore?

A year and a half earlier, when I first arrived in Vietnam, pilots in my squadron had searched for several Air Force F-111A aircraft lost on combat missions over the jungle. Six aircraft had been involved in a combat evaluation called Combat Lancer. Secretary of Defense McNamara wanted to demonstrate that his decision was superior to select an aircraft to be used by both the Air Force and Navy by deploying the aircraft in combat as soon as possible. Unfortunately, the first aircraft crashed only 11 days after it arrived in Vietnam. Another crashed two days after the first one, followed by a third vanishing a short time later.

To lose half of the F-111A force in a month was discouraging. It was not possible to get even a single clue about the first two losses, as the crews maintained radio silence on single-ship night combat missions. No wreckage from either aircraft was ever found. Neither aircraft appeared to have been shot down in the target area, a belief strengthened by the report of the third crew, who ejected. Their report, and examination of the wreckage, pointed strongly to gross failure of the horizontal stabilizer control system. The main control-valve rod inside the unit had failed, snapping in two at a welded joint. This had immediately driven the left horizontal stabilizer to the limit of its negative travel, causing sudden and violent roll and pitch-up, while slamming the control stick into the pilot's stomach. Although I didn't know exactly what failed in the F-111B I was flying, I knew that the history of surviving an incident in any model of the F-111 with mechanical malfunctions was poor. I would soon be making a number of the most critical decisions I had ever made in my flying career. A wrong decision meant that it would all be over.

Cautiously, I got wing flaps partially down, allowing our speed to be reduced. The aircraft still had over 11,000 pounds of fuel onboard—too much to attempt a landing. I contacted Mugu tower to determine the status of their arresting gear and what maximum weight their equipment would handle. If we jettisoned half of the remaining fuel, we would be just at the arresting gear's maximum capability. This was cutting it pretty thin.

Slowly I descended to about 1,000 feet altitude approximately 10 miles off shore and aimed directly at the runway at Point Mugu. The foam and spray of white caps, which had appeared so small from 5,000 feet, now seemed more threatening. The wind was shaking the plane as if it were driving over a washboard road. I started to jettison fuel and told Bush to lock his seat belt harness.

"Tell me when I'm down to 5,000 pounds, Bill," I requested.

He wasted no time and energy with a response. We were now committed to an arrested landing, and our altitude would soon be below the recommended level for safe ejection. We were betting the farm on things holding together for a few more moments.

The Mugu tower operator reported that the winds were a 90-degree crosswind from the left, 15 knots with gusts up to 25, and fire trucks were in place at both ends of the runway. Still flying the aircraft entirely with the electrical trim button on top of the control stick, I struggled to keep from the natural tendency to fly the aircraft with the stick. Our altitude was too low to risk entering a left-hand spiral again with the stick jammed up against the instrument panel.

The fuel jettison switch was turned off about 4 miles on final approach. The runway appeared large out the front windscreen, and I could see the arresting gear cable strung across the runway. We were just about home.

Though touchdown was gentle and I heard the tires squeak, the aircraft instantly leaped back into the air and the nose started to rise. From that point I had absolutely no control of the aircraft—Bush and I were along for the ride. The tail hook, however, caught the arresting gear cable and stopped the aircraft in mid-air. We came down directly on the nose wheel, which immediately collapsed. The aircraft slammed down hard, followed by the grinding sound of metal sliding across a concrete runway. My feet felt like they were crushed, but at least we were finally stopped.

In a fraction of a second, some of the hydraulic fluid released from the broken nose gear caught fire. I reached for the canopy jettison handle located at the top of the windscreen between the two seats and pulled it.

Almost immediately both canopies fired into the air as smoke and flames spilled into the cockpit. With the wind from my left, the fire wrapped around under the nose of the aircraft. Flames came in the right side of the cockpit and singed Bush's right arm and neck. There was plenty of smoke on my side, but no flames.

Bush screamed out some old Marine Corps cadence and leaned toward me to get away from the fire. Rather than struggling to manually unhook my shoulder harness, seat belt, oxygen connection, and radio cord, which would take many seconds even in the best of circumstances, I reached down with my right hand, squeezed the ground egress handle and heard a pop. All my connections to the F-111B automatically released.

I stood up in the cockpit, with parachute and survival kit still attached, and jumped over the canopy rail. Within seconds I was away from the aircraft. Looking back, I saw that Bush was still in his ejection seat, but a Navy crash crew was already spraying foam in his cockpit. The fire was quickly extinguished, and the fire crews helped Bush evacuate the cockpit. We had made it home.

That day I was wearing a military-orange cotton flying suit that could easily be seen in the water following an ejection. Fortunately, Bush had traded some of his flight equipment with his Marine Corps buddies and was wearing a newly issued khaki Nomex flying suit. This new fire-retardant flight suit was a lifesaver for him. Even though his right forearm and neck received third-degree burns, his flight suit did not catch fire as my cotton one would have.

As we walked around the F-111B aircraft surveying the damage, it was not evident to me that Bush had sustained serious burn injuries, nor did he say anything to me. His flesh burns were under his Nomex flight suit. His suit looked absolutely normal, with no charring or discoloration. Later he would receive skin grafts from his leg to mend his arm and neck.

We were not surprised to find the nose gear area of the aircraft severely damaged. It had experienced about 6 negative Gs when the aircraft stopped in mid-air after the tail hook caught the arresting cable and then crashed into the concrete runway.

Our surprise came when we viewed the left side of the F-111B. A large metal panel covering the top of the left wing sweep mechanism had ripped off the aircraft. The loss of the panel itself should not have caused any severe problem, but this jagged piece of metal, measuring about 2 feet by 3 feet, had embedded itself in the top of the fuselage. It looked like an ax stuck in a tree. Under the surface of the fuselage, in the area struck by the metal, were the control rods to the horizontal stabilizer, all severely bent. No wonder I had had control difficulties. The jagged piece of metal had just missed a main fuel line. If the fuel line had been punctured—I didn't even want to think about that!

Later Bush and I met with Navy and Hughes personnel to debrief our test mission. Four Hughes engineers, assigned to monitor the flight testing of this special AIM-54A Phoenix missile, sat across the table from us. Unaware of the extreme difficulties and problems we had experienced over the last few hours, they opened their data logbooks and began to ask questions.

"How did the missile work, Bill?" they asked.

Bush looked up. Slowly and deliberately he said, "We 'pickled' the missile."

The missile engineers started to write in their logbooks. They looked up somewhat concerned and innocently asked Bush, "What do you mean 'pickled'?"

"We dropped the damned missile in the ocean!" Bush shouted.

They looked at one another in disbelief and shrugged their shoulders. They closed their data books and left the room.

About a month after the accident, the manager of our flight test organization invited me to attend a meeting located in the headquarters building of Hughes Aircraft Company. The company senior officers met on a quarterly basis in what was called a policy board meeting. Lawrence A. "Pat" Hyland, vice president and general manager of the company, conducted the meeting. He reported directly to Howard Hughes, who was still living at the time.

When the meeting began, I was asked to describe the F-111B emergency and my crash landing. Then, to my astonishment, Mr. Hyland presented me with a letter and bonus award in the form of a check. The letter said, in part, "the officers of Hughes Aircraft Company join me in expressing sincere appreciation for the dedication, skill and courage shown by you, as the pilot of an F-111B airplane, in the resolution of an in-flight emergency. The consequences of an emergency, in which the longitudinal control of the airplane was severely limited, might have been a catastrophic loss of human life and an airplane/weapon system of vital importance to the PHOENIX flight test program. The cool analysis of this critical situation, the selected course of action, and flawless performance resulted in only minor personnel injury and a salvageable airplane/ weapon system."

The ceremonies were not yet over. Shortly after the policy board meeting, Grover "Ted" Tate, an old friend of mine from Edwards Air Force Base, arranged a lunch. Tate had been a flight test engineer for General Dynamics for many years, having flown test missions in the B-36 Peacemaker, B-58 Hustler, and F-111A Aardvark. He had a great sense of humor and later wrote four books about his flying experiences. At this time, he represented both Grumman Aircraft Company and General Dynamics as a technical consultant to Hughes, assisting our company in maintaining the F-111B. During the lunch he announced that the Navy had approved funds to repair the aircraft and expected to have it flying again within three months.

Tate presented a wooden plaque to me. Attached to the front of the plaque was the actual yellow canopy jettison handle I had used to blow the two canopies off the aircraft. That plaque is hanging in my den today. A brass plate below the jettison handle reads:

DREAMS THAT START OUT ON WINGS
OFTEN END UP WITH SORE FEET
FROM WALKING HOME
TO
GEORGE MARRETT
SAVIOR OF 972

CHAPTER 2

Jet Pilot

*When Hughes was a young man dating all the starlets in
Hollywood, he had a reputation for being quite a lover. One of his
close friends asked him one morning how he'd made out before
with a particularly luscious starlet.*

*"Terribly," replied Hughes. "I took her to Chasen's Restaurant
and ordered her the most expensive meal. We had two bottles of
the best champagne—at $45 a bottle. And, after the first few sips
she became very loving. I have never had loving like that."*

*"What's your complaint? Sounds like everything went just
great," said the friend.*

*"Well," said Hughes, "I think I could have made out as well
with a couple of beers."*

Favorite story of Mike Trupp, Director of International Relations, U.S.
Maritime Commissions

Even from the darkened sanctuary of his Beverly Hills Hotel bungalow,
Howard Hughes could hear the sound of aircraft engines as planes flew
on their landing approach to Los Angeles International Airport. By the
mid-1950s, although he was flying little, his love of aviation remained
strong and resulted in a second airplane movie. Hughes had acquired the
rights to a story called *Jet Pilot* and planned to make another spectacular
aerial film, a jet-age *Hell's Angels*. Like *Hell's Angels*, the story line was
uninspiring and merely an excuse to thrill the world with the sight of jets
streaking across the sky but now in living Technicolor. Hughes initiated
the project in order to capture his three top passions in one film: his love
for planes, his hatred for communism during the Cold War, and his at-
traction to well-endowed women.

Jet Pilot starred John Wayne as an Air Force colonel stationed at a
remote base in the Alaska wilderness—scant minutes away from the Soviet border. The story revolved around Janet Leigh, an attractive Russian
pilot, pretending to defect to the side of democracy in order to snare
Wayne for interrogation. Leigh, who was blonde and busty, was forced
down over the United States and Wayne captured her. Wayne performed

a search of Leigh as she did a striptease taking off her flying gear. She then took a shower and again teased Wayne while he watched in disbelief and excitement, wondering if this was some kind of commie plot. Meanwhile on the soundtrack, low-flying jets zoomed overhead and the roar of engines punctuated the appropriate moments of Leigh's motion. Eventually Wayne and Leigh marry and wing off in their F-86 Sabre Jets through moonlit skies on a poetic honeymoon flight.

Shooting of the film started in 1949 with the dramatic scenes. Hughes brought German Josef von Sternberg out of retirement to direct the film. Then Hughes decided he could do a better job himself and fired Sternberg.

Hughes dispatched film crews to air bases all over the country to film aerial footage of dueling jets. Always the perfectionist, he wanted the same background he had insisted on for *Hell's Angels*—huge, puffy, white cumulus clouds that reminded him of a woman's breast. As could be expected, the final product showed stunning aerial sequences of jet fighters rolling in the sky, sliding up alongside of each other. You could hear Wayne and Leigh banter over the radio—their planes seeming to make love with each other. It was pure Howard Hughes.

By January 1951, Hughes had shot 150,000 feet of film, enough for a 24-hour movie and over 10 times more than the finished product required. Hughes so loved every scene, he could not make up his mind which to include and which to delete. For six years he struggled mightily with the mountain of celluloid, trying to edit *Jet Pilot* to a manageable length. It was 1957 before the film was finally released, and it had cost more than $4 million.

At that time I was a student at Iowa State College in Ames, Iowa, majoring in chemistry and planning to become a research scientist. I was born and raised in the flatland of Nebraska and attended elementary school during World War II. As a boy I heard reports over the radio about aerial dogfights over Europe and dreamed of becoming a fighter pilot.

While a student, I had met Captain Harold "Hal" Fischer, a double jet ace who had flown the F-86A in Korea. He had given a presentation to the cadets in my Air Force Reserve Officers Training Corps class about flying combat. I was very impressed with him, wearing his formal military uniform, with silver Air Force wings and several rows of colorful ribbons pinned on his chest. I pledged to myself that sometime in the future I would fly a Sabre Jet.

After hearing the mass promotions for *Jet Pilot*, a classmate of mine and I drove 30 miles to witness the grand opening of the film. For me, the film was a career-changing experience. Seeing the jets zoom through the sky chasing each other around the clouds, I decided I wanted to become a jet pilot. Though the general public enjoyed the film, not everyone agreed with my positive reaction. Critics generally gave the film a poor review. In the end, unlike *Hell's Angels*, Howard Hughes lost money on *Jet Pilot*.

During my senior year in college, I met a young lady from my home town of Grand Island, Nebraska. Janice Sheehan was tall, slender, and had auburn hair. She had Irish and German ancestry and we were inseparable. After I graduated from college, we got married. I joined the U.S. Air Force in February 1958 and during the course of the next year, I soloed in the single-engine propeller Beech T-34 and received jet training in the Cessna T-37 and Lockheed T-33. Upon graduation from Air Force basic flying school at Webb Air Force Base, Texas, in April 1959, and receiving my Air Force silver wings, Jan and I packed our belongings again.

We had been married just a little over a year, but packing our household goods was getting to be routine. This was our third move in twelve months while I attended different Air Force flying schools. My next assignment would return us to the hot, humid South. There I would attend a six-month Air Force advanced flying school at Moody Air Force Base in Valdosta, Georgia, flying the F-86L Sabre Dog. The F-86L Sabre Dog was an advanced version of the F-86A Sabre Jet, which had been filmed in *Jet Pilot*. The plane was very successful in shooting down MiGs in the Korean War. Pilots flying the F-86 shot down about eight MiGs for every plane they lost, and damaged an equal proportion.

Like we had done a year earlier, our 1958 robin's-egg-blue MGA roadster made another trip out of Texas crossing the Gulf Coast states. Valdosta, Georgia, was located about 80 miles east of my Air Force primary flying school in Bainbridge, Georgia, where I had flown the T-34 and T-37 only six months earlier. The Moody Air Force Base local flight training area encompassed the Okefenokee Wildlife and Refuge Area, a huge swamp consisting mostly of illegal moonshiners and ferocious alligators.

The F-86L Sabre Dog version was a single-seat all-weather interceptor built by North American Aviation Company in El Segundo, California. Over 2,500 F-86s were produced during the course of seven years in the 1950s. The importance of the interceptor has always been overshadowed by the Korean War vintage F-86A day fighter, since most MiGs were shot down by that version. Although unglamorous compared to its day fighter brother, the Sabre Dog was responsible for several world speed records and defended the U.S. heartland during the early stages of the Cold War.

Modified with the Hughes Aircraft Company E-4 Fire Control Radar, 12-inch extended wing tips, 24 2.75-inch folding-fin air-to-air rockets, and an afterburner, the improved version of the F-86D Sabre Dog became the F-86L. It was a defensive fighter stationed at Air Force bases along both the east and west coasts and the northern border with Canada. Under control of Air Defense Command, the F-86Ls primary duty was to intercept and destroy enemy Russian bombers in the event of their attack on the continental United States.

My checkout in the F-86L consisted of ground school, simulator, and flying training. Simulator training focused on aircraft performance, emergency procedures, and airborne intercept tactics. Since there was no dual controlled F-86L aircraft produced for pilot training, passing the final simulator check stood between me and my first solo. After much study, as well as hours and hours sweating out the multitude of emergency procedures in the simulator, I finally passed my check ride and was scheduled for my first Sabre Dog flight.

Four years earlier a cousin of mine married a jet pilot, Captain Charles "Chuck" Teater, a veteran of World War II and Korea. He was a Sabre Dog pilot flying from a fighter squadron in Sioux City, Iowa. Chuck was the first jet pilot I met; by 1959 he was an instructor at Moody Air Force Base and would chase me on my first flight.

Climbing into the F-86L from the left side of the fuselage was easy enough. A pilot's step extended from the lower portion of the fuselage about 10 inches, where I placed my left foot. Two spring-loaded kick steps were located on the side of the fuselage and were used as both a handhold and a footstep. The cockpit was roomy and comfortable, as compared to the Lockheed T-33 I had just flown in flight school. The General Electric J-47 engine started easily and lit off with a noticeable thump and a yellowish-orange flame spurting out the tailpipe. From the cockpit the view was excellent; I sat much higher above the ramp than in the T-33. Looking back at the wing I became conscious of the drooping leading-edge slats and felt the odd excitement of a wing swept back at 35 degrees.

Unlike the F-86A used in Korea, my Sabre Dog had a combined one-piece movable stabilizer and elevator. The flight controls were light in both pitch and roll as I made a full sweep of the cockpit. I was ready to taxi.

When the control tower cleared me onto the runway I thought I could also hear my own heart beating. Into position I set the brakes, ran the engine up to military power (full-engine power without afterburner), and checked the flight controls one last time. I released the brakes and lit the afterburner, remembering to make sure the engine variable nozzle opened. My instructor warned me that if the nozzle didn't open, the backpressure in the engine would cause the RPM to slow down. Then the electronic fuel control would sense low RPM and add more fuel. The backpressure would build up more; the RPM would drop more; so even more fuel would be added to the fire. After 14 seconds of this scenario, the Sabre Dog engine could explode in a ball of fire or melt off the tail of the aircraft. I finally found the nozzle gauge on the instrument panel. By the time I looked up again I had exceeded the takeoff speed. Pulling back on the control stick as fast as I could, I made one of the fastest rotations and steepest takeoffs in the F-86L ever made at Moody.

I retracted the landing gear as soon as I could find the gear handle and started to climb. At 180 knots the leading-edge slats retracted into the wing from air pressure and Captain Teater joined with me in formation. We leveled off at 20,000 feet, and I got my first chance to maneuver the Sabre Dog like the North American designers had intended. Unlike the T-33, with its slow roll rate caused by the weight of two 230-gallon wing tip fuel tanks, the F-86L rolled smartly with just a small amount of aileron movement. Using 250 knots as an aim speed, I slowly rolled into a 3G turn. Both leading-edge slats started to creep open. Teater warned me that if only one slat came out during the maneuver the added lift on one side could cause the Sabre Dog to roll inverted and possibly fall off into a spin. My F-86L flew like a dream—I felt like I had flown the plane a long time.

Next I got to push the engine to military power, dive at 30 degrees, and accelerate to 400 knots. With a smooth application of 4Gs I looped the Sabre Dog going over the top at 150 knots. Following the loop, I practiced several Immelmanns and a Cuban Eight.

For the first time in my life, I was finally flying a jet fighter. The F-86L was similar to the plane John Wayne and Janet Leigh had flown in the movie *Jet Pilot*. To me, it was a dream come true. I rolled into a high-G descending turn and made believe I was closing in on a Russian MiG fighter. "Pow-pow-pow," I spoke to myself in my oxygen mask, making sure that I did not transmit over the UHF radio and outside my plane; Captain Teater might think I had lost my sanity.

Because it was a single-seated aircraft, I learned to fly the aircraft and operate the radar at the same time. This required high skill on the part of the pilot and good instrument proficiency. Operating the E-4 Fire Control system was my first exposure to a Hughes Aircraft Company product. Their system was quite complicated for its time and usually didn't work very well. The electronic units held a bunch of old-style vacuum tubes. These units were either degraded or failed on every flight. Hence, obtaining a long-range radar detection and lock on of a target aircraft was unusual. The probability of detection and lock on to an enemy aircraft was slim. It was a marginal weapon system in my estimation. I had to spend the majority of my attention with my head down searching for the target on the radar. It was very easy to get disoriented and forget to keep flying the F-86L.

Lieutenant Cloyce G. Mindel, one of my fellow students from Wisconsin, got confused on a night practice intercept mission, lost control of his F-86L, and crashed into the Okefenokee Swamp. This loss of a pilot friend due to an accident was the first of many I would experience in my flying career.

One entire training flight in the F-86L was devoted to reaching supersonic flight. Using afterburner, I climbed the Sabre Dog to 40,000 feet, leveled off, and accelerated to a speed of 0.9 Mach number. Still in full power, I rolled the aircraft inverted and pulled the nose straight toward the ground, aimed at an imaginary moonshiner's still in the heart of the Okefenokee Swamp. At about 30,000 feet, the F-86L exceeded the speed of sound and created a sonic boom for all the alligators to hear. For me, there was no physical sensation in the cockpit when I broke the sound barrier—all I could see was a jump in a needle on the Mach meter. In seconds it was all over: The boom ended, with most of the fuel depleted, and I flew back to the Moody Air Force Base landing pattern. For breaking the sound barrier, I received a North American Aviation *Mach Buster* card and tie tack. It was another rung in the ladder to becoming a fighter pilot.

In October 1959, with 77 flight hours in the Sabre Dog and the end of my advanced flying school program fast approaching, I anxiously awaited my first permanent military assignment. The assignments were based entirely on class standing, not on recommendations from instructors, as had been the case in basic flying school. All 39 graduating fighter pilots in my class gathered in the base auditorium. Thirty-nine assignments from fighters to bombers to tankers were listed in chalk on a blackboard, with appropriate location and aircraft type. The top-ranking F-86L pilot had his choice of any squadron and plane listed. After he chose, the assignment he selected would be erased from the board and the next-highest-ranking pilot would get his choice.

My position was number nine, high enough to assure I would get a fighter assignment. But I had raised my personal expectations: Now I wanted to fly the Century Series category of aircraft somewhere other than the hot and humid South. Century Series aircraft were the newest versions of fighters in the Air Force that would fly faster than the speed of sound in level flight, not in a dive as the F-86L did.

Luck came my way. Our MGA roadster would cross the entire United States, this time to California. My new squadron was the 84th Fighter Interceptor Squadron (FIS) flying the Mach 1.73 McDonnell F-101B Voodoo from Hamilton Air Force Base, just 25 miles north of the Golden Gate Bridge near San Francisco. I was anxious to leave for California but was thankful I had a chance to fly the famed MiG-killing Sabre Dog at least a few flight hours. Little did I realize then that I would cross paths with Hughes Aircraft Company in the future.

Jan and I drove our MGA roadster from Georgia to California in December of 1959. As we came down the western side of the Sierra Nevada range into the Sacramento Valley, we saw the winter greenery of the West Coast. What a pleasant change from the snow of our home state of Nebraska and the humidity of the South where I had attended flight school. Within a couple of days we rented a partially furnished two-bedroom house in Novato, a town a few miles north of the base. It was nothing spectacular, but we were now living in sunny California and I was finally going to become a jet fighter pilot.

I was eager to visit Hamilton Air Force Base and see first-hand the flight line, hangars, and supersonic aircraft. Hamilton was the home of the 78th Fighter Wing. The wing had achieved a distinguished combat record flying P-51 aircraft on missions from England over Germany in World War II. Two fighter squadrons were stationed on the base. One was the 83rd

FIS, equipped with the F-104A Starfighter. During the previous year, the 83rd FIS had set a world speed and altitude record with the aircraft. It was a red-hot Mach-2 interceptor armed with Sidewinder heat-seeking missiles. My squadron was the 84th FIS, which had recently given up their old Northrop F-89 Scorpions, ugly subsonic planes nicknamed gravel-gobblers due to their drooped nose and low air intakes, to start flying the F-101B Voodoo. The F-101B was a twin-engine, two-seated, 45,000-pound jet interceptor, about twice as large and fast as the F-86L Sabre Jet.

Development of an all-weather interceptor version of the basic F-101 Voodoo was first considered by the Air Force as early as the fall of 1952, but it was rejected at that time as being too costly. However, in the spring of 1953, the idea of the all-weather interceptor Voodoo was revived again, this time as a long-range interceptor to complement the relatively short-range F-86D and L. The idea was turned down again, because the Air Force's ultimate long-range interceptor was going to be the Mach-2 Convair F-106A.

However, late in 1953 delays in the F-106 program caused the Air Force to reconsider its procurement policy for all-weather interceptors. At that particular time, the subsonic F-89 Scorpion was the backbone of the Air Force long-range all-weather interceptor squadrons, with the supersonic Convair F-102A Delta Dagger just beginning to undergo flight testing. The F-102A had always been considered by the Air Force as only an interim interceptor, filling in the void until the far more advanced F-106 could be made available. However, the F-102A was experiencing teething problems on its own at that time and it appeared that its introduction into service might be appreciably delayed. In addition, the explosion of a hydrogen bomb by the Soviet Union in August of 1953 made it imperative that the Air Force find something other than the F-102A that would help fill in the gap between the subsonic F-89 Scorpion and the Mach-2 F-106 Delta Dart. So the Air Force contracted with McDonnell Aircraft to build the F-101B interceptor.

The fire control system on the F-101B was to be the Hughes Aircraft MG-13 system, an improved version of the Hughes E-6 system that had been fitted to the F-89D Scorpion. The armament consisted of two guided missiles equipped with conventional warheads and two rockets with nuclear warheads. No internal cannon armament was installed.

The F-101B retained the center and rear fuselage sections and the wing and tail surfaces of the F-101A. However, it had a revised forward fuselage housing the MG-13 Fire Control System, with automatic search and track mode, as well as a two-seat tandem cockpit with pilot in front and Radar Intercept Operator (RIO) in the rear. A retractable refueling probe in front of the pilot's cockpit and missile armament were also added. The internal fuel capacity was reduced to 2,053 gallons to provide more room for electronic equipment and armament. Armament consisted of either a Hughes Aircraft GAR-1 semi-active radar homing missile or a GAR-2 infrared-homing Falcon missile. These missiles were carried on and launched from a rotary armament door covering the fuselage bay beneath and behind the rear cockpit. A total of two missiles were attached in recessed slots on the exposed side of the door. After the missiles were launched, the door flipped over, exposing the two Douglas MB-1 Genie nuclear warhead rockets.

During flight testing, problems were encountered with the RIO's position in the rear cockpit. It had been badly designed, and little could be done except to make minor changes. The Hughes MG-13 Fire Control System turned out to be marginal, being merely a refinement of the E-6 Fire Control System fitted to the F-89, and could not effectively control the weapons of an interceptor as fast as the F-101B. A proposal to replace the MG-13 with the MA-1 system planned for the F-106 was turned down as being too costly.

By the summer of 1960 I had completed my training in the F-101B, had become combat-ready, and had started spending time on alert. Each of the four flights in the squadron were scheduled for three days of alert on a rotational basis. Four Voodoos were armed with two Genie rockets and two GAR missiles and on a one-hour scramble status. Two other F-101Bs were armed with just missiles and were on Hot 5 status, meaning they were required to be airborne in five minutes if called upon by Air Force headquarters.

That fall my flight was deployed to Tyndall Air Force Base, Florida, for live firing training. Six F-101B Voodoo aircrews departed Hamilton for the Gulf Coast with a refueling stop at Carswell Air Force Base, Texas. It was my first time to fly a Voodoo east of Arizona, Utah, or Montana.

When we arrived in Florida we sat through several briefings on the latest status of Air Force weapon development and our upcoming firing of an inert Genie rocket in the Gulf of Mexico offshore range. During the evening we went to the Officers Club bar and drank beer. While there I learned to eat raw oysters—quite a challenge for a boy from Nebraska. I didn't like the look of raw oysters and was reluctant to eat one. I did find the oysters went down more easily if you placed them on a cracker, added a generous amount of catsup, and drank some beer between each one.

Soon the day came to launch the Genie rocket. I had never fired a weapon from a plane before. A year earlier I had jettisoned a pair of fuel tanks off a T-33 when I experienced a fire warning light in weather over Oregon. So I looked forward to launching a weapon at an unmanned drone.

My RIO and I took off from Tyndall and were radar vectored to the turn-in point. We had briefed the mission several times on the ground and had a precise checklist to follow. Nevertheless, both of us were apprehensive and worried we would make a mistake and screw up the launch.

Fortunately my RIO got an early radar detection of the target and a solid lock on. I followed the steering commands displayed on my radarscope. Our launch was on a southeast heading so as to fire over the Gulf of Mexico and avoid populated areas. The ground radar controller started a countdown and I squeezed the red trigger on the flight control stick.

"Five, four, three, two, one, fire," commanded the voice on the ground.

The 800-pound MB-1 rocket dropped free and the motor lit off. I saw the white-colored rocket accelerate in front of me and soon picked up the drone just as I started the escape maneuver. Our launch was a scored kill; it was time to celebrate with more raw oysters.

In the years to follow, as a Hughes Aircraft test pilot, I would fire many Sidewinders, Sparrows, and Phoenix missiles at drones in the Pacific offshore weapon range. But I never ate raw oysters again.

During the 1960s there was great concern that the Soviet Union would launch jet bombers with nuclear weapons to attack the cities of the United States. The Cold War was at its peak during this time, and people took the threat of the Soviet Union making a first strike against the United States with nuclear-equipped bombers with great seriousness.

The F-101B aircraft I was flying out of Hamilton could carry two of the MB-1 Genie nuclear warhead 1.7-kiloton rockets. Each of the rockets had the explosive power of about one-tenth of the bomb that was used over Hiroshima and Nagasaki during World War II. These rockets were designed to be fired at incoming Russian bombers at around 200 miles from the Pacific Ocean coastline as the enemy aircraft flew toward our country.

After launching the Genie rocket, it was mandatory that we execute an escape maneuver to prevent ourselves from being injured by both the blast and the radiation of the nuclear explosion. We were particularly concerned about the blast effect at night, when our vision was extremely important for getting the aircraft back to our home base. Pilots felt that their vision would be lost if they happened to be looking in the direction of the blast at the moment of explosion.

Due to our concern, as junior pilots we asked our squadron commander and tactics instructors how we could possibly return to land with injured eyesight. These senior officers agreed that we indeed would have great difficulty flying our flight instruments at night with damaged vision. They came up with a very novel and inexpensive solution. This idea took the form of a standard civilian plastic eye-patch. The eye-patch was attached to an elastic string and could be worn over just one eye as we flew our aircraft. Our helmet and oxygen mask fit over the eye-patch. That way, if an explosion occurred, we would only lose one eye and could then remove the eye-patch from the good eye and fly the aircraft home using its vision.

The eye-patch was issued to us in a small red zippered vinyl bag that we could easily insert in our flying jacket and could access during flight. About this time Francis Gary Powers was shot down in a Lockheed U-2 aircraft as he was flying over the Soviet Union. We read in the *San Francisco Chronicle* that Powers was carrying a suicide kit, which he could use if he were captured. To impress our wives and girlfriends with the danger and responsibility the country had bestowed upon us junior aviators, we informed them that we also had been given a suicide kit, which we carried in a small red zippered bag. We had at least found one good use for the eye-patch. We looked for more.

Junior aviators spent a lot of time after flying at the fighter room bar in the basement of the Officer's Club. This was a bar a pilot could attend wearing a flight suit. It was a good place to discuss tactics with other pilots while drinking a couple of beers. Soon it became the custom to wear the eye-patch over one eye while drinking in the fighter room. To an outsider we looked quite strange—prime physical specimens, all wearing a patch over one eye.

As could be expected, the squadron commander joined us for a beer one evening. To his surprise, he found all of his aviators wearing an eye-patch. He made a mistake by asking one pilot why everyone was wearing a patch. The pilot explained to him that all the aviators were drinking heavily and planned to save one eye with which to drive home.

Before long, a directive was published requiring all eye-patches be turned into the supply office.

Gradually I accumulated more flying time and experience in the F-101B. Flight operations were getting to be routine, and I was even beginning to get bored with spending days and days on alert. By late 1962, our sister squadron, the 83rd FIS, was also flying the F-101B. They kept aircraft on nuclear alert 24 hours a day and 7 days a week, just as our squadron did.

Regulations were very strict concerning the inspection of aircraft with nuclear weapons on-board. While the pilot preflighted his cockpit, the RIO would stand at the top of the tall entrance ladder hooked to the side of the aircraft, gun at the ready, making sure the pilot made no mistake that might damage the rocket or cause a nuclear accident. Likewise, the pilot observed the RIO preflight his cockpit. All cockpit switches that armed the nuclear weapon were safety-wired to the OFF position. Electrical power could not be applied to the aircraft at any time during this process, and several Air Policemen surrounded this whole activity, also armed with guns.

Government rules at the time stipulated that for safety considerations no Air Force nuclear-equipped interceptor would fly over the continental United States unless we were at war with the Soviets. Complicated authentication codes and procedures were in place to prevent accidental flight.

Because we had an hour to get airborne if scrambled while on nuclear alert, the aircrew could go to the Officers Club and meet their families for dinner. Our flight commander carried a portable communications radio, and all aircrew stayed close together. We also spent many hours while on alert in the flight simulator and base gym.

In October 1962, the two fighter squadrons had one of the wildest parties at the Officers Club we had ever attended. Alcohol flowed freely, and both squadrons were anxious to out-do the other. Drinks were thrown on people until most of the dancing couples looked like swimmers. Then someone opened a pillow and doused the dancers with feathers. The dancers didn't miss a beat. Now dancing on broken bar glasses with feathers sticking onto their suits and party dresses, they continued into the early morning hour. It was a party to end all parties.

The next day our flight was on alert. It was expected that the alert crew would assist in cleaning up the club after the wild night. We slowly went through the motions, knowing this was only the start of our three-day alert cycle.

Suddenly a command on the radio ordered us to our planes. We drove in a couple of Jeeps to our aircraft and waited for further instructions. And then we waited longer. The military has always been a hurry-up-and-wait type of organization. Rumor had it that we were going to have a no-notice evaluation by our higher headquarters. If that were the case, headquarters would send a pilot to our base with a written order to our commander. The order would temporarily relieve us of our nuclear-alert requirements. The F-101Bs would be off-loaded of nuclear weapons, and the aircrew tested with written examinations and simulator evaluations. Aircrew assigned to each alert aircraft would then fly practice intercepts against Air Force targets that simulated the Russian enemy to determine how the aircrew would fare if it were a real war. It was critical for our squadron to score high on these no-notice evaluations.

A box lunch was brought to us as we stood by our aircraft. We had been standing near our F-101Bs for nearly six hours. With nothing else to do, I began a conversation with one of the Air Policeman standing guard.

"What would you do if we got scrambled?" I asked.

"Sir, I would hold my position," he exclaimed.

With the worldly view of a first lieutenant, I explained to him, "If we get scrambled with these nukes onboard our aircraft, we are definitely at war! The Bay Area is a prime target area; Russian nukes will soon be exploding on San Francisco. We can't possibly stop every incoming Russian aircraft. I can guarantee you the entire Bay Area would be in ashes."

To emphasize, I added, "If we scramble, your security job is over. Personally, I would get the hell out of here! Head northwest up in the hills to get away from the radiation and fallout."

About that time, the phone at the alert console rang. Our senior officer, a captain, answered.

The deputy wing commander spoke, "Get those planes airborne!"

The captain repeated the words for all of us to hear. Eyes widened and lips took on a thinness of extreme concern. The captain asked the commander to verbally pass on to him the required secret authentication codes.

The commander repeated emphatically, "Captain, I said get those planes airborne!"

Codes or no codes, it was clear the order was to be executed. For a second or so we all held our positions, unable to resolve the contradiction. As in the movie, *It's A Mad, Mad, Mad, Mad World*, we waited for someone to make the first move. The tension mounted. Then simultaneously, as in the movie, we each ran to our aircraft. I couldn't believe we were going to fly the F-101B with nuclear weapons loaded.

All the pilots started their engines and we taxied toward Runway 30. I noticed the 83rd squadron pilots were also taxiing, but toward the opposite end of the same runway we were planning to use. They were coming from the alert hangar, which was on the north side of the base. At this time, we were definitely going to fly, unless the deputy wing commander called us back at the last minute.

"I'll bet this is still part of an exercise and the maintenance personnel have off-loaded the nukes while we were cleaning the Officers Club," I thought.

The control tower operator boomed over the radio, "All aircraft cleared for simultaneous takeoff—each maintain the right side of the runway."

Pilots in our 84th squadron pulled out onto Runway 30 in single file and applied afterburner power to start takeoff. The 83rd squadron pilots did the same. The 83rd pilots were taking off on Runway 12, the opposing end of the Runway 30 we were using. The two squadrons' aircraft were headed directly at each other, separated laterally by only a few feet. Not even the Air Force Thunderbird Demonstration Team would ever be approved for such a risky maneuver. Now I knew we were at war!

One of the senior captains in my flight had attended the Interceptor Weapons Instructor School at Tyndall Air Force Base, Florida. He was now airborne in our flight acting as our deputy flight leader. He was an absolute stickler for regulations and details. I called him pain-in-the-butt since he discussed every tactic and maneuver like a lawyer. We clashed on most flying subjects. He was legally correct with his statements but living in a dream world, I thought. I believed a real war would never be fought using his strict approach to the military regulations.

As we flew northwest approaching the Pacific coastline, I kept looking back at San Francisco. Any moment now incoming Soviet intercontinental ballistic missiles would be exploding, and all our lives would be changed forever. I had left a wife and two-and-a-half-year-old son back home I might never see again. I turned around in the cockpit and looked back at Hamilton Air Force Base for what I thought could be my last time. Far off on the horizon the beautiful red Golden Gate Bridge was still shinning brightly in the late afternoon sun. I wondered what had happened to the Air Policeman I had been talking to. Did he take my advice?

Off to my side and slightly below me, I saw an F-101B with its landing gear still extended.

"One of our pilots must be having a gear problem," I called over the UHF radio.

I then noticed it was pain-in-the-butt, our deputy flight leader. He radioed that he couldn't get his nose landing gear to retract. I joined in close formation only about 10 feet off his left wing and quickly observed what had caused his problem. He had failed to remove the nose landing gear safety pin prior to takeoff. His nose landing gear would now remain extended for the duration of the flight.

To make things even worse, because the nuclear rockets were loaded internal to the aircraft and directly behind the nose gear, his entire radar and weapon system was automatically deactivated protecting his aircraft if his Genie rockets were launched. Here we were on the biggest potential combat mission that any of us could ever imagine in our wildest dreams, and pain-in-the-butt was already out of the battle.

He did have one possible use: Our tactics called for us to ram (fly directly into an enemy aircraft, make physical contact, and knock it down) if we were out of weapons or had a disabled weapons system.

I wondered if pain-in-the-butt would follow his cherished Air Force regulations and actually ram an enemy aircraft.

We orbited over the Pacific Ocean for an hour or so. Nothing happened except for radio communication between pain-in-the-butt and the ground radar controllers. The war now seemed to be centered on his problem. No one was looking for the enemy.

"Where the hell are the Russians?" I wanted to know.

This would have been a good time to make a caustic remark over the radio to pain-in-the-butt about the major mistake he had made. Instead I held my tongue; maybe I was developing the maturity to become a true fighter pilot.

Low fuel quantity was slowly becoming a critical factor as we continued to orbit. Around and around we turned at 35,000 feet, the city of San Francisco just a speck on the horizon. Suddenly, just like the order to scramble, we were given an order to fly north and land at a civilian field in Oregon.

As soon as I landed in Oregon, I opened an inspection plate on the underside of my plane. Sure enough, the two nuclear rockets were really on board. We were not playing games, nor was this the no-notice inspection we were all expecting.

Pilots and RIOs gathered around an old black-and-white TV set as President John F. Kennedy spoke to our nation about the crisis. We learned, with the rest of our country, about the Russian missiles being placed in Cuba. The entire Air Force was on maximum alert. Our Air Force Air Defense Command commanders wanted to disperse their fighter aircraft away from the missile threat in Cuba. Russian bombers were not flying across the Pacific Ocean to the United States...at least, not yet.

Once again we were back on ground nuke alert. Days and days went by until our wives could package clean flight suits and underwear and have them shipped to us on a military transport. Now time really dragged on and on. No flying. No parties. No gym. No war.

Slowly, the federal government resolved the Cuban Missile Crisis and our squadron commander made plans to return the F-101B aircraft and nuclear rockets back to Hamilton. As a safety precaution, he decided to have the rockets deactivated internally; place heavy-duty, nonbreakable safety wire on all cockpit weapon switches; and ferry each aircraft one at a time back to our home base so that there was no possibility of collision. The war was over; not a shot had been fired. But the crisis was the closest the United States and the Soviet Union came to an all-out nuclear exchange during the Cold War.

Pain-in-the-butt had time to remove his nose wheel safety pin before he flew home.

While I was flying the F-101B at Hamilton Air Force Base in the early 1960s, great improvements in air defense were being tested at Hughes Aircraft Company in Culver City, California.

"Get your affairs in order," Hughes test pilot Oliver E. "Ollie" Deal told his YB-58 test crew. "The YB-58 test flights will be very hazardous; you may not survive!"

When 40-year-old Deal spoke, people listened. He was the only Hughes test pilot with a Ph.D. degree. Not only was Deal highly educated, obtaining his advanced degree in physics from UCLA, he had also been a naval aviator in World War II, earning the Distinguished Flying Cross. During the Korean conflict he returned to active duty in the Marine Corps. Robert DeHaven, manager of the Hughes Aircraft Flight Test Division, hired Deal in 1955, impressed with his academic credentials. Since joining Hughes Aircraft he had flown the F-86D, F-100, F-102, and F-106 aircraft. So when Ollie Deal warned the Hughes engineers about the dangers that lay ahead, they did indeed listen.

In the early 1960s Hughes Aircraft Company acquired the sixth-built Convair YB-58 Hustler, Serial Number 55-0665, for flight test of a very unique and secret radar and missile weapon system. The B-58 was a Mach-2 Strategic Air Command bomber designed to drop a thermonuclear warhead on the Soviet Union. The Hustler was the first bomber with a delta wing and weighed 50,000 pounds empty and up to 175,000 pounds with weapons and fuel. The YB-58 was powered by four General Electric J-79 engines, which suffered reliability problems. At the time, several aircraft had been lost and their military crews killed during accidents early in the aircraft testing. Due to these accidents the B-58 fleet was restricted to subsonic flight for nearly a year and the aircraft often grounded. Ollie Deal had reason to be concerned about the safety of his crew.

During the late 1950s the Air Force drew up a specification to provide a fire control and missile system for the North American F-108 Rapier interceptor. The aircraft was to be capable of Mach 3, and its Hughes

ASG-18 pulse-Doppler radar control system, developed in parallel with the Hughes GAR-9 missile, would possess a look-down/shoot-down capability for head-on attacks against Soviet bombers if they chose to turn the Cold War into a hot one. As ground tests of the weapon system continued at Hughes, a decision was made by the Air Force in the late 1950s to cancel the program. The reason given for the cancellation was that the F-108 was simply too expensive for the Air Force, now that the primary Soviet threat to the U.S. mainland was its battery of intercontinental range ballistic missiles rather then its fleet of long-range bombers. Nevertheless, the Air Force wanted to continue the development and testing of the ASG-18 system and GAR-9 missile on a "stand alone" basis.

The missile component of the weapon system was to be much larger than the earlier Falcon missile. Designated the GAR-9, it had a design range of around 115 miles. The GAR-9 was 156 inches long, had a diameter of 18.2 inches, weighed 818 pounds, and would fly out to Mach 6. The large radar of the ASG-18 was to provide target illumination for the missile's semi-active radar guidance. The GAR-9 was powered by a solid grain propellant rocket motor and a low-yield nuclear warhead was envisioned. Since the weapon would be used for defense of the continental United States and could explode over friendly territory, later plans would be made for a non-nuclear warhead.

An Air Force crew flew the YB-58 into Culver City. Then nearly a year-long modification program was started. In order to fit the large ASG-18 radar in the plane, 7 feet had to be added to the nose of the YB-58. With a long nose the aircraft resembled the dog made famous in the Charles M. Schulz *Peanuts* cartoon, so the flight crew nicknamed the plane *Snoopy*. The ASG-18 radar had one of the largest antennas ever mounted on an aircraft up to that time. A special ventral pod was developed to carry and launch the GAR-9 missile. The new pod carried no fuel, just room for a large internal bay for the missile, its cooling system, and telemetry. When the modification was complete, an Air Force crew ferried the YB-58 to Edwards, where Hughes Aircraft test pilots could start the test program.

After several months at Edwards, management of the Flight Test Division was not pleased with the progress of the flight test in the YB-58. Between flight delays caused by aircraft groundings and Ollie Deal scaring the pants off the flight engineers, little had been accomplished. It was time to make a crew change. Another Hughes test pilot had also attended the YB-58 ground school at Convair's plant in Fort Worth, Texas, and he was brought in to get the program back on track.

Thirty-eight-year-old James D. "Jim" Eastham was born in El Dorado, Kansas. Eastham learned to fly in the Air Force and flew in the Berlin Airlift and in Korea. After graduation from college he worked for McDonnell Aircraft in St. Louis as an engineer and later as a test pilot on the Navy Banshee and Demon. In 1956 Eastham came to work for Hughes Aircraft Company and spent four years at Holloman Air Force Base, New Mexico, firing over 300 missiles from F-102 and F-106 interceptors. Jim Eastham took over duty as project pilot on the YB-58. On his first test flight, using a B-57 target flown by Hughes pilot Chris Smith, Eastham's crew collected more data than on all the total flights Ollie Deal had previously accomplished.

One day while Eastham was in his office at Edwards, flight engineer George Parsons came in and sat down. Parsons was a superb engineer who had flown in the F-89 years earlier. Parsons was concerned about the hazards Ollie Deal had talked about.

"Hogwash," said Eastham, trying to dispel the danger in Parson's mind. "Testing in the YB-58 isn't any more dangerous than what you did in the F-89."

But on the next flight with Eastham, Parsons would get some excitement. On takeoff in the YB-58 they heard a thump when one tire blew just before liftoff. Then, before they could start their acceleration to Mach 2, the YB-58 developed pitch oscillations. Eastham turned off the pitch damper and canceled the supersonic run. As they returned to Edwards they lost one of their four engines and had to make an emergency landing. As soon as Eastham stopped the YB-58 on the runway, he shut down the other three engines. He and Parsons exited the cockpit by climbing out on an escape rope. This flight had been as dangerous as Ollie Deal had predicted, but because of Eastham's skill as a pilot the two men returned safely.

On May 25, 1962, the first GAR-9 was launched from the YB-58. The Hustler was flying at 1.09 Mach and fired on a QF-80 drone at 23 miles during a head-on pass. The target was damaged and the test considered a success. Launches from the B-58 continued until February of 1964, with seven of eight successful.

While at Edwards, Eastham noticed that Hughes Aircraft management had sent their best mechanics to support the aircraft. Everyone, including the radar and missile engineers, was going "balls-out" to achieve success. Even top management of Hughes was vitally concerned about the progress of their flight test. Eastham wondered why there was so much interest in what was only an engineering experiment. With no follow-on production plan, how was the program staying alive? Through the grapevine he heard that Hughes Vice President Allen Puckett was talking to senior Air Force personnel about the success of the Hughes equipment. Rumor had it that something big was about to break.

Jim Eastham and his family were living in Lancaster, California, about 30 miles southwest of Edwards Air Force Base. One night in late spring of 1962 his doorbell rang. Louis "Lou" Schalk appeared at the door. Schalk, a graduate of the U.S. Military Academy at West Point, had attended the Air Force Test Pilot School in 1954 and had test flown the F-100, F-101, and F-104 aircraft. Five years later he joined Lockheed as a test pilot, flying the F-104 Starfighter. Unknown to Eastham at the time, Schalk had just made the first flight of the A-12, a top-secret, single-seat CIA spy plane.

"Come to work for me," asked Schalk.

"Doin' what?" answered Eastham.

"Can't tell you," said Schalk.

"I'm flying the YB-58," responded Eastham. "It doesn't get any better than that."

"What I have in mind is a hell of a lot better!" exclaimed Schalk.

Eastham went along with the challenge and met with Kelly Johnson, Lockheed's chief aircraft designer. Eastham told me Johnson put his "fat finger" in his face. Then Johnson said, "Keep doin' what you're doin'."

Johnson meant for Eastham to continue flying the YB-58 for Hughes Aircraft until Johnson could get the special clearance required for Eastham to fly in classified Area 51, the mysterious Groom Lake facility. Eastham already had a top-secret clearance, but the CIA required even more of a background check. Eastham possessed unparalleled knowledge in the field of flight testing missile and radar systems and was therefore the ideal test pilot/engineer to evaluate a brand new aircraft called the YF-12A Blackbird.

In the early 1960s, Kelly Johnson submitted a proposal to modify the A-12 airframe into a YF-12A interceptor. The Air Force agreed with his idea and contracted with Lockheed to build three YF-12As out of the A-12 production line.

The Mach-3 YF-12A was a monster of an aircraft, over twice the size of the Convair F-106, which was the Air Force's newest and most modern interceptor of the time. The Blackbird was 101 feet, 8 inches long, with a wingspan of 55 feet, 7 inches, and a height of 18 feet, 6 inches. Maximum gross weight was 124,000 pounds and the plane was powered by two Pratt & Whitney J-58 engines, each producing 31,500 pounds of thrust.

The A-12 fuselage would be extended 3 feet for a second cockpit to house a weapon system operator (WSO) and internal weapons bays that would carry three GAR-9 air-to-air missiles (later designated the AIM-47). The YF-12A differed from the A-12 in that it had a folding ventral fin under the rear fuselage to add directional stability due to a more rounded nose to enclose the ASG-18 radar. The cockpit in the YF-12A was slightly raised when compared to the A-12, so the pilot could see over the rounded nose when the aircraft was taking off and landing. It also had two ball-shaped infrared sensors below the cockpits and carried streamlined camera pods under the engine nacelles to photograph missile launches.

Eastham was now working for both Hughes Aircraft and Lockheed Aircraft without his immediate boss at Hughes being aware of this special arrangement. At times he would disappear, and management at Hughes, and his wife, had no idea where he was. Robert DeHaven, Eastham's immediate supervisor, did not know that he was working for Lockheed. DeHaven was very unhappy and threatened to terminate Eastham. It was the price Eastham would pay for being associated with a highly classified program and the opportunity to fly the world's fastest plane.

Jim Eastham immediately checked out in the Lockheed F-104, which was used as a chase plane for the A-12. Next he started to put together a pilot's flight manual for the YF-12A. Eastham made contact with all the Lockheed engineers who had designed the various systems in the Black-bird. Slowly he gathered information to write a handbook, which included system descriptions, as well as normal and emergency procedures. With all his study and knowledge, Eastham was chosen to fly the first flight on the YF-12A at Groom Lake. On August 7, 1963, Eastham successfully completed the flight with Lou Schalk flying as safety chase in an F-104.

In February 1964 President Lyndon B. Johnson announced the existence of the Blackbird program. Lou Schalk and Bill Park flew

YF-12As numbers one and two from Groom Lake to Edwards Air Force Base. This move diverted attention away from Area 51 and the CIA intelligence-gathering nature of the A-12 project.

By early 1964 I was a student in the U.S.A.F. Aerospace Research Pilot School; the name was later changed to the Test Pilot School. It was a 12-month program made up of 6 months teaching pilots how to evaluate the performance, stability, and control of aircraft. The last 6 months was space training to include a flight in a C-135 transport to perform Zero-G maneuvers, a centrifuge ride to 15Gs, and a zoom to 80,000 feet in an F-104 Starfighter. Colonel Charles E. "Chuck" Yeager was commandant of the school and leading the Air Force into the space age.

Because of winter rains, my class got behind in our flying schedule. In an attempt to catch up, weekend flights were flown. On a Saturday morning, after starting the engine of a T-33 trainer, I called the Edwards control tower operator and asked for permission to taxi. He responded with instructions to hold my position and the strangest order I had ever heard over the radio. The order was to refrain from looking at the center taxiway of the field. Unable to resist the temptation, I glanced through the windscreen and to my surprise saw the most sophisticated twin-engine streamlined plane I had ever seen. The aircraft in question was the YF-12A.

In the spring of 1964 the first airborne AIM-47 missile separation from an YF-12 was scheduled. Kelly Johnson didn't think a simple ejection mission was required. He was confident that his design was correct and opted for a launch with active propulsion. Eastham objected to that plan and voted for a separation test first. He felt it was too hazardous to launch a missile with a live motor before the ejection was filmed and studied. Eastham, as it turned out, was absolutely correct. During the separation test, the missile's nose-down position was not correct. Had the missile's rocket motor fired, the YF-12A would probably have shot itself down. Johnson and Eastham reviewed the movie of the ejection test, which had been filmed from a chase aircraft. When the missile came back up and struck the bottom of the YF-12A, Johnson let out a "wham!" and laughed. Eastham wasn't pleased with Johnson's reaction; the Blackbird could have been lost and he and his crew killed.

By the summer of 1964 Lou Schalk decided he had had enough of flight testing. He asked Kelly Johnson if he could be an aircraft salesman for Lockheed.

"Hell no!" said Johnson. "I'm the only salesman Lockheed needs."

Schalk left Lockheed to accept a position with North American Aviation, where he remained for 10 years before resigning to devote full time to the field of real estate.

After the AIM-47 missile ejection problem was solved, launches of missiles with telemetry began. The first test of the YF-12A aircraft and weapon system came on March 18, 1965. Jim Eastham and his WSO, John Archer, accelerated to Mach 2.2 at 65,000 feet and fired on a Q-2C drone flying at 40,000 feet. The mission was a complete success.

Wanting to capitalize on the success of the YF-12A test program and continue to divert attention away from spy activities in the A-12, the Air Force scheduled a world speed and altitude record attempt at Edwards. On Saturday morning, May 1, 1965, flying the number three YF-12A, Air Force pilot Colonel Robert L. "Silver Fox" Stephens and WSO Lieutenant Colonel Daniel Andre set a world speed record of 2,070 miles per hour and a sustained altitude record of 80,258 feet. On the same day pilot Major Walter F. Daniel and WSO Noel T. Warner set a new 500 km and 1,000 km closed-circuit record. The Air Force invited the press to cover the event and encouraged wide publicity. Little did the news agencies know that civilian Jim Eastham had developed the flight technique for establishing the speed record and in fact had previously flown about 100 miles per hour faster than the official record.

By early 1965 I graduated from the test pilot school and was assigned to the Fighter Branch of Flight Test Operations (Test Ops) at Edwards. Pilots in our group were flying the X-15 rocketship, YF-12, F-4C, F-104A, and the new F-111A. Some pilots had flown combat in World War II and Korea. It was an illustrious group, and I was pleased to be a junior member.

The previous December my test pilot friend Robert "Bob" Gilliland had made the first flight in the SR-71, the reconnaissance version of the Blackbird. Several times I flew as a safety chase in a T-38 or F-104 for Gilliland. Seeing the huge SR-71 up close was quite a thrill. I also flew with both Colonel Stephens and Major Daniel in a T-38 as they maintained pilot currency between their flights in the Blackbird.

Over the course of the next year and a half, six AIM-47 missiles were fired from the YF-12 at drones. Colonel Vern Henderson and Major Sam Ursini, two of my F-101B friends from Hamilton Air Force Base, were also now stationed at Edwards. They flew the last firing mission of the

YF-12A. Cruising at Mach 3.2 and 74,000 feet, their missile hit a QB-47 drone that was flying just above the terrain. The Blackbird and Hughes weapon system was a huge success.

With the completion of the missile launches, Air Force planners calculated that Air Defense Command would require 93 F-12B interceptors to provide a defensive screen that could protect the entire United States from the Soviets during the Cold War. However, in January of 1968, Secretary of Defense Robert McNamara, called "Mac the knife" by some, canceled the YF-12A program. It was reported that McNamara was against any program he had not thought of and developed. In the opinion of the Johnson Administration, more money was needed to fight the war in Vietnam and there was not a need for a high-altitude interceptor.

Kelly Johnson disagreed with the Johnson Administration when he said, "Every day a high altitude penetration of U.S. airspace occurs and we do not have an aircraft with the ability to fly up and eyeball the threat. This aircraft carries women and children…the Concord supersonic transport."

Maybe Jim Eastham said it best when he told me, "The YF-12A did everything technically it was designed to do."

"It was the best interceptor the Air Force was never allowed to buy!" he quipped.

Meanwhile at Test Ops I was learning to become a tactical fighter pilot rather than an interceptor pilot. I checked out in the new F-111A aircraft and performed wet-runway tests as a copilot. Because the plane was experiencing incompatibility problems between the engine and the airframe, General Dynamics, the manufacturer, went through a major redesign. Therefore our fighter branch was not able to accomplish either performance or stability and control testing, which was our mission. I did, however, accomplish testing on the autopilot and the General Electric air-to-ground radar.

During the late fall of 1967 I was making a grand tour of Europe. Although I was only a captain in the Air Force, an eight-passenger T-39 Sabreliner jet, usually reserved for generals, was my private mode of transportation. I was flying in glorious style.

I had recently completed several extremely dangerous test flights in the McDonnell F-4C Phantom, trying to determine why eight aircraft flown by Tactical Air Command (TAC) pilots had crashed while maneuvering at low altitude. In preparation for flying combat, F-4C aircraft were loaded with 25-pound smoke bombs and rocket pods. Pilots fired the ordnance on simulated targets in Air Force gunnery ranges. With a full load of fuel, the aircraft was being flown out of balance. As a result, the flight controls were so light that some pilots maneuvered the F-4C through airframe buffet and into a full stall, ending in loss of control and a crash. At Edwards I came up with a method to move the aircraft into balance. Test engineers and I also modified systems to alert the pilot when he was nearing a dangerous condition. After my testing experiences, I didn't think much of the F-4C as a fighter-bomber.

Senior officers in TAC were anxious to hear the results of my flight tests. I gave a detailed briefing to them at their headquarters at Langley Air Force Base in Virginia. Fearing that more F-4Cs would be lost, the commanders asked me to give more presentations to operational F-4C units all over the United States. Interest in my Phantom flight test results also came from the headquarters of the U.S. Air Force in Europe. A request came for me to brief the European headquarters staff and all the F-4C squadrons in England, Germany, and the gunnery range at Wheelus Air Base in Libya. So a T-39 executive aircraft and pilot was made available to transport me in high fashion.

During a refueling stop in Germany, I made a phone call to my boss back at Edwards. He had news for me; I had received military orders to go to war in Vietnam and would be required to start combat crew training in the Douglas A-1 Skyraider at Hurlburt Field, Florida, in a little over a month. The Skyraider was a tail-wheeled propeller aircraft that cruised at 165 knots and flew at very low altitude. It was painted in jungle camouflage markings and resembled the old P-47 Thunderbolt of World War II fame. I thought there must have been a mistake in those military orders—I was a jet pilot!

CHAPTER 3

Combat and the F-15A Eagle Fly-Off

Hughes only dated the most beautiful girls in the world. Once an unattractive female at his studio tried to get his attention while he was working by wiggling around and displaying her beautiful chassis. Finally, after she had hoisted her skirt as high as the law would allow, he blurted out without looking up from the script, "You're wasting your time, Miss. My weakness is airplanes."

Favorite story of David Swit, Publisher, Product Safety Letter

By May 1968, I had started to fly combat missions from Udorn Royal Air Force Base in Thailand. My job during the Vietnam War was to fly the A-1 Skyraider and rescue Air Force and Navy aircrew shot down trying to stop the flow of materiel and troops on the Ho Chi Minh Trail in North Vietnam and Laos. Pilots in my squadron also flew strike missions in the northern part of Laos in support of General Van Pao and his friendly ground troops. During my year of combat I flew 188 missions in support of the war. In the dry season (from October to May) the Pathet Lao communists would gain ground, but during the wet season (April to September) the friendly Laotians, with the help of our airpower, would regain the lost land. It was a static war, with the front line remaining about the same over the period of my year.

The war looked like a loser to me. Without our government's will to bomb Hanoi and the shipyards of Haiphong to prevent Russian equipment from flowing down the Ho Chi Minh Trail once and for all, this terrible skirmish that was causing the loss of a generation of pilots and planes was hopelessly doomed. I expected the overall results of the war to be a stalemate. It seemed like it would end with a negotiated settlement between North Vietnam and the United States, just like it did in the Korean War. I expected North Vietnam would take all land north of the 17th Parallel, and South Vietnam all land to the south.

Finally I came to the conclusion that I might have more opportunities as a civilian test pilot than I would if I remained in the Air Force. I had always considered myself more of an aviator than a military officer. I had joined the Air Force to fly and fight—I had done that, and now it was time to move on. So I resigned my commission in the Air Force to become effective upon completion of my year of combat in April 1969.

When I returned home to my wife and two young sons in California, there was an invitation for an interview from the chief test pilot of Hughes Aircraft Company. The company, located in Los Angeles, had an opening for a job as an experimental test pilot.

Howard Hughes was the original test pilot for his company. Back in the early 1930s Hughes formed a company in Glendale, California, to build a single-engine, retractable landing gear aircraft named the *Racer*. Hughes would go on to set a world speed record of 352 miles per hour and transcontinental speed record from Burbank, California, to Newark, New Jersey, in the *Racer*. In 1938 he set a round-the-world record of 3 days and 19 hours flying a modified Lockheed L-14 Super Electra.

In 1940 Howard Hughes purchased around 1,200 acres of land in Culver City, California, just 3 miles north of Mines Airfield, the present site of Los Angeles International Airport. He bought the agricultural land to build a factory to be used for construction of war materiel in anticipation of the United States' entry into World War II. During the war he designed and later built a twin-engine reconnaissance aircraft, designated the XF-11, on the site. He also built parts of the wooden H-4 Hercules Flying Boat, later called the *Spruce Goose* by the media, a name Hughes detested. For his own personal use, Hughes prepared an 8,000-foot grass strip on land next to his plant in which to operate his personal aircraft. Employees of the Flight Test Division maintained his aircraft and provided air transportation for him.

Several of the aircrew hired to fly with him in the Lockheed L-14 round-the-world flight stayed with his company. They formed the Radio Department of the Hughes Tool Company during the war. Receiving a couple of small contracts to build electrical equipment, the department grew in number of employees and capacity. After the war the department expanded into electronic weapons and would later become a multi-million-dollar enterprise as the Hughes Aircraft Company.

In May 1948 Hughes hired retired Air Corps General Harold L. George to be Vice President and General Manager. Fifty-five-year-old George was born in Somerville, Massachusetts, and learned to fly in World War I. After the war he specialized in aerial bombardment and later assumed command of the first squadron to be equipped with the B-17 Flying Fortress. During World War II he became commander of the Air Transport Command.

When George took over in the spring of 1948 the company was hardly a promising venture, having lost $700,000 on sales of $1.9 million the year before. The only serious work in progress was several low-priority research projects funded by the Air Force and led by two talented young scientists, Simon Ramo and Dean Wooldridge. Former classmates at Caltech, Ramo and Wooldridge had pursued independent careers in electronics research—Ramo at General Electric and Wooldridge at Bell Telephone Laboratories—before teaming up at Hughes Aircraft.

The Air Force turned to them to undertake several studies aimed at developing an electronic weapons control system for military interceptors, a combination radar set and computer that could find and destroy enemy planes day or night in any weather. The contracts amounted to only several thousand dollars. Nevertheless, they provided the basis for Hughes Aircraft's great leap forward.

By plunging into military electronics—a field largely ignored by the large and established defense contractors because of its low priority within the Defense Department and the modest funds set aside for research contracts—Hughes Aircraft got the jump on everyone else. Late in 1948, when the military suddenly became alarmed over the lack of an all-weather interceptor, the only promising electronic weapons system was the one being developed by Ramo and Wooldridge. The Air Force awarded an $8 million contract to Hughes Aircraft to build and install 200 units in the Lockheed F-94. Building rapidly on this success, Ramo and Wooldridge captured a contract to develop the Air Force's Falcon air-to-air missile. The 6-foot, 110-pound missile was to be part of a complete electronic weapons package that could find an enemy plane, automatically launch a missile, and then assure through radar impulses that the missile was guided to hit its target.

Following the success of the F-94 interceptor with its E-1 electronic weapons control system, Hughes Aircraft engineers were awarded an even more spectacular contract. They won a design competition for the MG-10 electronic weapon and navigational control system to be used in the Convair F-102 supersonic interceptor, a revolutionary plane intended to be the backbone of U.S. air defense strategy for years to come.

If the interceptor business made Hughes Aircraft healthy, the Korean War made it prosperous. When the war broke out in June 1950, Hughes Aircraft, by virtue of its pioneering work with electronic weapons systems, became the sole source for the entire Air Force interceptor program, and within two years the Hughes workforce had grown to 15,000. The once-modest research laboratory in Culver City, California, now bulged with more than 1,000 scientists. By 1952, Hughes Aircraft Company had employees in divisions focused on armaments and aeronautics; radar, missiles, advanced electronics, electron tubes, and field service engineering; with growing facilities for electronics and missile manufacturing. Revenues of the company, still a division of the Hughes Tool Company, surpassed those of the Oil Tool Division, the original company. And the rise in earnings was remarkable—from $400,000 in 1949 to $5.3 million in 1953.

The year 1953 marked a turning point. With the Korean War under way, Hughes Aircraft was the sole supplier of key Air Force systems. Ramo and Wooldridge expressed difficulty in working with Howard Hughes and quit to establish their own company. The Secretary of the Air Force issued an ultimatum: Reorganize Hughes Aircraft so Howard Hughes was not active in management, or lose its contracts. In response, Hughes incorporated the electronics portion of Hughes Tool Company under the name of Hughes Aircraft Company in December 1953. Its sole shareholder would be the newly formed Howard Hughes Medical Institute (HHMI), created to fund innovative medical research.

Lawrence A. "Pat" Hyland became Hughes Aircraft Company's Vice President and General Manager in late 1954. Hyland had a distinguished engineering record working in government laboratories between World War I and World War II, and later had risen to manage Bendix Corporation. He held scores of patents, but his primary charge then was returning Hughes Aircraft to a smooth business path. He took firm control of the company and reorganized it into three operating groups. The largest—Airborne Systems Group—comprised the Tucson, Arizona, missile manufacturing and El

Segundo, California, electronics manufacturing facilities. The strategy worked. Within five years Hughes Aircraft was the 11th largest defense contractor with over 20,000 employees.

The following year brought one of Hughes Aircraft Company's most renowned achievements, when the first working laser was activated at the Hughes Research Laboratories in Malibu, California. In 1963 Hughes Aircraft generated global headlines again with the launch of Syncom, the first geosynchronous orbital satellite.

By the late 1960s the company had grown to become the world's largest defense electronics company. At that time Howard Hughes had not been seen on the flight line for about 10 years. He was living on the ninth floor of the Desert Inn Casino in Las Vegas, Nevada, away from the public eye and in total seclusion. His Hughes Aircraft Company had grown to about 45,000 employees with sales now over $1 billion.

Late one afternoon in early May 1969, Charles A. "Al" McDaniel Jr. and Chris M. Smith, two Hughes test pilots and veterans of World War II, met me at the Los Angeles airport. Forty-nine-year-old McDaniel was born in Los Angeles and joined the Army Air Corps in 1942. He went through military flying school and started his testing career at San Bernardino Air Material Command. While there he evaluated modifications on the P-38 and service tests on the C-67 and BT-13B. After World War II he joined the National Guard at Van Nuys, California. In 1950 McDaniel joined Hughes Aircraft Company and tested early radar and missiles. He also flew Howard Hughes around the country.

Smith, age forty-seven, was from New York state and joined the Army Air Corps in 1943. Like McDaniel, he also attended flying school and then was an instructor in both basic and advanced cadet training. During World War II Smith was stationed in North Africa and Italy, flying the P-51. In late 1951 he also joined Hughes Aircraft and tested radar and missiles.

During that evening and next day in May 1969 I was introduced to the pilot staff made up of McDaniel, Smith, and two younger pilots that had recently been hired. I also received a tour of the Flight Test Division building and met the manager, Robert M. DeHaven. DeHaven was a World War II ace with 14 Japanese kills to his credit, flying the P-40 and P-38 and had been with the company for 21 years.

The Flight Test Division had contracts with both the Navy and Air Force and specialized in testing advanced airborne radar and long-range, air-to-air, and air-to-ground missiles. Next I visited the flight line and hangar to see the present fleet of military test aircraft. Two Grumman F-111Bs and a Douglas A3D were being used on Navy programs. A McDonnell F-4C and a Lockheed T-33 were being used on Air Force programs.

For Air Force programs, flight testing was accomplished over the Air Force Flight Test Center at Edwards Air Force Base, where I had flown as a test pilot prior to service in Vietnam. For Navy programs, flight testing was performed over the Pacific Ocean in the Pacific Missile Test Center, west of Naval Air Station Point Mugu.

Since I had flown the Air Force F-111A, the General Dynamics version of the plane, if I accepted employment I would fly the Grumman F-111B, testing the Hughes AWG-9 system and AIM-54 missile. Even though I was a former Air Force pilot, not a Navy pilot, my experience flying the F-111A would shorten the time required to become qualified to fly the F-111B. On the Air Force side of the ledger, Hughes Aircraft was testing an improvement to the Westinghouse radar installed in an F-4C. Hughes engineers had modified the radar so that it could detect and lock on to low-flying aircraft. I would be scheduled to fly the F-4C because I had tested the aircraft at Edwards only two years earlier.

The company was also in the early stages of working with the Air Force to develop the AGM-65 Maverick air-to-ground missile. An F-4D and F-4E would be loaned (official title was bailed) to Hughes for early development of the missile at Culver City. Later the development team would be moved to Holloman Air Force Base, New Mexico, where missiles could be launched in the White Sands Test Range.

But the most intriguing program on the horizon was the upcoming F-15 Eagle test program. Hughes Aircraft Company was in competition with Westinghouse Electric to build air-to-air radar for the Air Force's newest air-superiority fighter. Because of my recent combat experience and knowledge of Air Force test procedures, I was offered the opportunity to be the Hughes project pilot.

By mid-May of 1969, I accepted the offer to fly for Hughes Aircraft. In the next two months I bought a house with a swimming pool in Woodland Hills, located in the west end of the San Fernando Valley.

I moved my family to the new house and donated my military uniforms to Goodwill. I bought several business suits and a German Volkswagen "Bug" to commute 26 miles on the freeways of Los Angeles. I left the A-1 Skyraider propeller aircraft and war in Vietnam behind me and looked forward to becoming a civilian jet test pilot. It was the start of a new career.

The McDonnell Douglas F-15 Eagle is still one of the world's most formidable interceptor fighters. Although largely designed in the late 1960s and early 1970s, it remains the primary air-superiority fighter serving with the Air Force, and it will remain so until the end of the first decade of the 21st century. In service with the U.S., Japanese, Israeli, and Saudi Arabian air forces, the Eagle has scored an impressive number of air-to-air kills, perhaps approaching 100, with no known air-to-air losses.

The F-15 Eagle had its origin in the mid-1960s, when the U.S. aircraft industry was invited to study Air Force requirements for an advanced tactical fighter that would replace the McDonnell F-4 Phantom as the primary fighter aircraft in service with the U.S. Air Force. Such an aircraft needed to be capable of establishing air superiority against any projected threats in the post-1975 period.

Throughout much of the Vietnam War, the primary fighter in service with the Air Force was the F-4 Phantom, a large, twin-engine, two-seat aircraft. The Phantom had originally been designed in the 1950s to Navy requirements for a two-seat multirole fighter interceptor, intended to destroy enemy aircraft at beyond-visual-range (BVR), using a fire-control radar to detect threats and direct Sparrow semi-active radar-guided missiles against them. No cannon was installed because the wisdom of the late 1950s was that the internal gun was an obsolete holdover from the pre-missile age.

During the war North Vietnamese pilots were equipped with MiG-17s and MiG-21s, small, relatively unsophisticated aircraft designed for close-in dogfighting. In the years 1965–1968, the kill ratio in air battles against the North Vietnamese Air Force was only 1.5:1, much poorer results than the 8:1 ratio obtained in Korea by the F-86 Sabre Jet against the MiG-15. One of the reasons for this rather poor record was the restrictive Rules of Engagement over North Vietnam. These rules required a close-in positive identification of the enemy before missiles could be fired, negating the advantage of the Phantom's radar and long-range Sparrow missiles.

In a close-in knife fight against MiG-17s and MiG-21s, the Phantom was considerably less maneuverable and was at a relative disadvantage in this type of encounter. Another reason was that most Navy and Air Force pilots had little flight training in air-to-air combat, and they did not know how to exploit the strengths of their own aircraft against the weaknesses of the enemy's planes. As a result of the experience over North Vietnam, the Air Force concluded that they had better pay more attention to the possibility of close-in air-to-air fighting in the design of their future fighter aircraft, and not simply rely on long-range missiles to ensure victory.

In July 1967, the Soviet Union unveiled a new generation of combat aircraft at an airfield at Domodedovo near Moscow. Among these was the Mikoyan MiG-25 Foxbat, a twin-engine, twin-tailed fighter capable of a Mach 2.8 performance. The Foxbat was the Soviet's equivalent of our YF-12 Blackbird. The capabilities of the Foxbat sufficiently alarmed Air Force officials that work on the Fighter-Experimental (FX) was assigned a high priority. The Air Force now had a clear idea of what they wanted. The emphasis was to be on an air-to-air fighter rather than on ground-attack aircraft. The conception of the FX as being a 60,000-pound variable-geometry multirole aircraft was abandoned in favor of a 40,000-pound fixed-wing dedicated air-to-air fighter.

During 1968 the aircraft industry vacillated between considering a large, twin-engine aircraft with advanced radar with long-range missiles, and a small, MiG-21-sized, single-engine aircraft with minimal electronics systems but with an emphasis on maximum performance and high maneuverability. However, guided by the Air Force's unhappy experience with the F-104A Starfighter, a single-engine, high-performance aircraft with minimal electronics systems that the Air Force had found that it did not need, the twin-engine, advanced electronics option seemed more attractive.

The Air Force specified that the new fighter should have low wing loading with buffet-free performance at Mach 0.9, a high thrust-to-weight ratio, long-range pulse-Doppler radar with look-down/shoot-down capability, a ferry range sufficient to permit deployment to Europe without midair refueling, and a maximum speed of Mach 2.5. A twin-engine aircraft was preferred because of its higher reliability. The Air Force wanted a single-pilot aircraft; they felt the development of more advanced computer systems, radar, and electronics made a radar intercept officer unnecessary. The aircraft was to be superior in air combat to any present or projected Soviet fighters, both in close-in visual and in BVR air-to-air combat.

McDonnell Douglas proposed a large, single-seat aircraft with twin-fins and a pair of turbofan engines. On December 23, 1969, the McDonnell Douglas proposal was named the winner of the contract and the aircraft was designated the F-15. The company was authorized to proceed with the design and development phase, to build and test 20 full-scale development aircraft, and to manufacture 107 single-seat F-15s and two-seat TF-15s.

McDonnell had a tough time coming up with a name for the plane. James McDonnell, the founder of the company, had a penchant for the supernatural, calling his aircraft Banshee, Demon, Voodoo, and Phantom. When birds were considered, McDonnell listened but was only willing to consider certain ones that had an aggressive spirit. The name Eagle was suggested and people opened their dictionaries to study the bird. They found it to be a fowl that hunted in bad weather. Considering the radar capabilities that were being built into the aircraft and the desire to make it an all-weather plane, the name stuck.

The F-15 was ordered "off the drawing board"; there was to be no prototype and no competitive fly-off against other manufacturers' aircraft. This raised quite a controversy, with many in the press fearing another cost-overrun debacle. However, in response to criticism from Congress over cost overruns and lengthy delays that had occurred in both the C-5A Galaxy and F-111 programs, the Air Force introduced a set of demonstration milestones that the contractor had to meet before the next stage of funding could be issued. For the F-15 project, the milestones began with a fly-off competition between Hughes Aircraft and Westinghouse Electric for their radar, with a selection of a radar contractor by September 1970.

In the spring of 1968 Hughes and Westinghouse were each funded by the Air Force to build two engineering models of their proposed radar and compete for the radar contract. Both contractors would be loaned a twin-engine Douglas B-66 Destroyer aircraft to modify and in which to fly test missions out of their home plant. The plan called for about six months of testing at their facility and then a two-month fly-off competition conducted by McDonnell Douglas at Lambert Field in St. Louis, Missouri.

In mid-1969 an Air Force crew delivered a WB-66D, Serial Number 55-0391, to our airport at Culver City. The B-66 model we received was the final production version of the Destroyer. It was a weather-reconnaissance aircraft, carrying a crew of five. Three seats ejected upward, and two in the aft crew compartment ejected downward. Thirty-six of the weather-reconnaissance models were built in the Tulsa, Oklahoma, plant. Our plane was the second one manufactured; it was 13 years old.

After many years as a fighter-interceptor pilot, fighter test pilot, and combat attack pilot, Hughes Aircraft Company wanted me to become a bomber pilot. And to add insult to injury, I would become a bomber pilot on a fighter program. Hughes's flight-test management thought I would be the best person to represent the company, as the project pilot, because I had an Air Force testing background and had just returned from a combat tour in Vietnam. Richard Gralow, a former Navy test pilot, was my backup. Thirty-six-year-old Gralow had just joined the company a couple of months earlier. He was a graduate of the Navy test pilot school and had tested the AJ3 Vigilante. Gralow was also flying one of our Douglas A-3 bombers in flight tests at Hughes.

Our B-66 would undergo a six-month modification to accept the engineering model of the Hughes proposed F-15 radar. Our radar was an X-band (8–12 GHz) coherent, pulsed-Doppler system with look-down/shoot-down capability and was given the designation APG-63. It was designed with a maximum detection range of greater than 100 miles.

This radar had several different air-to-air modes, employing various pulse repetition frequencies (PRF), depending on the type of search that was being carried out. The long-range search mode used high and medium PRFs, which offered a compromise between the best air-to-air tracking of tail-on and nose-on targets, with the pilot selecting search ranges of between 10 and 200 miles. Medium PRF was the heart of our radar. Dave Kramer, a brilliant young Hughes electronics engineer, who had graduated from Case Western Reserve in Cleveland, Ohio, and gotten his masters at Princeton, had developed this unique waveform.

A velocity search mode using high PRF was intended exclusively for head-on, high-closure-rate targets. For short-range search modes, medium PRF was used. This was generally chosen for engaging short-range maneuvering targets, in situations where the Sidewinder missile or the gun was to be used. The radar also incorporated a nonpulse-Doppler mode using low PRF, which was useful only when "looking up," since it offered no clutter rejection.

Data from the APG-63 radar was processed digitally and fed to a central computer. This information was displayed to the pilot on either the vertical situation display (VSD) or on the head-up display (HUD). The VSD was a cathode-ray tube mounted on the upper left side of the instrument panel. That display was used mainly in the long-range phase of an engagement, displaying a cleaned-up radar picture and presenting target data such as altitude and ground speed. At shorter range and in combat, the HUD was used, which combined target information with vital aircraft performance figures like airspeed, altitude, and Gs.

Hughes Aircraft engineers built two complete sets of our radar. One system was installed in the B-66 and the other placed in a roof house, where it could be tested in a static environment. The electronic boxes could be swapped back and forth from the plane to the roof house. Also in-flight instrumentation was added to the B-66 so that our flight tests could be recorded and played back after landing.

The B-66 was originally envisioned as a replacement for the World War II–era piston-engine Douglas B-26 Invader in the tactical bombing role for both day and night operations. The Air Force thought that the B-66 would be more or less an off-the-shelf copy of the Navy A-3. The A-3 was a 70,000-pound class bomber designed to carry a 10,000-pound nuclear bomb about 1,000 miles and then return to a carrier.

The first step in the Air Force design was the elimination of the features of the Navy A-3 that were specific to its carrier-based role, such as folding wings, arresting gear, and catapult harnesses. Then the Air Force found a problem in the Navy design. The A-3 did not have ejection seats; the crew escaped the aircraft via a chute in the rear of the cockpit. Because the B-66 would be flying at low altitudes and at fairly high speeds, ejection seats for the crew members had to be provided. The use of ejection seats in turn required that the cockpit canopy be extensively revised to accommodate the escape hatches needed for the ejecting crew. In addition, the cockpit itself had to be extensively revised, with the pilot sitting forward and the navigator and gunner/reconnaissance system operator seated immediately aft of him.

Two engines were mounted in pods attached to under-wing pylons. Douglas preferred the Pratt & Whitney J-57 turbojet, which was used on the A-3, but this engine was already committed to other combat aircraft projects. These projects had a higher priority than the B-66, and the Air

Force didn't think the manufacturer could produce enough engines to meet the demand. This left the Allison J-71, which was built by a division of the General Motors Corporation. It offered a thrust of only 9,750 pounds but was deemed to be an acceptable alternative.

In the fall of 1969 I was sent to Shaw Air Force Base, North Carolina, to check out in the B-66 and become a bomber pilot. The four-week class was made up of eight Air Force pilots and me. After completion of the course the other pilots were sent to Vietnam. I was pleased I had already finished a combat tour and was now a civilian.

My flight instructor told me the B-66 was overweight and underpowered. Therefore, the takeoff roll was long and the airplane just limped off the runway. Additionally, the aircraft had poor asymmetric power characteristics. This meant that if an engine failed on takeoff, the pilot would have a very difficult time keeping the wings level and the nose pointed directly down the runway. The good engine would produce so much thrust that it would cause the B-66 to yaw into the dead engine. Then because of dihedral effect, the B-66 would roll over and crash.

Air Force instructors at Shaw came up with a novel procedure to prevent this possible catastrophe. They told me that if an engine came apart it typically failed about 45 to 60 seconds after the pilot selected full power. Unfortunately, this was about the time the B-66 was preparing to lift off, the worst possible time for a failure. The instructors recommended a B-66 Destroyer pilot lock the brakes after lining up on the runway, push the throttles up to full power, and run the engines for a full minute before releasing the brakes. If the engine failed before a minute passed, no harm would be done by simply sitting static at the end of the runway. And if the engines ran at full power for one minute, instructors reasoned that the engines would probably run for another minute, allowing a safe takeoff. It was a simple solution to a potentially deadly problem. Because the Hughes runway at Culver City was short and narrow by military standards (8,200 feet long by 85 feet wide), I decided to adopt their recommendation.

Even in the 1940s, when Howard Hughes purchased the land in Culver City, California, his grass-and-dirt strip was marginal from a piloting point of view. In the winter, rain caused the ramp to be flooded, making it difficult to repair aircraft. An Edison Electric power line crossed perpendicular to the main runway, requiring pilots make a decision to land before the obstruction or beyond it. Hughes leased fields surrounding the strip to a farmer so that the land would be taxed as agricultural rather than commercial to save money. The crops attracted varmints, which in turn attracted birds. Bird strikes were commonplace.

In the early 1950s, when jet aircraft were needed for avionic testing, the Air Force required that Hughes pave the field with asphalt. However, the surrounding land continued to be farmed with lima beans, attracting many varieties of birds.

When I arrived in the spring of 1969, Hughes Aircraft Company was operating military aircraft from the field on a waiver from the U.S. government. The government had many concerns about the ability to conduct safe flights at the airfield. Several of the engineering buildings were located too close to the runway, providing a hazard if a plane lost brakes on landing. Loyola University sat on top of the Westchester bluff that paralleled the runway. Noise complaints from school officials were commonplace every time a jet fighter took off in afterburner. The runway was only 85 feet wide—much less than the 150-foot Air Force standard. In addition, there were neither taxiways nor overruns.

To somewhat ease these operational problems, the Navy installed an optical "meat ball" (an approach aid used on aircraft carriers) next to the approach end of the runway. The Air Force loaned a chain link arresting gear to Hughes Aircraft and it was installed at the far end of Runway 23. The gear could be used for aircraft equipped with a tail hook for either aborted takeoffs or brake failure on landing.

Another severe hazard was that the Hughes airfield flight operations extended into both the Los Angeles International and Santa Monica airport air traffic areas. Hence, the chance of a mid-air collision with a civilian aircraft was very high. So the Air Force and Navy restricted operation of their military aircraft to day visual flight rules (VFR) operation. Only instrument flight rules (IFR) departures were allowed, and no night operation was permitted.

As soon as I returned to California I checked on the progress of the modification of the B-66. The racks, electrical wiring, and radar controls were just about finished. However, I was shocked when I found how much our plane weighed. Engineers calculated the weight of the plane at 49,000 pounds with zero fuel. If we added a full fuel load of 27,000 pounds, the takeoff roll would take practically three-quarters the length of the Culver City runway on a hot day. If the fuel load were greatly reduced, for a shorter takeoff roll, then our data-collecting time in the Edwards range would be less than an hour—not enough time to get the critically needed data. It was a real dilemma.

Finally, I selected a mid-range fuel load that would give us an hour and a half flight time but still marginal takeoff performance. As a result, we would be operating in a "dead man's zone." This zone would be a 10- to 15-knot interval during takeoff, centered around 125 knots, where if one engine failed I could not stop on the remaining runway. Likewise, I couldn't continue takeoff on the good engine and ever get airborne.

Further complicating this dangerous scenario was the fact that we had three upward ejection seats and two downward seats. All five crew members could not safely eject until the B-66 was at least 1,000 feet above the ground. Dick Belmont and Mike Haggerty were the two Hughes engineers who would occupy the downward seats in the aft crew compartment. One would operate the radar data processor and the other the data signal processor.

Belmont and Haggerty, both very talented engineers, didn't like the idea of sitting in downward seats while the three of us in the front seat sat in upward seats. In a humorous vein I told them I could put the B-66 in a 90-degree bank and we would all have the equal probability of survival.

In 1947 Howard Hughes had a similar decision to make when he made the first flight in the H-4 Hercules Flying Boat, nicknamed the *Spruce Goose* by the press. The completion of the flying boat was several years behind schedule and World War II was over. Senator Ralph Owen Brewster of Maine, a member of an investigating committee set up to determine the cause of uncompleted World War II contracts, was very critical of Hughes.

To satisfy his critics, Hughes taxied the giant plane in the Long Beach Channel on a Sunday morning with 31 passengers and crew members on board. Despite not having approval from the Civil Aeronautics Administration to fly the seaplane and the fact that he had few life vests and no rafts, Hughes was faced with a moment of truth. He would face his critics in the Senate and give them an answer: His great ship would either fly as he promised, or it wouldn't. If it didn't, he would be subjected to further criticism. Taking the biggest risk of his 20-year flying career, Hughes took off and climbed to about 25 feet above the water during his 30-second flight. Hughes had beaten the odds.

After much consideration I decided my odds favored an aborted takeoff in the B-66 as the best choice if I lost an engine. Even though we would roll off the end of the runway, crash through the boundary fence, and cross Lincoln Boulevard, it was a better choice than a low-level ejection.

A Mexican-style restaurant located on Jefferson Boulevard was about a mile directly beyond the end of our runway. I calculated that if I aborted a takeoff, while in the dead man's zone, we would come to rest in their parking lot. To make light of the danger, like Jim Eastham had done in the YB-58 years earlier, I told my crew we could crawl out of the burning plane, walk into the restaurant, and order a meal, assuming reservations were not required. I discussed this hazardous situation with the crew members each time we briefed for a mission.

When we arrived at the aircraft, one would always ask me, "Did you make a reservation?" I knew what he meant. Though the question was asked in a humorous vein, I knew we were all deadly serious about the potential loss of an engine at a critical time.

By early January 1970 the engineering model of our radar was installed in the B-66 and we were scheduled for a shakedown flight. On a cold winter morning Bob Mintz, our Hughes radar operator, and I took off from Culver City and flew to the Edwards Air Force Base range. While in Edwards's air space I completed a checkout of all the aircraft systems. My UHF radio failed and low clouds and drizzle covered the airfield back at Culver City, so I landed at Edwards. There the plane could be repaired; I didn't want to attempt a landing in the busy Los Angeles basin without being able to communicate on the radio. The gutsy and reckless Howard Hughes would probably have flown back to Culver City and landed, radio or no radio. But times had changed since he last flew at Culver City about 15 years earlier. Now the Air Force was watching us like a hawk and it was not a time to break Federal Aviation Administration (FAA) regulations. With an air abort on the first flight, our F-15 radar program got off to a poor start. Little did I realize then how bad the flight testing would be over the next eight months.

On the fifth flight of the test program I hit a bird on takeoff from Culver City. Flocks of birds were very common around the runway. Some were seagulls because of the nearness to the ocean. Some were smaller birds that fed on the bean fields, which were north and west of the asphalt runway. I saw a large black bird directly in front of me just as I rotated the B-66 for takeoff, but I couldn't keep from hitting it. All engine instruments appeared normal, so we continued the mission.

The bird struck the left side of the black radome. Fortunately the radome was undamaged, but the bird left a full-body imprint in grayish dust. It appeared the bird was hit sideways, with one wing down and the other up. The dust pattern looked exactly like the Eagle logo McDonnell had published in their F-15A advertisements. We took the incident to be a good omen. Our B-66 was not damaged, and we had already killed an airborne target with the radar. Maybe the bird strike was a sign from above that we would win the fly-off and radar contract.

Dick Gralow and I alternated flights in the B-66. By the end of April we had flown a total of 10 flights with very limited success. Something seemed to go wrong with either the radar hardware or software on every mission.

In the spring of 1970 even McDonnell was concerned about our lack of progress. They transferred Bob Hedin, a young McDonnell engineer with experience in radar, to monitor our progress and report back to St. Louis. Not only would Hedin attend our flight briefings and debriefings, he would occasionally fly in the aft crew compartment.

Finally, in early May we were able to make a flight where the radar detected a Lockheed T-33 target on each of three passes using high PRF and three passes using medium PRF. The T-33 was considered a small target, measuring about 2 square meters in radar cross-section. But even though we got detections, the radar would still not track an airborne target. Some of the flight crew wondered if we would even attend the fly-off scheduled to start July 1st. The radar performance was so poor we would be an embarrassment to our company. It would simply be a waste of time and money to attempt to compete against Westinghouse.

Wayne Wight and Ed Rosenmayer, two McDonnell radar operators, came to Culver City in early June. They were part of the McDonnell and Air Force team that would evaluate both the Hughes and the Westinghouse radar during the fly-off in St. Louis. They planned to fly a couple of flights in our B-66 and get familiar with the operation of the radar. Wight and Rosenmayer flew a few missions in the B-66, but our radar was still not working very well. Even our aircraft was starting to act up. An extended strut gave the anti-skid brake system a failure signal, so we had no brakes on one landing. The mechanics changed the seals on the struts to solve the problem.

Because the F-15A was a single-seat aircraft, a pilot would have to operate the radar by himself. Both the F-4 Phantom and F-101B Voodoo carried a radar operator who was dedicated to the task of making target detection and lock on. Therefore, it was important to get pilot feedback on the status of our radar. McDonnell Aircraft selected Robert "RB" Robinson to be their radar project pilot. Robinson was a retired Lieutenant Colonel from the U.S. Marine Corps. On November 22, 1961, he had set a world speed record of 1,606.505 miles per hour in an F-4H-1 Phantom over Edwards Air Force Base. Robinson was scheduled to get an orientation flight in our B-66 the end of June. I was very concerned about a world-class pilot flying our radar because we really didn't have much to show someone of his stature. As it turned out, his flight in the B-66 was also a bust.

By this time we were less than a month from the start of the fly-off. In communication with the McDonnell fly-off managers, we found that the HUD lock on mode of our radar would be evaluated. Because the B-66 was a bomber, Douglas Aircraft did not install a HUD in the plane. Nevertheless, I told Hughes management I could construct a HUD that would work for the upcoming competition. I took a coat hanger and twisted it to make a rectangle, which duplicated the size of the HUD. I taped the wire to the glare shield. Then I took another coat hanger and made an eyepiece, which got attached to the overhead light panel and was suspended directly in front of my face. This arrangement allowed me to visually maneuver the B-66 in such a manner as to place the T-33 target in any of the four corners of the HUD field of view. On my command, the Hughes radar operator could activate the auto-acquisition mode.

The two McDonnell radar operators and one pilot were impressed with my homemade HUD. We hoped this novel approach to a problem balanced the negative impression they experienced because of our poor radar performance.

On Saturday morning, the 27th of June, I took off for St. Louis. The second radar system black boxes, weighing about 700 pounds, were loaded in the aft crew compartment. Because of this added weight and the marginal takeoff characteristics of the B-66 operating from the Culver City runway, I could not make it to Lambert Field nonstop. I planned a short first leg to Altus Air Force Base, Oklahoma. Bob Mintz fired up the radar and looked for targets of opportunity as we cruised at 33,000 feet over Arizona and New Mexico. Because we were flying the same jet routes as commercial airliners, he tried to get some extra test points. The system was still performing poorly.

The drag chute failed when I landed at Altus Air Force Base. As a result, I used more braking than was normally needed at Culver City. After shutting the engines down, we refueled and prepared for the second leg. Military fire department personnel placed fans on both main landing gear brakes to accelerate cooling because they were hot from heavy use. Hughes management personnel were already at the McDonnell plant in St. Louis and anxious to know our expected arrival time. Finally, the brakes cooled down and we departed for St. Louis about an hour behind schedule.

The drag chute failed again upon landing at Lambert Field. I applied heavier brakes this time to clear the runway for commercial airliners landing behind me, and then taxied to the McDonnell ramp. A large group of Hughes employees and a scattering of McDonnell and Air Force people greeted us when we shut down. Our program manager planned a group photo, so we lined up in front of the B-66. Meanwhile, smoke started to emit from the right wheel brake. Eventually we had to contact the McDonnell fire department, and they rushed over with red lights flashing and sirens roaring. It was an inglorious arrival for the start of the fly-off competition.

The McDonnell Douglas Company had a personality of its own. Engineers who believed in putting everything on paper dominated it: procedures, memos, and rules. It was a company that gave great attention to detail, with a penchant for penny-pinching. During the two summer months of the fly-off their engineers dressed in short-sleeve white shirts with a tie. Most had short hair and carried a notebook under one arm. They were straight-laced and very conservative. Our Hughes crew was made up of more laid back engineers who wore open-neck, colorful shirts and had a great sense of humor. For the most part, they were brilliant in their specialty and were world class in designing and building radars. Some had long hair and a free spirit. All felt we had a superior product and if we could just get the radar to work as designed, we would be in the winner's circle.

McDonnell engineers had written an extensive flight-test plan for both Hughes and Westinghouse to follow. Over the course of two months, each contractor had the opportunity to fly two missions per day over 43 weekdays. All missions were flown over Missouri farmland using the T-33 as a small target. Each contractor was required to submit engineering data on 84 valid data passes. The passes varied from head-on, tail-on, look-down, look-up, and HUD auto-acquisition lock ons. It was an ambitious plan.

The bad luck we experienced in Culver City continued in St. Louis. Our first competition mission was another airborne abort due to loss of coolant in the radar. Likewise, our second mission was a bust because of excessive moisture around the transmitter unit.

The heat and humidity in July and August were about as uncomfortable as could be imagined. It took a toll on both our equipment and our people. A year earlier I had spent 12 months in Vietnam flying 188 combat missions and was somewhat acclimatized to the extreme heat and humidity of Southeast Asia, so I fared well. Many of the Hughes employees were not so fortunate.

There was also extreme pressure on all the Hughes employees to get their job done fast and not make mistakes. It was vitally important to fly every test flight as precisely as possible and get good radar data. I was very familiar with flying under pressure after my experience of rescuing downed pilots in war; I felt I knew how to pace myself.

Just when the radar seemed to be working, the B-66 aircraft developed problems. A week into the fly-off an inspector found a crack in a horizontal stabilizer hinge. We lost several days until a hinge was removed from a pickled B-66 in the Boneyard at Davis Monthan Air Force Base, Arizona, and was shipped to us. Then the left engine fuel pump started leaking. It was replaced by a unit obtained by flying one of the T-33 target aircraft to Tulsa, Oklahoma, to pick it up. Within a couple of days, the right engine alternator stopped functioning and was replaced by a serviceable unit expedited from Shaw Air Force Base, North Carolina. All these aircraft failures prevented us from flying many data missions.

Just as we started getting good radar data again, another problem developed. On the first of August we made a flight and air-aborted because the radar operator did not have control of the antenna. During post-flight maintenance inspection a mechanic found two turbine wheel blades damaged on the left engine. The B-66 was grounded and we ordered a replacement engine from the Air Force. Our mechanics worked around the clock to install another engine, and two days later I flew a functional check flight to evaluate the engine. When I returned to land at Lambert Field, I made a straight-in approach from the southeast. Coming in to land in that direction, I flew directly over a cemetery. It seemed symbolic of our failed efforts.

Even the radar set in the roof house experienced its own set of unique problems. Jim Easton, the Hughes Flight Test Radar Manager, received a B.S. in physics from Lafayette College in Easton, Pennsylvania. Easton prepared a demonstration for Dr. John L. McLucas, the Secretary of the Air Force. As McLucas was coming up the stairs to view our radar, a 3,000-psi hydraulic line powering the antenna burst, spraying coolant fluid on some visitors. McLucas was distracted by several Hughes engineers as the hydraulic line was taped and wrapped with a mountain of rags. It seemed that everything that could go wrong, did go wrong.

Probably the most amusing incident occurred to the technician who serviced our instrumentation system. Forty-two-year-old Eugene "Oops" Martin was responsible for loading tapes in a data recorder in the aft crew compartment of our plane. After a mission he retrieved the tapes and installed new ones.

Both Hughes and Westinghouse aircraft looked alike; they were standard aircraft taken out of the Air Force inventory and most of our modifications were internal to the plane. The planes were camouflaged in brown and green and had a white serial number painted on the tail. Our number was 391, and Westinghouse had 390. The only real difference that could be seen from a distance was the radome. Hughes used a black radome from an F-111B and Westinghouse used a white one from an F-4.

Oops Martin walked out to the flight line to exchange tapes and, by mistake, got into the Westinghouse aircraft. He didn't realize he was in the wrong aircraft until he saw unfamiliar instrumentation equipment. Fortunately, he got out of the plane without being discovered by Westinghouse, McDonnell, or Air Force personnel. Entry into the opponent's aircraft would have been a major violation of the rules.

Martin drew a humorous cartoon showing a Westinghouse employee kicking him off the plane. As it turned out, "Oops" was an appropriate name for Martin. He was an accomplished artist and drew about 20 cartoons depicting our never-ending difficulties or "oops." When the fly-off was completed, program management published Martin's cartoons in a booklet and distributed a copy to every Hughes employee who had worked in the competition.

Martin's drawings were not the first cartoons Hughes test pilots remembered seeing in the Flight Test Division. Another incident many years earlier had also caused them to laugh. Usually all kinds of cartoons, pinups, and aircraft photos can be found in military pilots' ready rooms. In the late 1950s one photo made its way onto those walls frequently. Variations of this photo ranged from the actual photograph to artists' conceptions to cartoonists' rollicking portrayals of a character that lived a rather obscure existence but who would leap into fame unknown to himself—all because of a simple wish he wanted fulfilled.

This gentleman's physical features, particularly his Popeye face, generated endless captions, allowing a chuckle to creep into the serious side of someone carrying out his military mission. The picture of the old gentleman, who almost faded into obscurity, hung in flight operations rooms and military offices, particularly those of fighter squadrons. The wrinkling skin, the craggy beard, the toothless gums, the willow-wisp body, and the piercing eyes were the epitome of a cartoonist's dream of a perfect subject. The sheer aura of the old gentleman's features was enough to generate instant laughter; he didn't have to speak.

Few people knew who the true character was. Hughes Aircraft Company test pilot Chris Smith was one who did. Smith told me about the incident that would propel the old man into fame, because he was standing there when it happened.

The person in the photograph was Fred "Freddy" Goslin, a janitor for Hughes Aircraft in the 1950s. In his earlier years he was a song-and-dance man who worked the old vaudeville circuit in upstate New York. Evidently nothing materialized from this venture, and after World War II Goslin moved westward, ending up in Los Angeles. Once again he tried to penetrate the entertainment world—again unsuccessfully. Somehow his meandering brought him to Hughes Aircraft, where he was hired as a janitor. By then he was in his sixties and had lost all of his teeth. The etched lines of his face were already deeply ingrained; later they would become his trademark.

Goslin's duties required him to keep the Hughes pilots' locker and personal equipment rooms clean and orderly. He would often be heard humming a ditty or two as he swept the floor. Goslin often expressed a keen desire to wear one of the jet pilots' helmets, fitted with visor, oxygen mask, and radio headset.

His wish wasn't fulfilled until his 65th birthday. Company policy made retirement mandatory when an employee reached the age of 65. On the day Goslin was to retire in 1953, he went to the pilots' locker room for his final good-bye. It seemed a shame that this old man with his near-pathetic features, who had punctuated the late afternoon hours with his quiet rendering of the songs that at one time must have been part of his vaudeville act, had to go.

Hughes Aircraft photographer Nick Allen was in the locker room. Allen told me he talked with Goslin for a while, just shooting the breeze. Somehow the conversation turned to the pilots' helmets hanging on the wall.

"I'll bet you'd look good in one of those," Allen said.

At that, and just for laughs, Goslin took a helmet off the hook and put it on.

"The helmet was much too big for him," remarked Allen. "Goslin was funny enough, but then he took out his teeth and started hamming it up."

This act caused an instant reaction: sidesplitting, hilarious laughter. Scraggy beard, piercing eyes that reflected a slight tinge of a smile, puckered lips curling over his toothless mouth radiating a "gummy" expression—all created a natural unrehearsed portrait that simply had to be recorded. Allen got his camera and took 12 quick photos, portraits that would later soar around the world. Goslin reveled in the hilarity; at last his act had caught on. After that, Goslin made his final good-bye, turned, and strutted off into retirement with a gleam in his eyes. For a few minutes, he had visualized himself as a jet pilot.

A couple of years later word drifted back to Hughes Aircraft that Goslin had become a singing waiter at one of the lesser-known Hollywood bistros. He then faded into oblivion, reportedly dying in his seventies without being aware of his fame.

Allen selected the photo he liked best and named it "the Old Geezer." The man's countenance generated captions from pilots who saw some humor in their duties. "Sleep tonight! Your Air Force is awake!" was the caption Allen first put on it. Before long "Testing is fun," and "Ready, willing, and able," or "Sleep well tonight, your borders are well guarded!" were but a few of the other captions that brought an instant guffaw as one gazed at the aging face.

Copies of the photograph were found in the Flight Test Division building and the Customer Relations lobby. More copies were distributed to visiting military personnel. Soon other doctored versions made their way back to Hughes Aircraft. Company test pilots traveled to military installations worldwide and often came in contact with hilarious variations of the photo—all of this humor because a lone, obscure janitor, who had once tried to sing and dance his way to fame, had momentarily been a make-believe jet pilot and a sharp photographer was present to record it for posterity.

After the engine change on the B-66, the aircraft was ready to fly. In each of the next five days we ground-aborted with more radar problems. As we approached mid-August, with just two weeks left in the fly-off, we completed a mission with our first medium PRF radar track. Finally we were on the road to recovery. Over half of our data passes were completed in the last 14 days of the fly-off. I flew 13 missions in the last week of competition, 3 in one day. We came on like gangbusters at the end. At a final summary, we satisfactorily presented to McDonnell and the Air Force about 80 percent of the data passes they requested. On the rare occasion when the aircraft was in commission, the weather was cooperating, and the radar was performing as designed, we had a beautiful system that met all the Air Force design criteria.

On September 2nd I flew the B-66 back to California, with a refueling stop at McConnell Air Force Base, Kansas. When I arrived over Culver City fog covered the runway, so I landed at Point Mugu. Coming back home proved to be just as difficult as the flight to St. Louis and the competition there. The fly-off was officially over; all we could do was to wait for the announcement of which company had received the contract award. I returned to flying the F-111B, evaluating the AWG-9 system and AIM-54A missile.

Late in September McDonnell announced that Hughes Aircraft was awarded a $105 million contract. A top McDonnell executive told Hughes Senior Vice President Johnny Black he was very impressed with the Hughes employees who worked on the fly-off competition. The executive witnessed first-hand the multiple problems we encountered and the difficulties we fought to overcome them. He remarked to Black that the Hughes team didn't give up. In his estimation, problems would come up in the future and if the same team worked as hard as we did in the fly-off, McDonnell and Hughes would both succeed.

As soon as I heard Hughes Aircraft had won the contract, I walked down the ramp to shake hands with all the B-66 aircraft mechanics. They were the unsung heroes of the competition. Then I walked over to the F-15 engineering offices to find Bob Hedin, the McDonnell technical representative. He was not in, so I obtained a roll of toilet paper and strung it over his fluorescent flights. A photographer took my picture sitting behind his desk to preserve the historic moment.

Dick Gralow and I continued to fly the B-66 into 1971, when he left the company for another job. After he left, Hughes test pilot Chuck Blake went through the Air Force training at Shaw Air Force Base and backed me up. Thirty-eight-year-old Blake had flown the reconnaissance version of the F-101 Voodoo in Vietnam. He had worked for Hughes Aircraft for about three years. Blake and I then exchanged flights until I flew our final flight in late November 1971. That year we flew 96 flights, and by then the radar was performing great. It was definitely a winner.

The Air Force master plan was to transfer the B-66 to McDonnell in St. Louis so they could install and test pre-production F-15 avionics in the aircraft. A McDonnell pilot was sent to California for that purpose. I watched as the aircraft lumbered down our Hughes runway, heading west on takeoff and piloted by another test pilot. As the plane gained altitude over the Pacific Ocean, the pilot of the Destroyer started a gentle turn to the east, heading toward St. Louis. It was sad to see the old bird depart, and I said what I thought was my last farewell.

Years later I heard from Don Roudenbush, the F-15 Marketing Manager, that Hughes Aircraft Company ended up with over $9.5 billion in sales on the initial F-15 radar order and follow-on contacts for 1,500 F-15 aircraft purchased by the U.S. Air Force, Israel, Japan, and Saudi Arabia. The F-15 radar was very profitable for Hughes Aircraft, and the Air Force received an aircraft and weapon system that would be in their inventory for at least 35 years.

Five years after the F-15 radar fly-off I ferried a Navy A3D to Davis Monthan Air Force Base for it to be placed in the Boneyard for permanent storage. After signing the transfer of ownership papers, I was given a tour of the storage site. To my surprise, I saw our old B-66 sitting in the desert. Again I was face-to-face with this once very familiar companion. She had not aged gracefully. The brown and green camouflage paint was faded due to the intense Arizona sunshine. One tire was flat, causing the plane to lean on its side so much that one wing tip practically touched the sandy ground. Many of her inspection panels were loose or completely missing. The years had been hard on her.

The flight crew entrance hatch on the bottom of the fuselage was left open. Using stairs attached to this hatch, my aircrew and I had climbed into the cockpit nearly 200 times. Slowly I ascended the stairs once again, remembering how well we had cared for this cherished friend and how important it had been to all of us at Hughes Aircraft in the past.

The flight instruments in the cockpit were still intact, all complete and easily readable. I did find one toggle switch on the instrumentation panel left in the ON position. With all the radar and flight instrumentation black boxes removed, the switch had no function anymore. However, I did gently turn the switch OFF; it seemed the proper thing to do.

I noticed a large black checkmark painted on the side of the fuselage. It had not been on the B-66 when I last flew it. A civilian employee of the Boneyard explained to me that the checkmark indicated that the plane was scheduled to be cut up and salvaged. Its days were now definitely numbered. Again I said a sad farewell to this old friend and walked away. I did not look back.

Author George J. Marrett and childhood friend Bob Preston are ready to fly in World War II (1943). (Courtesy of George R. Marrett.)

Howard Hughes's world-speed-record *Racer* parked at Hughes airfield in Culver City, California (1945). (Courtesy of Hughes Aircraft Company.)

Hughes Aircraft Company facilities and 8,200-ft airfield in Culver City, California, as seen from the air (1972). (Courtesy of Hughes Aircraft Company.)

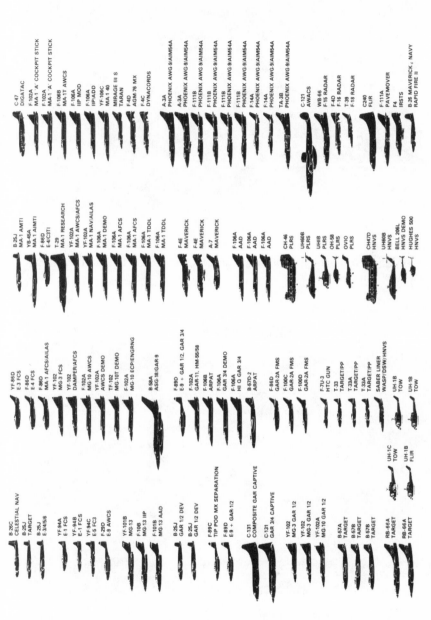

Test and support aircraft that were flown for Hughes Aircraft Company test programs from 1948 to 1987. (Courtesy of Hughes Aircraft Company.)

Test pilot James D. Eastham standing in front of Lockheed YF-12 Blackbird (1962). (Courtesy of James D. Eastham.)

Eleven mechanics standing in front of seven flight test aircraft parked on Hughes airfield ramp (1956). FRONT ROW: Harold Graf, Ken Brown, Joe Bergesch, and Lou Tyler. BACK ROW: Ed Mauss, Charley Bocksy, Pete Mauss, Ed Hudson, Pat Mullin, E. Epstein, and Homer Johnson. AIRCRAFT FROM FRONT TO BACK: F-102A, F-100, F-86D, F-102A, YF-94, TF-102, and F-89 (Courtesy of Hughes Aircraft Company.)

Test pilot George J. Marrett standing in front of
Grumman F-111B SeaPig (1969). (Courtesy of
Hughes Aircraft Company.)

Test pilots Chris M. Smith, Charles A. McDaniel, and George J. Marrett standing in
front of Grumman F-111B aircraft. Test pilot William Davies sitting in cockpit
(1969). (Courtesy of Hughes Aircraft Company.)

Westinghouse Electric (390) and Hughes Aircraft (391) WB-66D aircraft parked on ramp at McDonnell Aircraft, Saint Louis, Missouri, during F-15 radar fly-off (1970). (Courtesy of Hughes Aircraft Company.)

WHICH WAY DID HE GO GEORGE, WHICH WAY DID HE GO

Cartoon of George J. Marrett during F-15 radar fly-off drawn by Eugene R. Martin (1970). (Courtesy of Eugene R. Martin.)

Photo of Fred Goslin, known as the "the Old Geezer" (1953). (Courtesy of Nick Allen.)

Cartoon drawn from "the Old Geezer" photo (1960). (Courtesy of Nick Allen.)

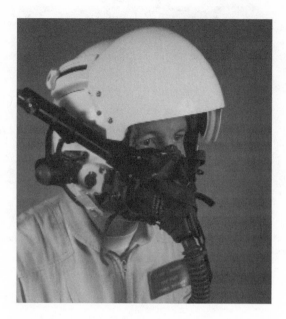

George J. Marrett wearing Helmet-Mounted-Display redesigned as a bifocular unit (1973). (Courtesy of Hughes Aircraft Company.)

Hughes engineer Otis Dodd and pilot George J. Marrett standing in front of McDonnell F-4D used on the AGM-65 Maverick missile test program (1970). (Courtesy of Hughes Aircraft Company.)

AIM-54A Phoenix missile launched by George J. Marrett from F-14A Tomcat at Foxbat target (1972). (Courtesy of Hughes Aircraft Company.)

Douglas TA-3B used to test AWG-9 radar and AIM-54A Phoenix missile (1974). (Courtesy of Hughes Aircraft Company.)

Hughes Aircraft Company managers Barney E. Turner (Manager of F-16 Radar Program), John H. Richardson (Senior Vice President), Fred P. Adler (Electro-Optical Group President), George J. Marrett (test pilot) and Meade A. Livesay (Radar Systems Group President) standing in front of F-4D Phantom test aircraft and agreeing to win the F-16 Radar Program (1975). (Courtesy of Hughes Aircraft Company.)

Cartoon of George J. Marrett as the "K-Mart Cowboy" drawn by Eugene R. Martin (1976). (Courtesy of Eugene R. Martin.)

George J. Marrett deplaning from T-39D Sabreliner test aircraft, with four-foot extended nose, during F-18 Hornet Radar Program (1978). (Courtesy of Hughes Aircraft Company.)

Crew Chief Bruce Bromme standing in front of A3D *Dumbo* aircraft used to test early Stealth bomber radar (1973). (Courtesy of Hughes Aircraft Company.)

Carl Garrett (NFO) and George Marrett (pilot) during a walk around inspection of number four built F-14A. (Courtesy of Hughes Aircraft Company.)

CHAPTER 4

The Impossible Journey

As Howard Hughes often remarked, "Money isn't everything, but what it isn't, it can buy."

While flying the B-66 on the F-15A radar program in early 1970, I had also successfully flight tested a unique air-to-air radar in an Air Force F-4C Phantom jet flying from the Culver City airport. For eight months, Hughes Aircraft engineers had made great progress in modifying and improving a production Westinghouse Electric radar that was standard equipment on the F-4C fighter. The Westinghouse radar had difficulty "looking down"; it could not distinguish an airborne target from the ground because of interference called ground clutter. A program called DynaCords was funded by the Air Force to determine if Hughes Aircraft engineers could correct this problem. Since we had successfully completed the tests and the program was finished, it was time to transfer the aircraft and radar to the Air Force at Eglin Air Force Base, Florida, for them to evaluate our progress.

At the same time, Hughes maintained a facility at Holloman Air Force Base, 6 miles west of Alamagordo, New Mexico. There we were testing our new tactical, air-to-surface guided missile, called the AGM-65A Maverick, at the Air Force Missile Development Center on an F-4D, F-4E, and A-7D. The Maverick missile was designed as a TV-guided launch-and-leave tank and armor killer.

Chuck Blake was the Hughes test pilot permanently assigned to our Holloman facility. In the summer of 1970 Blake was ill, so a back-up pilot was needed to conduct several Maverick missile test flights starting the following Monday.

William "Bill" Jessup and I were the back-up pilots. Jessup, age 36 from Reno, Nevada, was a former U.S. Marine. He had attended the Navy test pilot school and flown the OV-10 Bronco in combat in Vietnam prior to coming to work for Hughes. Both of us had been test pilots with Hughes for about a year.

I volunteered for the cross-country mission. Since we needed to ferry the DynaCords F-4C to Florida and also fly the F-4D Maverick missions at Holloman, schedulers came up with an idea to kill two birds with one stone.

If I departed Culver City early on Sunday morning, I could fly our DynaCords F-4C to Eglin with a refueling stop at Holloman. Then I would fly in a commercial Delta jet from Eglin to Atlanta, change to another Delta jet, and fly to Dallas. In Dallas, I would transfer to American Airlines for a flight to El Paso and then take a chartered Cessna airplane to Alamagordo, New Mexico.

This plan would require me to fly across the entire United States in the F-4C and return about two-thirds of the distance by commercial flight—all in one day. It was a very ambitious plan, something Howard Hughes might try. To complete this impossible journey with success, I would have only a few minutes on the ground at each stop. Any hiccup and I would miss my next connection.

Thirty-four years earlier Howard Hughes had purchased a Northrop Gamma single-engine aircraft from Jacqueline "Jackie" Cochran to attempt his impossible journey, a transcontinental nonstop record flight from the West to the East Coast. Hughes departed at 12:15 p.m. Pacific Standard Time from Union Air Terminal at Burbank, California, on January 13, 1936. Taking advantage of strong tailwinds prevalent in the winter months over the southern United States, he flew at 15,000 feet altitude. Shortly after takeoff, however, his radio antenna broke off, denying him communication with people on the ground.

North of Wichita, Kansas, Hughes ran into turbulent weather. The Gamma bounced around so strongly that the needle of its compass fell off. Without a radio or compass, Hughes was forced to fly by sight only and follow road maps spread out on his knees. He landed in darkness at the airport in Newark, New Jersey, 9 hours, 27 minutes, and 10 seconds after leaving California. For his transcontinental speed record in the Gamma, Hughes was awarded the Harmon International Trophy as the outstanding aviator of 1936. In a ceremony held in the Oval Office at the White House, President Franklin D. Roosevelt presented Hughes with a 30-inch-high trophy. The award was named for pioneer aviator Clifford B. Harmon. The only other Americans to have won the award were Charles Lindbergh and Wiley Post.

To give me the best shot at completing my transcontinental air race, a Hughes Aircraft maintenance crew would "turnaround" (inspect and refuel) my F-4C at Holloman and another Hughes crew would be waiting for me at Eglin. Most of our aircraft mechanics were former military types, well trained and dependable. As civilians, they would be paid double time for working on Sunday. I hoped it would be an easy trip, but it did seem like an impossible journey.

For our DynaCords F-4C test missions in California, a Hughes flight-test engineer sat in the rear cockpit and operated the radar and instrumentation. Since testing would not be accomplished on the ferry flight, I flew the aircraft solo.

Many flight restrictions were in effect operating out of our private Hughes Airport at Culver City. Because the field was located in a residential area between the Santa Monica Airport and Los Angeles International, our flights were restricted to day operation, sunrise to sunset. The airfield did not have any instrument landing aids; all flying had to be conducted using visual flight rules. If I took off at the stroke of sunrise, 5:45 a.m. Pacific Daylight Time, and had an average 50-knot tailwind across the United States, I would arrive at Eglin with about a half-hour to spare before my Delta jet was scheduled to depart—definitely an impossible journey in our post-9/11 terrorist era.

At 4 a.m. on a Sunday morning, I left my house in the San Fernando Valley and drove eastbound on the Ventura Freeway. It was the lightest traffic I had encountered in my year of commuting on the freeways of Los Angeles. I drove several miles on the San Diego Freeway without seeing another vehicle either in front of or behind me.

When I arrived, my F-4C was sitting on the ramp, fueled and ready to go. External electrical power was applied, and I preflighted the back seat of the Phantom. I aligned the inertial navigation system and inserted all my waypoints to Holloman. I closed and locked the rear canopy and started the twin General Electric J-79 engines. Then I taxied to Runway 23.

At the first glimpse of the sun's rays on the horizon, I applied afterburner on both engines and thundered down the Culver City runway. The students attending Loyola University on the bluff overlooking our runway were off for the weekend. Unfortunately, I was creating an early Sunday morning wake-up call for the thousands of homes surrounding the university and condominiums in Marina del Rey.

Cruising at 37,000 feet, I traveled effortlessly over Southern California, Arizona, and into New Mexico. Right on schedule, I started an enroute descent from 80 miles west of Holloman Air Force Base. Visibility was unlimited over the high New Mexico desert.

I landed the Phantom and spotted our Hughes mechanics waiting for me in front of Base Operations. Johnny Miller, the senior crew chief on the Maverick F-4D, was among them. Miller had been a mechanic in the Air Force before joining Hughes and was very conscientious. He was 10 years younger than I, with a round face; he was slightly bald and a good 50 pounds overweight. But looks could deceive: Miller was a sharp mechanic and I could count on him for a quick turnaround.

I left my parachute harness, leg restraints, oxygen mask, and helmet in the cockpit and ran over to Base Operations to file a flight plan for the next leg. Returning to the F-4C, Miller said he had found a slight hydraulic leak in the right landing gear and had tightened a fitting. The Phantom was refueled and ready to go.

Both engines were started and I asked for taxi instructions from Holloman tower. While taxiing, I reconnected my parachute harness and leg restraints, attached the oxygen fitting, and glanced at the instrument panel. No one had been in the cockpit since I had left it 10 minutes earlier; all the switches and controls should be as I had left them.

It was Sunday morning. The Air Force units were taking the day off, so I had the airfield to myself. With no other aircraft in the traffic pattern and calm winds, the tower operator gave me clearance to take off even before I reached the runway. Feeling confident that my cross-country flight was ahead of schedule, I rolled onto the runway and lit the afterburners.

The leg to Florida was about twice the distance of my flight from California. The weather forecast for Eglin called for multiple thunderstorms and low clouds with rain. It was fortunate that I was slightly ahead of schedule; I might need the extra time on this long leg.

As the Phantom broke ground, I raised the gear handle and started an immediate turn to the East. All three landing gear—two main and the nose —stayed down. The three green landing gear lights, which confirmed the gear was still down, were now staring back at me. I brought the throttles out of afterburner, increased my climb angle to reduce speed, and lowered the gear handle. So far I had not felt any movement of the landing gear, either up or down. Slowing down to 220 knots, I recycled the gear handle up and down several times. The hydraulic pressure looked normal. Why wouldn't the gear retract? A gear malfunction would be a major problem—the trip to Eglin was looking doubtful.

As I re-entered the Holloman traffic pattern, I asked the tower operator to look at my landing gear and confirm its position.

"Hughes 817," he reported, "your maintenance crew requests you check the landing gear circuit breaker."

On the right cockpit subpanel were five circuit breakers, important for the pilot to have control of in flight. Most of the Phantom circuit breakers, about 150 in number, were in the rear cockpit, beyond my reach. I found that the landing gear circuit breaker was OUT; it definitely had been IN on my flight to California. I pushed the circuit breaker in, retracted the gear handle, and heard an immediate *thump-thump*. The three green gear lights were extinguished.

"Gear is up," I relayed to the tower, adding power again and starting to climb to higher altitude.

As a safety precaution, Miller had pulled out the landing gear circuit breaker before working on the hydraulic leak in the wheel well. In the rush to get the F-4C refueled, he had forgotten to push it back in. I had missed it also as I quickly scanned the subpanel while taxiing to the runway.

"That was a close call," I thought.

Because of the circuit breaker I had lost precious minutes and wasted nearly a thousand pounds of fuel. Whatever time I had saved on the flight from California and quick turnaround was now gone.

Flying over Texas and the Gulf States, I looked at the clock, looked at my fuel quantity, and looked at the clock again. I would lose three hours due to the difference in time zones, making my commercial flight connection at Eglin extremely close.

Huge cloud buildups were in my path over southern Alabama and western Florida. Air traffic control radar vectored me around the biggest thunderstorms, and I flew in and out of the clouds. Finally I was cleared to start my descent and instructed to expect a ground control approach. This approach required more time and fuel; it was going to be a cliffhanger. The Phantom bounced around in the turbulence, and the sky became dark as I entered thicker clouds. Rain pelted the F-4C in the descent until I broke out of the clouds a couple hundred feet above the runway. I landed the Phantom in the rain, deployed the drag chute, and braked to taxi speed.

Clearing the runway, I saw a Delta Airlines jet parked in front of the civilian terminal, now only 15 minutes before my scheduled departure time. Fortunately the Hughes maintenance crew was in place. Bruce Bromme, our crew chief, used hand signals to guide me to a parking spot in front of Base Operations. Bromme was one of our senior mechanics and had been employed by Hughes Aircraft for over 20 years. He was a superb mechanic—absolutely the right guy for the job. During the late 1940s he owned an Indianapolis 500 race car that competed in the annual Memorial Day event. Now he raced sprint cars at Ascot Park Raceway in Gardena, California.

In the back seat of the F-4C I had stored all the military records concerning this Phantom. About 12 manuals documenting the complete history of this six-year-old aircraft formed a stack over a foot high. Bromme transported me in a rented pickup truck to the Air Force Maintenance Office so that I could deliver the manuals and sign all the forms transferring the F-4C back to the military. Time was counting down.

We sped across the ramp to the commercial terminal and stopped next to the parked Delta jet. Through the rain I rushed into the terminal, still wearing my military flight suit with G-suit attached. I carried my parachute harness, oxygen mask, flight helmet, and a small hang-up bag.

The terminal was crowded, with a long line of people in front of the single Delta Airline agent. If time were available, I hoped to change out of my wet flying gear and into civilian attire. The line was moving slowly, so I stepped forward to inquire if I had time to change clothes.

The Delta ticket agent was a young man in his late twenties; he was tall, thin, and looked like Jim Nabors, an actor who played the Marine Corps private from Mayberry on the television program *Gomer Pyle, U.S.M.C.* As a matter of fact, he even sounded like Nabors, with his southern Alabama accent and hillbilly talk. He had a show-your-teeth kind of smile and was working slowly—very, very slowly. I broke in front of the line and held up my ticket so he could see it.

"Do I have time to change clothes and still make my flight?" I asked.

"Golly gee," he responded. "You shore do."

For a passenger terminal, the men's room was very small, having just one toilet, one urinal, and one lavatory. I removed my harness and G-suit, watching the Delta jet through an open window. Other passengers used the restroom as I struggled to find enough room to change. In the heat and humidity, my clothes were wet as soon as I put them on. Then I realized the pilot on the Delta jet had started the engines. I raced to slip on my shoes and saw the jet taxi away. After all I had gone through in the previous 10 hours, I was going to miss my connection.

I charged up to the ticket counter and demanded to know why I had been given bad flight information.

"Surprise, surprise!" said the Gomer Pyle–looking ticket agent. "Your flight hasn't even arrived yet; all our planes are running two hours late because of the weather." For me, it turned out to be an impossible journey.

Since my flight out of Eglin was delayed for several hours, I missed all the other connections that had been reserved for me that day. I got as far as Dallas that Sunday evening and spent the night in a motel. Finally I arrived Monday mid-morning at Holloman Air Force Base, New Mexico.

The base dated back to World War II, when it was called Alamagordo Army Airfield. During the war, the field had served as the training ground for 20 different bomber squadrons flying B-17s, B-24s, and B-29s. After the war the future of the base was uncertain. However, in 1947 a new era began when Air Material Command announced the airfield would be its primary site for the test and development of unmanned aircraft and guided missiles. For the next 25 years the site, which became known as the Holloman Air Development Center and later the Air Force Missile Development Center, was the location from which missiles were launched, including the Hughes air-to-air Falcon.

Before I could fly the afternoon Maverick test mission, I was required to fly a range checkout flight with one of the Air Force test pilots, Lieutenant

Colonel Robert L. "Bob" Jondahl. Jondahl had graduated from the Air Force Test Pilot School in 1962, two years before I attended. He had a round face, was nearly bald, and stood with a crouch, leaning over at such an angle that he looked like he was going to tip over. This was the first time I had met Jondahl, but I did know several of his classmates from test pilot school.

My mission would take me into a part of the White Sands test area that I had never flown before. Air Force regulations required that I fly in a T-33 accompanied by a military test pilot and prove that I understood the range boundaries and regulations concerning flight test with Air Force missiles. At my home field in Culver City, Hughes Aircraft leased a T-33 from the government to be used as a small cross-section radar target. I was qualified as a pilot to fly our T-33 and had over 2,000 flight hours in the plane. The Holloman T-33 was very similar to our aircraft; Jondahl suggested I fly from the front cockpit.

It took just a few minutes of flying time to familiarize myself with the weapon range I would fly over for my afternoon mission in the F-4D. Jondahl pointed out several features as we flew, but he lacked enthusiasm and was anxious to return to Holloman.

After we landed, we debriefed our flight in the Hughes Facility Manager's office. Jondahl appeared tired and fatigued. He spoke slowly and seemed to have a hard time finding the right words to describe what he wanted to say.

Colonel Jondahl left the Hughes office and returned to the flight line. I remarked to our Facility Manager's secretary that maybe Jondahl was not feeling well. She called me over to her desk and quietly whispered in my ear that she and Bob had just started dating. They had been out together the night before—and were up into the early-morning hours.

Robert Jondahl and our secretary were married a few months later. Both had been married before and had several children from previous marriages. The following summer, Jondahl rented a Cessna light aircraft for a family vacation. Several of their children were to fly with them, including our secretary's son, who was attending the Air Force Academy in Colorado. With all of their family aboard, Jondahl attempted a heavy-weight takeoff from an airfield in Colorado Springs on a day with the temperature above 100 degrees Fahrenheit. A heavyweight takeoff can be dangerous enough, but on a hot day from a field with an elevation over 6,000 feet, it was suicidal. Jondahl barely got the plane airborne but never did accelerate to climb speed. He crashed, and all on board perished.

When I got airborne at Holloman, flying the F-4D with a Maverick missile on the left wing, memories of my combat experiences the previous year in Vietnam came back to me. Acting as Forward Air Controller, flying the A-1 Skyraider, I had spotted several large caves occupied by North Vietnamese soldiers located near the town of Sam Neue in the northeast corner of Laos. The caves had an entrance about the size of a three-car garage, and were reported to house enemy tanks and military vehicles. To this day some people feel that American pilots who are listed as missing in action are still being held in those caves.

My Skyraider did not have a weapon that I could use to destroy a cave. Standard 250- and 500-pound gravity bombs came in at too steep of a dive angle to enter the cave opening. Rockets and guns needed to be launched very near the target if they were to be effective. Enemy guns were too intense to consider a close-in pass.

Some Air Force F-4C squadrons carried a weapon that looked like a natural to use against a cave: the Martin Marietta AGM-12A Bullpup. The Bullpup was developed in the 1950s as an air-to-surface, radio-guided missile. Its maximum range was about 4 miles—the closest weapon the Air Force had at the time that could be considered to have a "standoff" capability. After launch, the pilot would steer the missile with a hand control located on the left side of the cockpit. By moving the hand control left and right, up and down, signals would be transmitted to the missile fins. The missile had to be guided by the pilot all the way to impact.

It was very difficult to employ the missile in combat because the pilot had to steer the missile, fly his own aircraft, and watch for enemy ground fire, all at the same time. I never saw a Bullpup come close to a cave entrance; most F-4 pilots were lucky to hit the mountain around the cave.

The Hughes Aircraft AGM-65A Maverick was a great improvement over the Bullpup, because it had a television camera in its nose and could lock onto the target. The image from the camera was projected on a 4-inch-square, green TV monitor mounted on the pilot's instrument panel. The pilot could control the movement of the TV camera up and down and left and right with a hand control located next to the throttles. When a target was observed in the center of the crosshairs, the pilot depressed a button on the handle and locked the missile to the target. At this point, the Maverick was fired and continued to track the target by itself until impact. On launch the pilot would lose the target image on the TV monitor, but he was now free to maneuver his aircraft to avoid ground fire.

The AGM-65A was designed around a 1 foot in diameter, 8 foot long, scaled-up Falcon airframe. It was propelled by a Thiokol solid rocket motor and steered by a set of small cruciform tail fins. Internal to the missile was a 125-pound high-explosive shaped charge. Maximum aerodynamic range was about 12 nautical miles; realistic range was nearer to 8 miles. The missile was fired from an under-wing station by using either a LAU-88 launcher (which could hold three Mavericks) or LAU-117 launcher (which held one Maverick).

For my test mission, tanks were arranged in single file on the White Sands test range. From an altitude of 12,000 feet, I could see them through the Phantom gun sight located above the instrument panel. We had developed a general rule of thumb: "If you could see a target with your naked eye, you were within range to attack it." My targets were radio controlled and moving at a predetermined speed over the white sand. I locked the inert missile to the lead target and flew over the tank at 50 feet while the on-board instrumentation recorded the data. Later we would replay the videotape and analyze the missile results.

The viewing angle of the AGM-65A missile TV camera was three degrees. This was an extremely narrow field of view. To appreciate how narrow that was, it can be compared with the view a pilot can normally see with his own eye scan. Without moving his head, a pilot can scan about 120 degrees horizontally. Flying a Maverick with a three-degree field of view was like looking through a soda straw. It was difficult to find a target unless the pilot lined it up very near the aiming pipper on the gun sight. Widely spaced targets could not be seen unless they were in a line coming directly toward or away from you.

Ten years earlier, when I was stationed at Moody Air Force Base, Georgia, I had flown the F-86L Sabre Dog equipped with the Hughes Aircraft E-4 radar Fire Control System. When vectored by ground controllers, I flew practice intercepts on simulated enemy aircraft. It was important to maintain strict control of the Sabre's heading, altitude, and airspeed by reference to the flight instruments. Then I would quickly glance at the radar display, looking for a radar return, or "blip," on the monitor. If I concentrated too long on the radar display, the F-86L would wander off altitude and heading. This could be quite dangerous; a pilot could lose control of the aircraft and crash. It took a fast crosscheck of all flight instruments and the radar to complete a successful pass.

Remembering my F-86L radar passes, I stressed in my written report of the Maverick test flight that the TV display not be used to initially find enemy targets. I recommended a pilot keep his head up, visually acquire the target through the windscreen, then—and only then—put his head down to watch the television monitor. At that time he could lock on the target and fire a missile. I emphasized in my report that pilots must not fly around with their head down, trying to find targets on their television monitor. That method would be a good way to hit another aircraft or lose control of the aircraft and crash into the ground. In effect, it was an easy way to kill oneself.

During a two-year test program run by Hughes at Holloman Air Force Base, about 30 Maverick missiles were fired. The missile was so effective that only one or two were scored as a miss. In fact it was so successful the Air Force was anxious to use it in combat.

In the final months of 1972, during the U.S. involvement in Vietnam, the AGM-65A Maverick missile was fielded experimentally during the Linebacker offensive against North Vietnam. Ninety-nine missiles were fired with an 88 percent success rate.

The Maverick missile was officially introduced into squadron service with the F-4E Phantoms of the 334th Tactical Fighter Squadron Eagles in June 1973. Maverick finally gave the Air Force its long sought-after air-to-surface, launch-and-leave guided missile capability.

News of the success of our Maverick missile launches at Holloman was traveling fast in the flight-test community. David B. Lindsay, a newspaper publisher, owner of the Cavalier Aircraft Corporation and a former World War II P-51 pilot, had recently designed an aircraft as a replacement for the A-1 Skyraider, which was still flying combat missions in Vietnam. Lindsay envisioned a modified P-51 airframe with a Lycoming T-55 turboprop engine and under-wing weapons stations, which could carry up to six Maverick missiles. The new aircraft would be called the Enforcer and could be a close air support (CAS) substitute for the Fairchild Republic A-10 Thunderbolt, which the Air Force had just chosen for that mission.

In early 1971, David Lindsay contacted Robert DeHaven, manager of the Flight Test Division. Lindsay thought that if the Maverick missile was included in his proposal to the Air Force, he might have a better chance of selling his Enforcer concept.

DeHaven joined Hughes Aircraft Company in 1948. Then age 26, he would go on to play a critical role in flight testing at Hughes Aircraft. Born in San Diego, he attended Washington and Lee University in Virginia but left to join the Army Air Forces in February 1942. After earning his silver pilot wings, DeHaven took P-40 training in Florida. By early 1943 he was sent to Port Moresby, New Guinea, where he was assigned to fly the P-40 in the 49th Fighter Group.

Lieutenant DeHaven shot down his first Japanese aircraft in the summer of 1943 and became an ace by the end of the year. During battles in New Guinea he downed 10 enemy aircraft with the P-40, one of the highest scores for Army Air Forces pilots, other than the American Volunteer Group (Flying Tigers). As the Japanese were pushed back toward their homeland, the P-40 pilots were slowly left out of the war. In the summer of 1944, his squadron transitioned to the P-38, which had the range to allow them to reach the enemy. By the fall of 1944, DeHaven led a mission in the P-38 and became one of the first pilots to return to the Philippines. Within seven days he acquired 4 more victories, bringing his total to 14 confirmed kills and 1 damaged. For his military service, he was awarded the Silver Star with one oak leaf cluster and the Distinguished Flying Cross with two oak leaf clusters. After the war DeHaven joined the Air National Guard at Van Nuys, California, and flew the P-51 Mustang.

The Enforcer would be the world's only jet-turbine, propeller-driven CAS aircraft. It carried ordinance on all 10 of its under-wing weapon stations. The load included two 1,000-pound bombs; two night-flare dispensers, each containing 16 two-million-candlepower flares; two 19-round 2.75-inch anti-tank rocket launchers; and four 7-round 2.75-inch white phosphorus marking rocket launchers. The Enforcer was designed with six M-3 50-caliber machine guns with 2,000 rounds of ammunition hidden inside the wings. Fuel was carried in two 120-gallon tip tanks and self-sealing 92-gallon fuel tanks within the wings.

The Enforcer would have many unique improvements compared to the P-51 Mustang. Armor plate would be installed on each side of the cockpit.

The pilot escape system would be an adaptation of the Stanley Yankee Escape System, which I had flown in the A-1 Skyraider in Vietnam.

According to Lindsay, the Enforcer would have the smallest silhouette, lowest infrared signature, lowest noise level, fastest acceleration, and highest survivability of any attack aircraft in the Air Force inventory. Unfortunately, the entire ordinance originally designed to fly on the Enforcer were weapons that dated back to World War II. Combat in Vietnam had showed that CAS aircraft needed standoff, smart weapons, which would be fired high above the enemy's guns and still achieve a high probability of hitting their targets. Installation of the AGM-65A Maverick on the Enforcer might just make the difference in winning a competition against the A-10 Thunderbolt II.

Lindsay asked DeHaven to determine if Hughes Aircraft Company might want to team with him to sell the Enforcer concept using the Maverick missile. He also felt that DeHaven might be able to contact Howard Hughes and have him put in some "good words" about the Enforcer.

DeHaven was the chief test pilot of Hughes Aircraft Company. He used his position and authority as manager of the Flight Test Division as though he were Howard Hughes. DeHaven made arbitrary decisions and demanded compliance of his employees. He had no direct contact with Hughes, so he could not help Lindsay with an introduction.

Because of my previous experience in flying combat missions in the A-1 Skyraider in Vietnam and my association with the Hughes Maverick missile flight-test program, DeHaven felt I should travel to David Lindsay's facility in Florida, evaluate his progress to date, and report back.

When I arrived, I found that the first of two Enforcers were under construction, still many months from completion. Lindsay was very optimistic that the Enforcer would catch on with the Air Force or some foreign country.

"With the Air Force in a fuel crunch, missile crunch, and a dollar crunch," he said, "I believe the Enforcer is an aircraft whose time has come."

Lindsay suggested that I pilot a couple of flights in his personal P-51D to compare the flying qualities of the Mustang with the Skyraiders I had flown in Vietnam. I jumped at the chance for a flight. However, it wasn't really fair to compare a lightweight P-51D without ordinance, flying over the nonhostile shoreline of Vero Beach, with some of my gut-wrenching combat experiences with the A-1 in Southeast Asia. Nevertheless, I could see that a heavily modified Mustang flying with several Maverick missiles would be a great improvement over the old Skyraider.

When I returned to Culver City, I reported my impression of flying the P-51 to DeHaven. He had flown the P-51 in the California Air National Guard and was familiar with the aircraft. I found the Lindsay Mustang to be one of the best aircraft I had ever flown. Flight controls were as light as the jet fighters I was flying, and visibility out the front windscreen and bubble canopy was unparalleled.

DeHaven and I discussed the opportunity for Hughes Aircraft to join David Lindsay in attempting to sell his Enforcer concept. Lindsay had invested several million dollars of his private funds in the venture. He wanted Hughes Aircraft to contribute money also. The Air Force had committed to an all-jet Air Force. Selling a modified World War II turbo-prop fighter, even if it was only one-fifth the cost of an A-10, would be an uphill battle. Finally we concluded that for every Maverick missile sold to the Air Force for the Enforcer, one would be subtracted from the A-10 inventory. This strategy would do nothing for Hughes Aircraft; we would be in a neutral position. So, DeHaven did not recommend to his senior management that we take part in the program. Furthermore, DeHaven was a self-promoting person and was reluctant to take a position unless it would advance his chance for promotion.

Eventually David Lindsay completed two Enforcers using modified Mustang airframes. A flight-test program was completed, but one aircraft crashed after losing its tail in flight. The program did not lead to a production order.

Ten years later, several highly placed friends of the Enforcer lobbied for the aircraft and obtained a $12 million development program, even in the face of heavy Air Force opposition. Now owned by Piper Aircraft Company, the new Enforcer would have a number of changes over the original Enforcer to make it a more combat-effective weapon.

Two aircraft were built and tested in 1984. After all the modifications had been completed, little of the original Mustang remained; in effect, it was a new aircraft. As before, the Air Force declined to order any production models. The two Enforcers are now spending their twilight years in aviation museums.

Just over 33 years ago, in summer and fall of 1973, the Middle East was seething with tensions. Six years earlier, in June 1967, Israeli forces conquered vast swaths of land controlled by Egypt, Syria, and Jordan. Officials in Cairo and Damascus had failed over the years to persuade or force Israel to relinquish its grip on the land and, by 1973, the stalemate had become intolerable. Egypt's Anwar Sadat and Syria's Hafez al-Assad meticulously planned their October 1973 offensive. They hoped to reverse Israeli gains of the earlier war and put an end to Arab humiliation. The war was set to begin on the holiest of Jewish religious days, Yom Kippur.

On October 6, 1973, a day that was the Jewish Day of Atonement, the Egyptians and the Syrians launched a surprise attack against Israel. The attack caught Israel almost totally unaware. Although there were signs of imminent attack, Israeli analysts did not believe that the Arabs would actually invade until they had reached strategic parity.

The Arab states had trained well and Moscow had supplied equipment on a colossal scale, including 600 advanced surface-to-air missiles, 300 MiG-21 fighters, 1,200 tanks, and hundreds of thousands of tons of consumable war materiel. On paper, the Arabs held a huge advantage in troops, tanks, artillery, and aircraft. This was offset, in Israeli minds, by the Jewish state's superior technology, advanced mobilization capability, and interior lines of communication. Despite unmistakable signs of increasing Arab military capability, Israeli leaders remained unworried—even complacent— and were confident in Israel's ability to repel any attack.

On the southern front, the onslaught began with a 2,000-cannon barrage across the Suez Canal, the 1967 cease-fire line. Egyptian assault forces swept across the waterway and plunged deep into Israeli-held territory. At the same time, crack Syrian units launched a potent offensive in the Golan Heights. The Arab forces fought with efficiency and cohesion, rolling over or past shocked Israeli defenders. Arab air forces attacked Israeli airfields, radar installations, and missile sites.

Grievously heavy on both sides were the losses in armored vehicles and combat aircraft. Israeli airpower was hit hard by a combination of mobile SA-6 and the man-portable SA-7 air-defense missiles expertly wielded by the Arabs. The attacking forces were also plentifully supplied with radar-controlled Russian ZSU-23-4 anti-aircraft guns. Israeli estimates of consumption of ammunition and fuel were seen to be totally inadequate. However, it was the high casualty rate that stunned Israel, shocking not only Prime Minister Golda Meir but also the legendary General Moshe Dayan, Minister of Defense. The shock was accompanied by sheer disbelief at America's failure to comprehend that the situation was critical. Voracious consumption of ammunition and huge losses in tanks and aircraft brought Israel to the brink of defeat, forcing the Israelis to think the formerly unthinkable as they pondered their options.

Half a world away, the United States was in a funk, unable or unwilling to act decisively. Washington was in the throes of not only post-Vietnam moralizing on Capitol Hill but also the agony of Watergate, both of which impaired the leadership of President Richard Nixon. Four days into the war, Washington was blindsided again by another political disaster—the forced resignation of Vice President Spiro Agnew.

Not surprisingly, the initial U.S. reaction to the Egyptian invasion of Israel was one of confusion and contradiction. Leaders tried to strike a balance of the traditional U.S. support of Israel with the need to maintain a still-tenuous superpower détente with the Soviet Union and a desire to avoid a threatened Arab embargo of oil shipments to the West.

Nixon, in response to a personal plea from Golda Meir, had made the crucial decision on October 9 to resupply Israel. However, four days would pass before the executive office could make a final decision on how the re-supply would be executed. Initially, planners proposed that Israel be given the responsibility for carrying out the entire airlift. Israel attempted to elicit interest from U.S. commercial carriers, but they refused to enlist in the effort, concerned as they were about the adverse effects Arab reaction would have upon their businesses.

The United States dithered in this fashion for days. Then, on October 12, Nixon personally decided that the Air Force Military Airlift Command (MAC) would handle the entire airlift. But there was still a problem to contend with: None of the governments of the countries in which MAC's overseas bases were located would allow the American airplanes to use them while carrying cargo destined for Israel, out of fear of Arab reprisals. Tel Aviv's Lod/Ben-Gurion air complex was made available as the off-load point.

"Send everything that can fly," President Nixon ordered.

The president did not want to involve the U.S. military, but the American airline industry refused to submit bids to contract to carry the cargo. He had no choice but to order MAC to begin an airlift called Nickel Grass. MAC inquiries with commercial carriers received the same negative response. Then it was suggested that MAC fly the material to Lajes, a base on the Portuguese Azores islands in the Atlantic. The threat of an oil embargo frightened U.S. allies. With a single exception, they all denied landing and over-flight rights to the emergency MAC flights. The exception was Portugal, which, after hard bargaining, essentially agreed to look the other way as traffic mushroomed on their field. Daily departure flights grew from 1 to over 40 in a few days. This was a crucial landing field for MAC, which could not have conducted the airlift the way it did without staging through Lajes. Even before permission was granted, the first Lockheed C-5 Galaxys and C-141 Starlifters were on their way to Lajes.

In 1973, after three years of service with MAC, the C-5 had turned into a pretty reliable airplane. Most of the problems that had occurred in the first production models had been rectified, and the airplane was becoming considerably more reliable. The C-5 was on the verge of proving its value to the skeptical press.

By October 1973 all MAC C-5s had been consolidated at Dover Air Force Base, Delaware, on the East Coast and at Travis Air Force Base, California, on the West Coast. The de-escalation of the war in Vietnam had lessened the demand on MAC's C-141 fleet.

The loads were to come out of several arsenals at diverse points within the United States. MAC immediately dispatched C-5s and C-141s from each of its bases to onload points near the various arsenals, then sent them to East Coast bases for refueling in preparation for the flight to Lod Airport outside Tel Aviv.

After our Hughes Aircraft Maverick test facility was closed at Holloman in the fall of 1971, many of the engineers, pilots, mechanics, and support personnel were transferred to Point Mugu, California. Hughes was developing and testing the AWG-9 system and AIM-54A Phoenix missile on the F-14A Tomcat for the Navy at Point Mugu. Bill Jessup and I were now flying the Tomcat.

An urgent request came from the Air Force: Hughes Aircraft was needed to support the Maverick missile deployment to Israel. Our government did not want the world to see Air Force blue-suiters loading and arming Maverick missiles on Israeli F-4 Phantoms. Likewise, they didn't want Air Force pilots briefing Israeli pilots on flight procedures and tactics used to fire the Maverick. So a scheme was devised to substitute military contractor personnel who had similar experience to those in the Air Force. They would wear civilian clothing and be less visible to the press than military airmen.

Test pilot Bill Jessup was selected for this unique assignment. He was given 24 hours' advance notice that he would be traveling to Israel and staying for an indeterminate time. By the next day, he got his passport updated and was given several vaccinations for exposure to illnesses in the Middle East and five thousand U.S. dollars. Jessup flew in a commercial airliner to Tucson International Airport in Arizona. Four hundred AGM-65A Maverick missiles, which had been produced at the Hughes Aircraft missile plant located next to the Tucson Airport, were transferred across town to Davis-Monthan Air Force Base and uploaded on a C-5. Within a few hours Jessup and the missiles departed for Israel.

The airlift began in mid-October and continued for 32 days, until the first ships began arriving in Israel from the United States. Fortunately, like the Berlin Airlift, the operation was pretty much routine, though the first crews flying into Lod Airport were apprehensive due to threats of interception by the Arabs. The routes from Lajes to Lod lay in pretty close proximity to countries that were unfriendly toward Israel.

Some crews, mostly those in C-141s, reported spurious radio transmissions, and some unidentified aircraft were reported during the airlift. But the U.S. Navy had several carriers positioned along the route of flight to provide fighter protection if needed, while the Israeli Air Force picked up each airplane 190 miles out and escorted it safely into Lod. Jessup told me it was comforting to see the fighters flying cover for the C-5.

Cargo carried included artillery shells for tanks as well as anti-tank missiles, armor, and other military cargo. Unlike the Berlin Airlift, Nickel Grass was a military airlift designed to prevent the defeat of a nation the United States considered to be a friend.

While Nickel Grass was going on, the Soviets were running their own airlift to support the other side. Using AN-12 and giant AN-22 turbo-prop transports, the Soviet air force flew 930 missions into Cairo and Damascus to bring in 15,000 tons of weapons over a 40-day period. The Russian planes operated in close proximity to the routes used by the MAC transports. Often the same air traffic control center was controlling American and Russian airplanes at the same time.

There were conversations between the American and Russian crews on the radios. One thing the MAC crews learned was that their Soviet counterparts were as apprehensive of the Arabs as they were. Both sides were afraid Arab fighters would attack a MAC transport, which would prompt retaliation against the Soviets from the Israelis. Washington officials had allegedly also told Moscow that if any American planes were attacked, U.S. fighters would enter the fray.

The continuous flood of U.S. war materiel enabled Israeli forces to go on the offensive in the latter stages of the war. In the north, Israel's ground forces recovered all territory that had been lost and began to march on Damascus. In the Sinai, tank forces led by Major General Ariel Sharon smashed back across the Suez, encircled the Egyptian Third Army on the western side of the canal, and threatened Ismailia, Suez City, and even Cairo itself.

Egypt and Syria, who had previously rejected the idea of a negotiated settlement, now felt compelled on October 22nd to agree to the arrangement hammered out by Washington and Moscow, with the goal of preventing the total destruction of the trapped Egyptian army. Israel was reluctant to comply immediately, wishing to gain as much as possible before a cease fire.

Fortunately, after several abortive efforts, an effective cease fire finally took hold October 28. Israel had suffered 10,800 killed or wounded—a traumatic loss for a nation of some 3 million persons, plus destruction of 100 aircraft and 800 tanks. The Arab nations suffered 17,000 killed or wounded, 8,000 prisoners held by the Israelis, and the loss of 500 aircraft and 1,800 tanks.

The airlift officially ended November 14. By then, the Air Force had delivered 22,395 tons of cargo—145 missions by C-5 Galaxy and 422 missions by C-141 Starlifter. The airlift had been a key to the victory. It had not only brought about the timely resupply of the lagging Israeli force but had also provided a deadly new weapon put to good use: the Hughes AGM-65A Maverick missle.

The Maverick missiles were an outstanding success, killing over 82 percent of their assigned targets. They worked flawlessly in the clear desert skies, just as they had been designed and tested to do at Holloman. Israeli pilots were quick to capitalize on the stand-off capabilities of the missile.

The Israelis' only complaint concerned the missile's total destruction of tanks and armored vehicles. Mavericks were designed to penetrate the vehicle's relative weak top and completely destroy them with a shaped charge. The Israeli military would have preferred that only the operators be killed and the vehicle just slightly disabled so that it could be repaired and used by them again.

Hughes engineers were concerned that the Israeli military would steal classified technical information on our missile and use it to produce their own weapon. These weapons could then be sold to foreign countries that might not be friendly to the United States.

Bill Jessup was very impressed with the Israeli pilots. He felt they were well trained, were motivated to defend their country, and got the most out of their aircraft and the Hughes Maverick missiles.

CHAPTER 5

Ace of the Test Range

*Howard Hughes is the only man to be arrested for indecent
exposure while fully clothed.*

Little did Hughes Aircraft Company test pilot Bill Jessup and I realize the
uproar we were causing at Naval Air Station (NAS) Miramar in California. Jessup was practicing touch-and-go landings in the newest and
most powerful Navy fighter in the fleet, the Grumman F-14A Tomcat.
He was flying the fourth aircraft manufactured at the Grumman factory in
Calverton, New York, an early pre-production model, Bureau Number
157983, using the call sign Bloodhound 204. The Tomcat had been delivered to our Hughes flight facility at NAS Point Mugu, 100 miles northwest of Miramar, for us to test and develop our company's AWG-9
system and launch AIM-54A Phoenix missiles. Before Jessup and I were
cleared to fly solo, Navy regulations required that we each obtain five
hours in the F-14A and complete five landings with a Grumman instructor sitting in the rear seat.

I was acting as a safety chase, flying our company-leased T-33. It
was late January 1972. Jessup had taken off from Point Mugu and
completed air work in the Tomcat offshore over the Pacific Ocean. He
then chose to fly a navigation leg to Miramar and practice touch-and-go
landings like Howard Hughes had done so many times in the past.

Only two weeks earlier, both of us had been at Miramar to fly a Navy F-4J Phantom, practicing in-flight refueling from a Douglas A-4 Skyhawk. The Navy used the probe-and-drogue system, new for me because I had been an Air Force pilot. In-flight refueling with an F-4J was a Navy requirement before we could "tank" with the Tomcat.

NAS Miramar sat atop a broad, open mesa about 15 miles northeast of San Diego, California, where the weather provided excellent flying nearly year round. Miramar's longest runway was located on the south side of the base and oriented in a northeast-southwest direction. This was the runway most often used and the one on which Jessup was making landing after landing. I flew a loose chase position, watching for any symptoms of failure in the brand-new F-14A.

Each time Jessup landed, I noticed a long, windowless concrete building that paralleled the runway just to the north. The building, probably a thousand feet long, had a sign painted on it with capital letters 20 feet high displaying:

"WELCOME TO FIGHTERTOWN, U.S.A."

The large, well-equipped base was home for all the Pacific Fleet F-4 and F-8 fighter squadrons when they were not deployed on aircraft carriers at sea. Miramar was best known as home of the Navy Fighter Weapons School, also called Top Gun. To a Navy fighter pilot, Top Gun was the ultimate flying assignment.

What had caused the commotion was the sight of our F-14A. The first Tomcat was not expected to arrive at Miramar for another six months. Tomcats would be assigned to VF-124, the Replacement Air Group squadron that would train all West Coast pilots and Naval Flight Officers (NFOs). Little did we know that phones were ringing all over the base. Every sailor on the field heard that a Tomcat was in the landing pattern. Many were driving to the flight line to get a glimpse of the F-14A, which caused a traffic jam on base. The Tomcat was the newest fighter to come into the Navy inventory, but only a handful were built at that time and all except ours were still at the Grumman manufacturing plant in Long Island, New York.

Jessup decided to practice these touch-and-go landings on the spur of the moment. Like Howard Hughes, he had not briefed me or anyone else back at Point Mugu prior to takeoff about his plans. Hughes flew multiple touch-and-go landings in every aircraft he built, bought, or borrowed. It is extremely important that a pilot checking out in a new aircraft learn to safely take off and land. But Hughes took this practice to an extreme, sometimes flying close to 40 touch-and-goes on one flight. Typically Hughes did not inform his copilot, tower personnel, or his mechanics of his intentions. He just flew until low on fuel and then landed.

Meanwhile, the Commanding Officer of Miramar questioned his staff about the Tomcat. Where did it come from? Why was it here? What was it doing at Miramar? Who was flying it? His staff had no answers; they were likewise caught by complete surprise.

In the past Howard Hughes liked nothing better than surprising people. He surprised newsmen when he made the first flight in the H-4 Hercules in Long Beach Harbor. He again surprised engineers working on the Convair 880 program when he arrived unannounced and wanted to fly. In the Howard Hughes tradition, Jessup was surprising the Navy brass at Miramar.

Flying chase on the F-14A I was transfixed by the appearance of the aircraft. It was a mean-looking machine, with a small fuselage and canopy, as well as large shoulder-mounted variable-geometry wings that could sweep from 20 degrees to 68 degrees. Hanging under the wings were two monstrous rectangular engine intakes, canted slightly outboard. Also canted outboard at a more rakish angle were the twin vertical stabilizers.

The Tomcat was one big fighter. "Tomcat" was selected as a nickname partly to pay tribute to Navy Admiral Thomas Connolly. Connolly was such a strong supporter of the F-14 program that the aircraft was referred to as "Tom's Cat," and the name stuck. Later pilots referred to the F-14 as the "turkey" because of its extreme flight control surface movements on carrier approach, similar to those of a wild turkey.

The tunnel on the underside of the fuselage between the engines was nothing more than a huge flat area with depressions for semi-submerged AIM-7 Sparrow missiles or pallets that would hold our AIM-54A Phoenix missiles. Production Tomcats would carry a new M-60 Gatling gun buried in the nose. Our number four aircraft had the gun removed and replaced with instrumentation, which would be used to record our future missile launches.

The Tomcat was 62 feet long and, with the wing swept back at 68 degrees, it had a wingspan of a mere 38 feet. With the wing swept fully forward 20 degrees the F-14's wingspan was 64 feet. Its eight internal fuel tanks carried 16,400 pounds of fuel. Empty, the Tomcat weighed just less than 40,000 pounds. With a full load of internal fuel and a typical combat load of two AIM-9 Sidewinders, two AIM-7 Sparrows, two AIM-54A Phoenix missiles, and a full load of 20mm ammunition, the F-14A weighed about 60,000 pounds. With six Phoenix and two Sidewinder missiles and external fuel (two fuel tanks holding 3,800 pounds of fuel hung from the center wing station), the F-14A tipped the scale at 68,000 pounds.

The Tomcat's two Pratt & Whitney TF-30-P414 turbofan engines could boost it out to Mach 2. At a maximum cruise wing and engine setting, the F-14A could achieve a remarkable range of 1,700 miles on internal fuel only.

Like Howard Hughes, we were unaware of the havoc we created. Jessup and I finished the checkout and returned to Point Mugu. It was now my turn to fly the Tomcat.

As a former Air Force pilot, the Navy F-111B was the first Grumman aircraft I had ever flown. The Navy canceled the F-111B program in 1968 after building just seven aircraft. But the Navy allowed Hughes test pilots to continue to fly the plane so that the AWG-9 system and Phoenix missile could be better tested before the first F-14A came off the production line.

In the previous two years, I had flown the Grumman F-111B about 300 flight hours and launched seven AIM-54A missiles at drone targets. I clearly recalled the failure of an over-wing panel, which caused me to make an emergency arrested landing at Point Mugu earlier. That crash landing was the closest call I had encountered in my 10 years of flying; I wasn't sure I cared for Grumman built aircraft.

But these considerations were not foremost in my mind in February 1972, when I approached the Tomcat for my first flight. That flight is still vivid in my memory, even after nearly 34 years have passed. It was especially poignant for me because I had spent the previous two years as the project test pilot on the Hughes APG-63 radar. During that time, Hughes modified a B-66 bomber to accept our version of a radar for the Air Force's newest fighter, the F-15A Eagle. I made the first flight of our B-66 from the airport in Culver City and flew most of the development flights, including the two-month fly-off competition against Westinghouse. Our company won the production contract and was part of the Air Force and contractor team assembled to create the newest and most powerful fighter in the Air Force inventory. Unfortunately, I did not get the opportunity to fly radar development flights in the F-15A; McDonnell test pilots would accomplish all that flying. The fighter capability of the F-15A Eagle was expected to be very similar to the F-14A. So getting a chance to fly the F-14A seemed to me to be payback for winning the F-15A radar contract but not getting an opportunity fly the Eagle.

Grumman test pilot Harold C. "Hal" Farley Jr. was assigned the task of keeping me alive during my first flight in the Tomcat. Farley graduated from the Navy test pilot school in 1964, the same year I attended the Air Force test pilot school. He and the other Grumman test pilot at Point Mugu, S. M. "Pete" Purvis III, had just checked out in the Tomcat themselves and had only a few flight hours in the F-14A. Grumman had just received the number five and number six aircraft at Point Mugu, which Farley and Purvis used, for weapon separation tests. A Tomcat flight simulator was still a year from being operational, so Jessup and I simply sat down with the Grumman pilots, read the flight manual, and discussed the various systems (hydraulic, electrical, pneumatic, flight control, etc.) of the Tomcat. It was the blind leading the blind.

Farley rode in the rear seat of the F-14A and looked over my shoulder to make sure I didn't get us into trouble. The Tomcats were not dual-controlled, so Farley didn't have a control stick or throttles in his cockpit. He had to have faith I could handle the Tomcat. Farley had reason to be concerned on our first flight in the number four F-14A: Grumman had had their share of trouble getting the Tomcat in the air for the first time.

In late 1970, Grumman's chief test pilot, Robert K. "Bob" Smyth, and the project test pilot, William "Bill" Miller, had been living with the first built aircraft for a year. Grumman guaranteed the Navy that they would make a first flight before the end of 1970. On December 21, 1970, the shortest day of the year, with only nine minutes of daylight left, Smyth made the decision to fly. He sat in the front seat, with Miller in the back, and blasted off in afterburner, making two big circles around the Calverton airfield at an altitude of 3,000 feet. He landed exactly at sunset. The first flight, although greatly shortened from the original plan, was successful. The aircraft was towed into the hangar, and the test team took time off for Christmas. The expanded first flight would take place later.

The next flight of the Tomcat took place from Calverton nine days later, on December 30, 1970. It was a brilliant clear winter day, but it had a far more dramatic conclusion.

This time Bill Miller flew from the front seat, Bob Smyth in the back. The test plan called for flying the F-14A to 15,000 feet and moving the landing gear, flaps, and wings through a complete cycle. Then, after gaining more confidence in the plane, they would climb to 30,000 feet, conduct flutter tests, and accelerate to Mach 1.2.

A half-hour after they were airborne, Miller felt an oscillation through the rudder pedals. Flying at 13,000 feet, they headed back to Calverton and were about to bring the flaps up when the chase pilot said he saw smoke coming from the Tomcat. In fact it was hydraulic fluid, which looked like smoke as it vaporized in the air stream. As the chase plane came in for a close look, the F-14A lost the combined hydraulic system. For a time it looked as though their luck was holding. An emergency nitrogen bottle was activated to lower the landing gear at four miles from the airfield, but fate evidently held all the aces that day and the secondary hydraulic system failed seconds later. With control limited to the Combat Survival System, Miller nursed the crippled F-14A toward the safety of home base.

Miller nearly made it, but with barely a mile to go it became apparent that he was losing the battle to retain control. The Tomcat began a series of porpoising movements, getting larger on each cycle. There was no alternative but to eject. Smyth went first, while the aircraft was just 25 feet above the treetops. Miller's departure was even more dramatic: He ejected from the Tomcat less than half a second before it struck the ground.

The ensuing investigation revealed that resonance caused metal fatigue and was the root cause of the hydraulic system failure. It was discovered that the revolutions per minute of both the engine and the hydraulic pump were on the same frequency. This caused the hydraulic lines to vibrate. Within seconds, the vibration reached such intensity that failure was inevitable, allowing precious hydraulic fluid to escape and causing swift and irretrievable loss of flight control. Hence, the first F-14A was a total loss.

I completed my first flight in the F-14A flying multiple touch-and-goes, just like Jessup and Howard Hughes. On my second and last training flight in the Tomcat, with Hal Farley again in the back seat, I refueled in-flight on a Navy A-6 over the Pacific Ocean. I completed my five flight hours and five landings and was considered qualified by the Navy to fly test missions. Unusual for a former Air Force pilot, I received "sea wings."

In late April of 1972, Bill Jessup fired the first instrumented Phoenix missile (a missile with warhead removed and replaced with a telemetry unit) from our Tomcat at a radio-controlled drone target in the Navy test range off Point Mugu. It was a head-on shot at medium altitude and medium speed against a drone, also at medium altitude and medium speed. Like shooting a free throw in basketball, it was an easy flight from a crew point of view but important in order to get the program off to a good start.

In the next year and a half, we were scheduled to fire many Sidewinders, Sparrows, and Phoenix missiles to prove the capability of our AWG-9 system. Next we would be firing from the edge of the missiles' envelope. Some missiles would be fired at drones programmed to represent a Soviet Foxbat, a Backfire, or an enemy cruise missile. Other missiles would be launched at a range of 120 miles (expected to be a world record for air-to-air missiles), at high-altitude targets flying up to 80,000 feet, at low-altitude targets skimming only 50 feet above the sea, at multiple target raids, at targets using electronic counter measures, and at targets of various sizes from small unaugmented drones to remotely piloted F-4 Phantoms. Each shot was critical; we were aware that any failures could put the program in jeopardy. The next missile launch was mine.

By the first of June of 1972, Hughes Aircraft received the ninth built aircraft, Bureau Number 157988, from Grumman. This aircraft would use the call sign Bloodhound 209 and had had many improvements built into it at the Grumman factory over our number four aircraft. The most important feature was engine inlet ramps, which were activated to move during supersonic flight. This would be the aircraft used during our high-speed AIM-54A Phoenix missile launches.

With two test aircraft in our flying stable, we checked out a third Hughes test pilot. Chuck Blake, our former AGM-65 Maverick missile test pilot who had flown two years for us out of Holloman, now moved back to Southern California. With just 40 hours in the Tomcat, I acted as the instructor pilot for Blake in flying the F-14A. It was my time to fly in the rear seat with no flight controls and have faith the front-seat pilot knew how to fly the plane.

My missile launch was designated the PP-17 mission, or otherwise known as the "Foxbat shot." At the time the Russian MiG-25 Foxbat was the fastest and most modern fighter in the U.S.S.R. inventory. It had a speed and altitude capability similar to our SR-71 Blackbird, which was over-flying North Vietnam. The Navy F-4Bs and F-4Js could not defend the fleet against the Foxbat threat. Therefore, it was extremely important for the Navy to obtain a defense against the Foxbat, the reason the PP-17 mission was scheduled early in the development program. The Foxbat mission was a big step up from our first launch, more like a three-point basketball jump shot than a free throw.

A Beech AQM-37A Stilleto drone was augmented (that is, electrically enhanced larger than its actual physical size) to represent the radar signature of the Foxbat. The drone would be flying directly toward us at Mach 2.2 and 80,000 feet altitude. I would fly the number nine F-14A at Mach 1.2 and 45,000 feet altitude and launch the Phoenix missile at 35 nautical miles from the drone.

Bill Bush and I were scheduled for the Foxbat shot. We had flown together many times in the previous three years. Bush was with me when I had had the near-disastrous close call in the F-111B two years earlier.

On June 21, 1972, Bush and I practiced the Foxbat shot against a manned Navy target in the Pacific range, flying subsonic in the number four Tomcat. The number nine aircraft was out of commission for repair. As soon as it was returned to flight status, we would attempt the difficult mission. Then we heard disturbing news that another F-14A had crashed on the East Coast. All Tomcats were grounded until the Navy completed an accident investigation.

The second F-14A accident produced tragedy, involving the death of Grumman test pilot Bill Miller, the pilot who had so narrowly cheated it in the crash of the first prototype. The accident occurred on June 30, 1972, exactly a year and a half to the day after the first accident. Miller was rehearsing, in the number ten aircraft, for a charity air display at the Patuxent Naval Air Test Center, where he had been performing carrier suitability trials. He was flying alone and had already completed a number of high-speed maneuvers when he was seen to be passing low over the water. Witnesses in a fishing boat nearby spoke later of seeing the Tomcat pull up suddenly, but too late to avoid the tail hitting the water. The aircraft hit at about 350 knots and exploded. Some thought Miller was distracted by something in the cockpit. One opinion was that he had had trouble sweeping the wing and looked down. It was a hazy, smoggy day, with no horizon, and no one was in the rear seat to warn him of impending danger. Best guess was that he simply flew into the water.

Navy's senior management was anxious to keep the F-14A program on schedule. Rear Admiral Leonard "Swoose" Snead, the F-14 program manager at the Naval Air Systems Command in Washington, DC; Captain John Weaver, the Navy's Phoenix program manager; and Captain Clyde T. Tuomela, deputy program manager in charge of test and evaluation, met to discuss the impact of the accident on further flight test. Within a few days, they decided the accident was probably pilot error and allowed us to continue preparations for the Foxbat launch.

If an aircraft was lost over the ocean, it was important to know what happened. So an over-water telemetry instrumentation system was installed in both of our Tomcats. Using this system, signals from the F-14's engines, flight controls, and hydraulic system were transmitted back to Point Mugu and monitored in real time by Grumman engineers. If they detected a problem, the pilot would be notified immediately. Were a severe problem to occur, causing us to crash into the Pacific Ocean, they would still have data to evaluate. For national security, it was extremely important for flight testing to continue.

July 21, 1972, was a very special day. That day we conducted the most intricate test yet of the F-14's weapon system by firing a missile on the Foxbat mission. During our pre-launch briefing, Bush and I recognized the importance of our flight. We also sensed the pressure on everyone in the program to have a successful launch. On the one hand, this mission could become a very historic flight if our launch were successful. On the other hand, if it were not successful, we would again hear rumors that the program was in jeopardy and could be canceled. We were keenly aware of the importance of our launch; our jobs could also be riding on the results.

The AIM-54A Phoenix was a large and complicated missile. It was 13 feet long, and 15 inches in diameter, with a 3-foot wingspan and a weight of 975 pounds. Its warhead, of the annular blast fragmentation type (continuous rod), weighed 132 pounds. In the long-range mode, which we would use that day, the missile used an autopilot and semi-active, mid-course guidance with active radar for terminal guidance. The rocket motor would ignite after it came off the launcher. The missile would climb to over 80,000 feet, accelerate to a speed in excess of Mach 4, and, after burnout, conduct its terminal guidance in a descending trajectory converting altitude into high-speed maneuvering. Navy aircrew nicknamed the missile the "Buffalo" because of its size, so heavy that a Tomcat can't carry six of them if the aircraft is to return and land on a carrier.

By the time Bush and I completed our preflight inspection, there was a crowd of anxious observers watching our missile engineers check the Phoenix missile mounted on the Tomcat's right wing. Ground electrical power was applied to the aircraft after we completed our pre-engine start checklist. After start, the electrical power cable was disconnected and we checked the missile and radar on internal F-14 electrical power. Bush went through exhaustive checks, leaving nothing to chance.

"Mugu tower, Bloodhound 209 ready to taxi to arming area," I called on the UHF radio.

I taxied from the parking ramp and started down the taxiway toward the engine run-up and arming area at the takeoff end of Runway 21. The pilot of a Navy F-4B photo chase aircraft followed me, with Hughes photographer Rudy Vonich occupying the rear seat. Vonich had a high-speed 35mm camera and planned to take multiple photos of our Phoenix missile as it was fired from my Tomcat. The arming crew was waiting for us and directed me to swing the Tomcat around, heading toward the Pacific Ocean. If an accidental firing took place, the missile would at least be aimed at the ocean. I braked to a halt, I set the parking brake, and Bush and I placed both our hands on top of our helmets. This motion signaled to the arming crew that we were ready to have them arm the missile and would not activate any armament switches while they were working under the plane.

Moments later I accelerated down the runway, lifted off, retracted the gear, and turned seaward toward the firing range. Over the UHF radio, I checked in with Plead Control, the Navy range controller, who would vector us to our hold area. The Navy F-4B photo chase aircraft joined in formation and visually checked the status of my plane and our Phoenix missile.

Meanwhile, Bush continued to run electronic self-tests on the AIM-54A. The missile was checked, rechecked, and then checked again. When we reached 35,000 feet, I throttled back to a loitering speed to conserve fuel for what might be a long wait for the drone to get in the proper position. We had fuel for only one supersonic pass; I didn't want to waste any. The AQM-37 drone was launched as soon as we took off and confirmed to ground controllers that our radar and missile were operating properly.

During the early 1970s, the Russians manned several trawlers that cruised off shore in the Pacific Ocean. They were officially classified as fishing ships but in reality were electronic "snoopers." The trawlers would be monitoring our UHF radio communication frequency, so we kept radio contact with our ground controllers to a minimum and used secret codes to relay test information.

Finally the drone was in position, about 100 nautical miles west of Santa Barbara, California. I was 150 nautical miles southwest of Los Angeles, some 120 miles southeast of the drone. The radar controller commanded me to turn the Tomcat to my launch heading of 320 degrees.

When we fired the Phoenix missile, it would cross Control Area 1176, a major commercial air route from Los Angeles to Hawaii. Navy controllers would coordinate with the FAA to make certain the air route was clear before we would be given the final clearance to launch. Even though the missile would cross the air route at 80,000 feet, we could not take the chance that a Boeing 747 with 300 passengers was flying through the air route and would be blasted out of the sky by an errant missile.

With everything a go, I lit the F-14's afterburners as soon as I rolled out on launch heading. Over my right shoulder I quickly glanced at the F-4 and observed the pilot light his afterburners. I started a gentle climb to 45,000 feet as soon as the F-14 was supersonic. So far everything was going as planned.

Bush and I started through the pre-launch checklist, calling out our actions in sequence to each other over the intercom. At Mach 1.2, I pulled the throttles back to a minimum afterburner position and checked my fuel quantity. We were now closing on the drone about a mile a second. At 50 miles' separation from the drone, the controller gave us a call that the range was clear and we were cleared to fire on his countdown. I gave one last look at the F-4; he was in perfect position.

"Five, four, three, two, one, fire," called the radar controller as we approached 35 miles from the target.

I felt a metallic thump, as the right wing became about 1,000 pounds lighter. A white bullet shot out from under the Tomcat and accelerated directly in front of me, maybe 50 feet lower in altitude. About 1,000 feet distant, the missile started a 45-degree climb, and a small white contrail streamed behind it. My Tomcat flew directly through the contrail, causing the F-14A to shake and rumble like crossing railroad tracks in a car.

"Good data," called the controller, meaning the Hughes engineers were getting satisfactory readings on missile telemetry.

As the controller continued to call out the distance to the target, I checked my remaining fuel. The needle was moving lower on the fuel quantity gauge; I was approaching minimum fuel. It was a temptation to pull the engines out of afterburner; it was a long swim to Point Mugu if I ran out of gas. The nose of the Tomcat had to remain on firing heading so that the AWG-9 system could illuminate the target drone. At 5 miles' separation, the Phoenix missile's own radar would go active and steer the missile to impact. We were still speeding along at Mach 1.2 and 45,000 feet altitude. The controller counted down the distance from the missile to the drone.

"Bloodhound 209, cleared to RTB [return to base]," he transmitted on the radio.

We had done our part, now it was time to fly home and find out the results.

When we taxied into the parking space, I could sense from the smiles and handshakes of the Hughes engineers that the launch was successful. Though it was only necessary for the Phoenix missile to come within what was a classified distance for the mission to be considered a scored kill, the missile actually hit the drone, causing it to disintegrate. Needless to say, our launch was scored a hit. The Navy and Hughes engineers were extremely pleased with the results. But many other launches were scheduled for the weeks to follow, and our attention now focused on them.

It wasn't until three months later that I fully realized how successful the launch was considered by the Navy program office and media. A color photo of our F-14A, at the very moment the Phoenix missile was ejected and the rocket motor ignited, was printed on the cover of the October 16, 1972, issue of *Aviation Week and Space Technology (AW&ST)* magazine. Rudy Vonich had taken a spectacular photograph that captured the essence of the combined Tomcat and Phoenix firepower. We knew the Russians probably subscribed to *AW&ST*; they would think twice before they flew a Foxbat over an American carrier with a Phoenix missle loaded F-14A onboard.

Four years later Soviet pilot Viktor Belenko defected with a Foxbat and landed in Japan. In the book *MiG Pilot*, written by John Barron in 1980, the author quoted Belenko's concern about flying combat against the Tomcat. Belenko realized that the F-14A's radar detected an enemy aircraft at three times the range possible with his equipment. Also, the Phoenix missile had a lethal range nearly five times the distance of Belenko's missiles. Our Foxbat launch may have been an important factor in his decision to defect during the Cold War.

Later, on vacation in Cairo, Egypt, I saw a book in the Hilton Hotel gift shop showing our missile launch on the cover. It was amazing how far and wide the launch photo was distributed. Anyone interested in airborne weapons, be they friend or foe, would certainly know the awesome firepower of the AWG-9 system and Phoenix missile.

My greatest thrill came 11 years after the launch, while visiting the National Air and Space Museum in Washington, DC. There, I saw the same photo next to an inert Phoenix missile on display. Thousands upon thousands of people visit the museum each year to see the Wright Brothers' aircraft, Lindbergh's *Spirit of St. Louis*, and Yeager's X-1. They would now see and learn of the fantastic capability of the F-14A and Phoenix missile. I was proud of the part I had played in their testing and development.

In 10 years of flying AWG-9 system development tests and AIM-54A Phoenix missile launches, I accumulated more than 300 flight hours on 205 test missions in 15 of the pre-production F-14A test planes. During that time, I shot down five drones with missiles and considered myself a "test range ace." The last of the Grumman feline fighter line was a tremendous improvement over the overweight, underpowered, side-by-side seating F-111B Sea Pig. The Tomcat was by far the best all-around fighter I ever flew.

The F-14A Tomcat was exported to only one foreign customer, the Imperial Iranian Air Force. The government of Mohammed Reza Pahlavi, the Shah of Iran, was granted a large amount of military assistance by the U.S. government in the hope that Iran would act as a bulwark against Soviet expansions southward, into the region of the Persian Gulf. In addition, Iranian oil revenues made it possible for the Shah's government to purchase massive amounts of Western-manufactured arms, including advanced fighters such as the F-5 and F-4.

In May of 1972 President Richard Nixon visited Iran, and the Shah mentioned to him that MiG-25 Foxbat aircraft of the Soviet Air Force had regularly been flying unimpeded over Iranian territory. The Shah asked Nixon for equipment that would intercept these high-speed intruders, and Nixon told the Shah that he could order either the Navy F-14A Tomcat or the Air Force F-15A Eagle. Both Air Force and Navy program managers made several trips to Iran to give presentations on their respective aircraft.

Grumman put up a quarter of a million dollars to send an F-14A to the Paris Air Show in May 1973, reasoning that its performance there would be duly noted by the group of high-ranking Iranian Air Force officers who they knew would be present.

Time went by and the Shah had not made his selection. Finally, a flight demonstration of both aircraft was scheduled at Andrews Air Force Base near Washington, DC in July 1973. All the Air Force and Navy brass were assembled when the Shah's motorcade arrived on the flight line. Grumman test pilot Don Evans put the Tomcat through its paces, and McDonnell test pilot Irv Burrows did the same with the Eagle. Both flew spectacular flights, but following the demonstration the Shah walked directly to the F-14A, ignoring the Eagle parked nearby.

The next month the Shah selected the F-14 Tomcat. Bill Bush and I had shot down a Foxbat-type drone exactly a year earlier using the AIM-54A Phoenix missile. Maybe the Shah had read about our successful launch in *AW&ST* magazine?

The initial Iranian order covered 30 Tomcats, but later 50 more were added to the contract. Their Tomcat was virtually identical to the U.S. Navy version, with a few classified features of our AWG-9 system omitted.

Having landed the Iranian deal, worth more than $1 billion to the Grumman Aircraft Company, they had to find a way to make it work. It entailed far, far more than simply building and ferrying 80 Tomcats to Iran. The Iranians had never had such a sophisticated aircraft and weapons system. Grumman's contract called for them to teach the Iranians how to fly and maintain the entire F-14A weapon system. To do this, Grumman mounted a major effort to train hundreds of their employees who were to be sent to Iran. Each person had to complete a course in the Persian language, plus 40 hours of transcultural orientation—how to adapt to life in Iran.

Two Naval Flight Officers, who would later be employed by Hughes Aircraft and fly with me in the Tomcat at Point Mugu, were part of the initial Grumman cadre sent to Iran. Eugene S. "Mule" Holmberg retired from the Marines after a 20-year career as an NFO flying the F-4. Robert "Bob" Bero joined the Navy and left military service after one tour in the Tomcat. Both were hired by Grumman and assigned duty teaching and flying with the Iranian pilots in their country.

Most of the Iranian pilots had flown the F-4 before qualifying in the F-14A Tomcat. However, the Iranian F-4s carried another pilot in the rear cockpit, so they were not familiar with the crew concept practiced in the U.S. Navy, with a pilot and an NFO. Whereas U.S. Navy crews shared responsibility for their performance—good or bad—the Iranians had a difficult time understanding that concept. They were all very defensive and chose to blame each other rather than work together.

Other basic cultural differences were observed. Some Iranian pilots refused to fly upside-down. Some were fearful that the Russian bear would extend its arm and claw from the border, grab a Tomcat in flight, and throw it to the ground. As a result, Iranian pilots were reluctant to fly near the Soviet border. American aviators classified these misperceptions as superstitions. It was hard to train aircrew that had such basic misunderstandings of life and aviation.

While going through basic Air Force flying school in Texas, one Iranian pilot drove his van on a two-lane highway. Thirsty for a beer, he placed his van on cruise control, got out of his seat, and walked to the back to obtain a brew. The van continued down the road for a while, and then rolled over several times, ending in the ditch. The pilot thought cruise control included vehicle steering—not just speed control. He was not a good candidate to whom to teach higher levels of weapons electronics.

The first of 80 Tomcats arrived in Iran in January 1976. By May 1977, when Iran celebrated the 50th anniversary of the Royal House, 12 had been delivered. At this time, the Soviet Foxbats were still making a nuisance of themselves by flying over Iran, and the Shah ordered live firing tests of the Phoenix be carried out as a warning. This was shortly after the radar of an F-14A detected a MiG-25B Foxbat reconnaissance aircraft transiting the country at a height of 65,000 feet and at a speed of Mach 2.

Several Iranian flight and ground crews arrived at Point Mugu to practice and launch two AIM-54A missiles in the Pacific test range. They would fire at Beech BQM-34E target drones using their own aircraft and flight crews, an all-Iranian show.

At the time, test pilots at Hughes Aircraft had been flying a Navy twin-engine 80,000 pound TA-3B Skywarrior, Bureau Number 144867, modified with the AWG-9 system, for seven years. It was one of the last A-3s built and had a more streamlined wing and higher thrust engines than the early models. Originally the plane was flown out of the Culver City airport, supporting the test program while we were flying the F-111Bs at that location. When our two F-14As arrived in 1972, the TA-3B was transferred to Point Mugu. The Skywarrior carried a pilot and four crew members, perfect for troubleshooting our radar in flight.

The Iranian crews practiced their missile-firing checklist over and over in our Skywarrior until they could accomplish it without error. I found it dull flying the TA-3B on pass after pass, but the Shah had ordered the launches be successful. The Shah should not have worried; we didn't carry beer in the Skywarrior.

Actually the Iranian launch geometries were not considered to be very difficult. The speed and altitude of both the shooter and drone were center-of-the-envelope conditions, somewhat like shooting fish in a barrel.

The first Iranian launch was conducted in August of 1977. The NFO in the F-14A acquired the drone target at a distance of 101 nautical miles and flying at 50,000 feet. The Iranian F-14A was flying at 40,000 feet and at a speed of Mach 0.8. The Phoenix was launched when the two were 35 miles apart and the target destroyed. It was a ho-hum mission by the standards in which the Navy was holding us, now five years after our first Phoenix missile launch.

The second Iranian launch was a little more difficult, with the BQM-34E target traveling at only 500 feet, while the F-14A was at 25,000 feet and again at a speed of Mach 0.8. The Phoenix was fired at a distance of 25 nautical miles, and once again the target was destroyed.

The Iranians made their point to the Soviet Union. With the F-14A and Phoenix missile in their inventory, they were once again in a position to guarantee the security of their own boundaries against anything that a potential enemy could put up against them.

Iran ordered 714 Phoenix missiles, but only 284 were delivered at the time of its revolution. These Phoenix missiles were of reduced capability as compared with those we delivered to the U.S. Navy.

Toward the end of the 1970s, there was increasing chaos in Iran. On January 16, 1979, the Shah fled the country, and on April 1, an Islamic Republic was declared, with the Ayatollah Khomeini as the head of state. The Imperial Iranian Air Force was renamed the Islamic Republic of Iran Air Force (IRIAF). The new government rapidly took on an anti-Western stance, denouncing the United States as the "great Satan." Following the Islamic revolution, massive numbers of contracts with Western arms suppliers were canceled by the new government, including an order for 400 AIM-54A Phoenix missiles. Relations with the United States became increasingly strained, especially the occupation of the U.S. embassy in Teheran by militant students and the holding of 52 Americans hostage. The United States responded with a cutoff of all political and military ties to Iran and the imposition of a strict arms embargo.

This arms embargo against Iran imposed by the West caused a severe spare parts and maintenance problem. Even the best-equipped units were often poorly trained and could not operate without Western contractor support. The political upheavals and purges caused by the fundamentalist revolution made the situation much worse, with many pilots and maintenance personnel following the Shah into exile. As a result, by 1980 the IRIAF was only a shadow of its former self.

This embargo was to have an especially severe long-term effect on the Tomcat fleet, because the embargo prevented the delivery of any spares. In addition, by August of 1979, all 79 of the F-14A Tomcats had supposedly been sabotaged so they could no longer fire Phoenix missiles. According to various accounts, this was done either by departing Grumman technicians, or by Iranian Air Force personnel friendly to the United States shortly after the fall of the Shah, or even by Iranian revolutionaries in an attempt to prevent operations by an Air Force perceived to be too pro-Western.

The Iran-Iraq war began on September 7, 1980, with an Iraqi air attack on six Iranian air bases and four Iranian army bases. It was followed by an Iraqi land attack at four points along a 700-kilometer front. Before the war ended in 1988, somewhere between 500,000 and a million people were dead, between one and two million people were injured, and two to three million people became refugees. Although little covered in the Western media, the war was a human tragedy on a massive scale.

Airpower did not play a dominant role in the Iran-Iraq war, because both sides were unable to use their air forces effectively. Fighter-versus-fighter combat was rather rare throughout the entire course of the conflict. During the first phase of the war, Iranian aircraft had the fuel and the endurance to win most of these aerial encounters, either by killing with their first shot of an AIM-54A or else by forcing Iraqi fighters to withdraw. Initially, Iranian pilots had the edge in training and experience, but as the war dragged on, this edge was gradually lost because of the repeated purges within the ranks of the Iranian military, which removed experienced officers and pilots who were suspected of disloyalty to the Islamic fundamentalist regime or those with close ties or sympathies with the West.

As Iranian capabilities declined, Iraqi capabilities gradually improved. After 1982, Iraq generally had the edge in most of the air-to-air encounters that took place, with Iran losing most. The Iranians could not generate more than 30–60 sorties per day, whereas the number of sorties that Iraq could mount steadily increased year after year, reaching a peak as high as 600 in 1986 to 1988.

It remains unclear exactly how many air-to-air kills were scored by Iranian Tomcats during the conflict, as records were repeatedly tampered with during and after the war, mainly for political, religious, or personal reasons. This has led to considerable confusion.

Post-war analysis concluded that F-14A aircrew had fired a total of 71 AIM-54s and had lost 10 more rounds when the F-14s carrying them had either crashed, had defected, or were shot down. Evidence suggests the F-14A accounted for 130 confirmed and 23 probable kills. Of those, at least 40 were scored with AIM-54s, 2 or 3 with guns, around 15 with AIM-7s, and the rest with AIM-9s. In one instance, four Iraqi fighters were shot down by a single Phoenix missile. There were two cases of two Iraqi fighters being destroyed by the same missile.

More important, the Tomcat provided the ultimate deterrence against marauding Iraqi fighters. Not only did it down many Iraqi jets, it forced many more to abort their mission before reaching their target. The simple fact was that where F-14s operated, there were no Iraqi fighters. No air-defense system has ever proven so effective.

As with the controversy surrounding the exact number of kills claimed by the F-14, the precise number of losses suffered by the Tomcat force is also open to conjecture. Some reports claim 12 to 16 F-14s were lost. Some were shot down in aerial combat and several lost in accidents, mainly due to engine or flight-control failures. At least eight others were badly damaged but returned to service after the war.

Even though it is extremely difficult to get exact figures on the aircraft lost during the Iraq-Iran war, the approximate exchange ratio would seem to favor the F-14 about eight to one. This result was not overlooked by the Soviets and could have played a factor in their Cold War plans.

Regardless of the number of F-14 aircraft Iran keeps in commission at the present time, they are not considered of any military significance in the post-2000 era.

CHAPTER 6

Bombing the Blue Eel Railroad Bridge

Howard Hughes says that money never bought him love, but it sure put him in a strong bargaining position.

Favorite quip of Stan Jennings, Jennings Publications

For nine years I had been a test pilot with the Air Force and Hughes Aircraft, but during that time I had never been in such a predicament. By that time I had flown many hazardous flights as an Air Force pilot, including wet runway tests in an Air Force F-111A, high-G stalls in the F-4C Phantom, and combat in Vietnam. As a Hughes test pilot I had launched missiles from the F-14A Tomcat, flown an overloaded B-66 from the short Hughes runway, and made a crash landing in an F-111B Sea Pig. Then I was selected to test a new cockpit instrument display. When I thought about testing a cockpit display, it sounded easy—any pilot could do it.

"How could you get hurt testing a display?" I said.

Then I found out.

In 1973 I found myself flying a simulated ground attack test mission from the rear cockpit of a Navy aircraft stationed at Point Mugu. I had never flown the tandem-seated Douglas TA-4C Skyhawk attack aircraft before. A Marine major, a test pilot who was flying in the front cockpit, gave me a short briefing on the operation of the ejection seat and procedure to close and lock the canopy. That's all.

As if performing flight test from the rear cockpit of an aircraft was not enough, I wore a special flight helmet that held an electronic unit directly in front of my right eye. This unit, called a helmet-mounted display (HMD), was attached to an electrical cable holding me so firmly that I looked like I was on death row and scheduled to be electrocuted.

The HMD tests were a very unusual hybrid program. The Air Force Aerospace Medical Research Laboratory, located at Wright-Patterson Air Force Base in Dayton, Ohio, funded the tests. That organization had the responsibility to evaluate new high-technology cockpit instrument displays for inclusion in Air Force planes. The Display Laboratory of Hughes Aircraft built and ground tested the HMD, and the Navy at Point Mugu provided the aircraft and weapon sensors. The Marine major flew the first tests of our equipment—and he didn't care for it. That's where I entered the picture.

The Marine major could have been selected for the part of the aviator in the movie *The Great Santini*, which came out in 1979, six years after our flight tests. In the movie, Robert Duvall played the part of a gung-ho Marine colonel who played tricks on his fellow aviators, flew fighter aircraft through illegal maneuvers, and treated his wife and kids as if they were in the military service. He was colorful and full of himself.

Evidently the Marine assigned to test our equipment came out of the same mold as the colonel in this movie. He had a typical Marine haircut, with only about an eighth of an inch of blond hair showing. His flight suit fitted him like it had been tailor-made, and his flight boots were shined to a high gloss. I didn't know how good a pilot he was, just that he had made up his mind that it was impossible to complete a successful weapon delivery pass using our Hughes HMD. He passed that opinion on to anyone who would listen. There were no shades of gray in his opinions; he was a black and white person.

Like Howard Hughes, the Marine was an in-control type of person. In aviation affairs, Hughes alone set the goals, directed the design and construction, and then personally flew the mission. He alone controlled all aspects of the flights. The Marine project pilot was out of the same mold.

The Marines' back-up test pilot was Navy Lieutenant Kent Ewing. I wished that he were the prime military test pilot for the program. Kent had a twin brother, Jon, who was an Air Force pilot. Jon Ewing and I had been stationed in the same squadron in Vietnam, flying combat missions in the A-1 Skyraider. Jon was a superb pilot, and I figured his twin brother was the same. But flying with Jon Ewing's brother Kent was not a choice the Navy gave to me; my flights would be with the *Great Santini* look-alike.

The Hughes HMD consisted of a miniature cathode-ray tube (CRT), about the size of a quarter, mounted on the right side of the flight helmet. The video image on the face of the CRT was routed to a position directly in front of the pilot's right eye. This image was projected on a half-silvered mirror so that the pilot could still see through the display to the outside world. A polarizer filter was rotated to reduce the amount of light coming into the display. In its full closed position, a pilot could only see the CRT image. In its open position, the pilot could see the outside world and a very dim CRT image. The CRT and electronic cable increased the weight of the helmet by about four pounds. Since it was too hazardous to wear the HMD on takeoff or landing, the unit was disconnected and stowed on the subpanel next to my right knee.

Engineers from the Hughes Display Department envisioned that a pilot would use his left eye to fly the plane, check his cockpit instruments, and watch for enemy ground fire. He would use his right eye to find a target on the display. After he found the target, he would move a cursor on the display with a hand control and lock on to the target.

The HMD would display a TV image from either an Air Force air-to-ground Maverick missile or a Navy Walleye bomb. Each weapon had a TV camera in its nose. Prior to our testing with the HMD, the image was displayed in the TA-4C on a 4-inch by 4-inch monitor on the aircraft's main instrument panel.

Before my flight, the Marine major and I met in the Navy flight planning room and discussed the results of his previous flight tests. He said he could not see the target image on the CRT if the polarizer was full open (allowing outside light to come to his eye). The major explained to me that it was like projecting a movie on an outside window of your house. The image was so faint he could not find the target.

Also, he had difficulty keeping his right eye on the target. If he relaxed, his left eye would overpower the right eye and he could only see the outside view. He had limited success making long, high-altitude descents to large targets in the open. But he had no success against more difficult and combat realistic targets. For smaller targets hidden in canyons, a steeper dive angle was required. If he dove on these targets, the time to find the target in the display was so short that he could never lock on. Other pilots had flown with him and reported similar results.

While flying to the test area, I had a chance to experiment with the HMD. My first reaction was one of surprise that such a fine picture could be displayed in front of a pilot's eye from a CRT about one inch in diameter. This favorable impression was countered somewhat by a resistance to extra equipment hanging on my head. I made a three-and-a-half G turn to the left and then to the right. The helmet fit was fine, and the display remained centered around my eye. However, my eyelashes did brush against the face of the CRT, which I found to be annoying and to produce early fatigue.

With the HMD attached to the helmet, I lost all visibility out the right side of the canopy from my three o'clock to six o'clock position. From my previous experience flying combat in Vietnam, I knew it was very dangerous to be unable to check for other aircraft and ground fire from both the left and right sides of the cockpit. Also, always making a left-handed entry into a weapon delivery pass allowed gunners to estimate the proper lead required to shoot. Flying the Skyraider, I mixed up the direction of the weapon delivery passes in both entry and escape.

The first target I flew against was a cement plant located 25 miles northwest of Palmdale, California. We started at 15,000 feet altitude over Palmdale and made a gentle, wings level, steady descent directly at the target. My dive angle was steep enough that I could observe the cement plant with my left eye through the front windscreen over the major's head. When I had the aircraft stabilized, I switched my attention to the right eye and looked for the target. The rear seat did not have a lock on capability, so I had to tell the major where to move the cursor on the display. Once locked on, I switched back to my left eye to make final dive corrections. I locked on, intentionally broke lock, and relocked several times on each pass. On every subsequent pass the task became easier—a learning curve was involved. Then it was time to make a pass on the dreaded Blue Eel Railroad Bridge without getting messed up and killing myself by flying into the ground.

We departed the cement plant and flew to a position northwest of the town of Tehachapi, California. Deep in a canyon was the Blue Eel

Railroad Bridge surrounded by hilly terrain and pine trees. From my experience in Vietnam, I agreed with the major that it was a more realistic tactical target. After several attempts, I finally locked onto the bridge. Once I developed a technique, I locked on every time. I hated to show up the major, who was also a possible customer; maybe I was just lucky. It was quiet in the cockpit on the way home; the major did not say a word.

While debriefing with the Hughes engineers, they came up with a possible reason for my success. A phenomenon known as biocular rivalry probably helped me find the target. This phenomenon occurred when the pilot's dominant eye tended to cause him to use that eye more than the other.

I was left-handed—and right-eye dominant. The major was right-handed—and left-eye dominant. Most people have a dominant eye opposite their dominant arm. By holding one finger at arm's length, a person can check their eye dominance. Viewing with both eyes, place your finger directly on an object across the room. Then close the right eye and see if the finger remains on the object. Then try the same procedure closing the left eye. Whichever eye stays on the object is the dominant eye. This eye-dominant characteristic helped me concentrate on the display with easier target acquisition.

I agreed with the major that the HMD system had major drawbacks. The Hughes Aircraft engineers went back to their drawing boards. Several days later, while commuting to work, I came up with an idea. If the attachment holding the CRT to the helmet were rotated down about 30 degrees, using the display would be like looking through the bottom portion of bifocal glasses. This modification would improve cockpit visibility to the right and allow pilots to use both eyes to view the outside world and instrument panel.

The Hughes Display Laboratory engineers liked my idea. Within a couple of weeks they revised the CRT attachment housing, allowing the display to angle down 25 degrees. That position was the maximum angle it could be lowered before the CRT interfered with the pilot's oxygen mask. I renamed the display the "bifocular" HMD, a name I found amusing. Later I got to test the HMD in the TA-4C one more time. The new bifocular approach was far superior to our previous method, and I was sure it would gain better pilot acceptance. The major could now lock on to the Blue Eel Railroad Bridge.

By the time I retired in 1989, Hughes Aircraft Company had annual sales of $2 billion in infrared devices and high-technology displays for their deployment. This thermal imaging equipment has been used by our Army, Navy, and Air Force. Now our military services prefer to fly and fight at night because of the superb electronic equipment that had its genesis many years earlier at Hughes Aircraft Company.

CHAPTER 7

Flying Dumbo

The story goes that a worried doctor finally got Howard Hughes on the phone to find out if he was in good health. Hughes explained that he was as healthy as could be expected for a man his age but that he had simply decided to drop out of sight.

"Well, you'd better be careful," the doctor said. "Where I come from, a person who acts and dresses like you is called a bum."

"It's all in the definition," replied Hughes. "If I were a poor man, I would be a bum, but since I'm a rich man, I'm a recluse."

The red warning light in the cockpit immediately caught my attention. It was dusk; the sun was setting over the Pacific Ocean. I was flying a twin-engine 75,000-pound Douglas A3D Skywarrior bomber on a classified test mission. This Navy aircraft, Bureau Number 135411, was one of the earliest Skywarriors built.

Six thousand feet below me was a super-secret submarine range, and we were trying to detect subs speeding along just below the surface of the water with a new high-technology Hughes Aircraft radar. The radar was referred to as a Synthetic Aperture Radar, or SAR for short. The program was called Multi-Mission Radar (MMR), funded by the Navy to create long radar strip maps. These maps would look like the actual terrain and islands we were flying over. It was in the early 1970s; I was flying out of the Hughes private airfield in Culver City.

The A3D aircraft had two direct current generators, either one with enough electrical power to handle all the plane's requirements. The red warning light indicated that one generator had dropped off the line and was not giving any power to the aircraft. If the second generator failed, all the cockpit lights and intercom communications with four Hughes engineers in the back of the aircraft would be lost—not a pleasant thought at night.

Most likely the two generators were simply out of synchronization. If I lifted a red plastic guard that covered the failed generator toggle switch and switched it from ON to OFF and back again to ON, it would probably reset and come back on-line. It was a very simple procedure. Unfortunately, the toggle switch was located about 10 feet behind me, in a crawlway leading to the aircraft's bomb bay. It was impossible for me to reach the switch from my seat, and it was unwise to unlock my seat belt and shoulder harness, take off my parachute, and crawl back, leaving the flight controls and throttles unattended.

In Navy service, the A3D was designed for a crew of three: pilot, navigator (who also served as a bombardier), and plane captain (called a crew chief in the Air Force). All three sat in a pressurized cockpit in the nose of the aircraft. In time of war, the plane captain would depressurize the cockpit, open an entrance hatch, and climb into the bomb bay to arm the nuclear device. The plane captain was also schooled in the operation and repair of the A3D. He knew more about the aircraft systems and emergency procedures than most pilots.

In my particular case, it would have been useful to have a Navy plane captain help me solve my electrical emergency. But all I had onboard was four Hughes Aircraft electrical engineers, and ironically none of them knew anything about the A3D electrical system.

In an effort to save weight, Ed Heinemann—the Douglas Aircraft Company's chief designer of a host of successful warplanes, including the World War II SBD Dauntless and Korean War A-1 Skyraider—elected to forgo ejection seats for the A3D. By installing a crew escape chute, similar to the one on the Douglas F3D Skynight, 3,500 pounds of weight would be saved. The escape chute required all three crew members to unlock their shoulder harnesses and lap belts, jettison an escape hatch from the bottom of the fuselage, and jump down the escape chute, deploying their parachutes when free of the Skywarrior. This was a difficult and timely procedure. The lack of ejection seats later earned the Skywarrior a label, with A3D grimly denoting "All 3 Dead." Flying the A3D was hazardous enough without getting out of my parachute and climbing through the bowels of the plane.

Because fleet A3Ds were painted battleship gray and were so enormous, Navy aircrew nicknamed the aircraft *the Whale*. Hughes Aircraft made a substantial number of modifications to our A3D to prepare the aircraft for testing of the ground map radar. To house a gigantic radar antenna in the nose, a 6-foot diameter, round, black plastic radome was constructed and attached to the existing aircraft nose structure. This change earned our plane the nickname *Dumbo*.

Hughes modification engineers locked the bomb bay doors in the closed position. Several metal racks, used to hold electronic black boxes, were then screwed to the top of the doors. Four aircrew seats were also attached to the floor so that Hughes Aircraft engineers could operate and test the radar during flight.

Life in the bomb bay was anything but easy for the engineers. While the bomb bay doors were locked, they didn't completely seal. From inside the bomb bay a person could see light from the outside world through small cracks. It was an eerie sight to sit in the bomb bay, dark because there were no side windows, and watch the earth move through the cracks. During flight, some of the engineers became disoriented if I banked the Skywarrior too steeply during turns because they did not have an outside visual reference.

Several fuel lines ran from the ceiling of the bomb bay through the wings and into the under-slung engines. Although the lines did not leak, they did give off a noxious smell, which became irritating after spending several hours airborne. I was glad I didn't have to sit in the bomb bay.

As the pilot, I sat on the left side of the cockpit and had the only set of flight controls. The Navy didn't believe in wasting weight for a co-pilot; the A3D was called a single-piloted aircraft. The navigator/bombardier sat on the right side of the cockpit, behind a set of his instruments. The Navy bomb and navigation equipment was removed from our A3D and replaced with electronic instrumentation used to record the results of our radar passes. The Hughes instrumentation engineer, who rode in this position, had the best seat in the house. He had a good view out the Skywarrior's bubble canopy and oxygen was available from a mask if fumes drifted up from the bomb bay.

Over the intercom I explained to the aircrew that a red warning light had illuminated and that I would attempt to reset the generator. Pointing to the toggle switch, I asked the Hughes instrumentation engineer, who was sitting in the bomb/navigator seat, to reset the generator. Because of this semi-emergency, he was frightened and had a glazed look on his face. I wasn't sure he understood my instructions. I repeated the simple procedure several times, and he slowly crawled back into the unlit passageway. It was obvious to me that he didn't know where the generator panel was located, as he disappeared all the way into the bomb bay. After a few minutes passed, I asked the radar engineers sitting in the bomb bay to send him back to the cockpit.

Soon he reappeared and climbed the escape chute stairs back to my position. While in the bomb bay, he had caught his helmet intercom cord on a metal rack and ripped off the plug-in connector. Now he could not re-connect into the aircraft intercom. I lost communication with him except for screaming in his ear over the sound of the twin jet engines. His glassy eyes were now even glassier. I could tell that he had not comprehended a word I said; it was better for him to get back in his seat and cause no further problems.

I aborted the mission and landed at the Navy base at Point Mugu. In discussion with the other Hughes pilots who flew the A3D, we realized how dangerous it was to fly the plane without having someone else onboard that understood the A3D systems. Were a serious emergency to take place, the pilot could not get out of his seat to activate some switches, handles, and circuit breakers. These controls were all at arm's reach in the F-4C, F-111B, F-14A, and B-66, the other aircraft I had flown for Hughes Aircraft.

Twenty years earlier, Howard Hughes had made his emergency in the XF-11 worse. He released his seat belt in an attempt to move in the aircraft to a position where he could determine the cause of excessive drag on his plane. Hughes was still unstrapped when the plane crashed, and he suffered severe injuries.

A change in our procedures was mandatory. Finally, after much discussion with the other Hughes Aircraft test pilots, we decided it would be easier to train one of our aircraft mechanics to operate the radar instrumentation than to train one of the Hughes engineers in the hydraulic, electrical, and pneumatic systems in the A3D.

Bruce Bromme, a mechanic who had previously been the crew chief on the DynaCords F-4C, was chosen to fill the position. From then on,

Bromme flew with us and was prepared to assist the pilot if an emergency occurred. In fact, we never had another emergency during the rest of the program. Usually Bruce Bromme was sound asleep while we radar mapped Southern California—a good sign.

By January 1975 I had flown *Dumbo* on 127 test missions during a period of about four years. We had produced incredibly realistic radar ground maps for the Navy. However, our A3D Skywarrior was 25 years old, being the seventh aircraft produced in the early 1950s out of a total of 283 manufactured. It was getting harder and harder to find replacement parts for older A3Ds like ours, and minor aircraft problems were occurring on most test flights. The Navy was running short of money to fund our tests. Though they were very pleased with our overall results, they decided to terminate our program and schedule the last flight.

By that time in my flying career, I had flown several aircraft to the military storage facility located at Davis-Monthan Air Force Base just outside Tucson, Arizona. Pilots called this facility, made up of thousands of acres in the hot and dry Arizona desert, the Boneyard. Due to the low humidity there, aircraft do not corrode as fast as they would in other parts of the United States and therefore can be returned to active duty in the future. Some were cocooned—or pickled, as was the military phrase—so that they were better protected from the elements and returned to active service more easily.

Our A3D Skywarrior performed well for us at Hughes. We had few in-flight emergencies, and neither the ground mechanics nor the engineers were injured working on the plane. But with the age of our aircraft and lack of Navy funding, it was time to plan the last flight to the Boneyard.

Hughes engineers removed all the radar black boxes from the A3D and stored them in a warehouse in case they were needed in the future. The radar electrical connectors were covered with plastic and the wiring cables secured to bulkheads so that they would not bounce around in-flight and interfere with the aircraft flight controls. Because Davis-Monthan was about an hour's flight time away, only a partial fuel load was loaded on the aircraft. *Dumbo* would probably never fly again; there was no need to land the plane with a lot of fuel remaining in the gas tanks.

Instead of our normal crew of six, only Mike Glenn, a 30-year-old Hughes flight-test mechanic, would accompany me on *Dumbo*'s last flight. Glenn, a short, feisty Navy-trained mechanic, had worked his way up in the Hughes maintenance department from a flight line mechanic to a shift supervisor. Glenn also flew in the Navy Reserve as a crew member in the Lockheed P-3 and was very familiar with our particular A3D aircraft. If an emergency occurred while airborne, Glenn could get out of his harness and parachute, then slide into that small passageway to assist me in handling the emergency.

Final photographs were taken of *Dumbo* on the Hughes flight line for our historical records. Every test engineer who had flown in the A3D lined up in front of the plane for this last picture. Some wanted to touch *Dumbo* for the final time. Dick Ollis, our Flight Test Division modification engineer, couldn't believe our A3D was really leaving because he had worked on it for 10 years. Everyone said goodbye to our cherished friend; the event seemed to be a cross between a going away party and a memorial service.

As we flew to Arizona, Glenn and I reminisced about some of the humorous experiences we had had in flying *Dumbo*. I remembered the time one of the Hughes radar engineers accidentally got the D-Ring of his parachute caught on a metal rack and popped his chute, which then spread over the floor. Other engineers were walking on his chute as they moved around the bomb bay. The engineer wanted me to land immediately. I instructed him to gather the chute in his arms and sit quietly in his seat; we were not going to waste precious data-gathering flight time because of his foolish mistake. Our test mission was too important to abort the flight and land. After that incident, an engineer never popped a chute again; they treated their flight equipment with better care.

Glenn recalled the time we could not land at our home field in Culver City because of strong Santa Ana condition winds. I knew it would be extremely dangerous to attempt a landing with strong crosswinds, so I selected a Navy base—NAS Lemore, about 100 miles north of Los Angeles —for landing. Civilian fields were not equipped with the proper fuel, engine start carts, or security agents to support a military aircraft with classified equipment. So if a pilot could not land at our home base of Culver City, Hughes procedures were to take a Navy plane to a Navy base and an Air Force plane to an Air Force base. Because it was late in the day, I knew we would be spending the night at Lemore.

After we landed I found that the four engineers onboard had left their wallets and money in their business suits back in the locker room at

Culver City. It never dawned on them that we would land anywhere other than our home field. Glenn and I had spent enough time in the military service to know that a person could get stranded from time to time in the flying business. We both carried a flight jacket, money, and a small toiletry kit. A little preparation went a long way. The engineers were not prepared and had a miserable night.

For our flight to Davis-Monthan Air Force Base we carried a large cardboard box containing all the aircraft records that had accumulated since *Dumbo* was built. Every repair, modification, or change that had been accomplished on the engines or airframe during its entire life was documented on these military forms.

As we leveled off at 33,000 feet altitude and followed the airways to Arizona, *Dumbo* seemed to be performing the best that I could remember. With just the two of us onboard, all test equipment removed, and a partial fuel load, the aircraft was very light in weight, so we cruised effortlessly through the California sky. The engines sounded smooth, with all the engine instruments in the green; the plane didn't seem antiquated and decrepit at that moment. Maybe the old girl knew she was headed for the graveyard and as is a military custom, wanted to look sharp at the end.

Glenn and I talked about removing parts of the aircraft after we landed and keeping them as souvenirs. On the center of the flight control yoke was a 3-inch plastic disc with the Douglas Aircraft Company logo displayed; it looked inviting to me. I also thought about taking the pilot's flight operating instruction manual and checklist; if the A3D never flew again, it would not be needed. Glenn eyed the aircraft bureau number placard mounted on the instrument panel. He felt it would look good on a pen set.

We descended slowly into the hot desert air. Plenty of fuel remained, so we flew over Davis-Monthan at 5,000 feet and viewed the multitude of discarded military airplanes below us. Parked in rows, wingtip-to-wingtip, was the history of military aviation over the previous 25 years. Most of the planes would be cut up and trucked off to a salvage yard. The metal would be melted down and converted to some commercial purpose, never to be an airplane again.

I thought *Dumbo* deserved respect for its years of service as a Navy bomber during the Cold War and its use as a flying test bed for Hughes. I made a landing as smooth as humanly possible, unlike the typical crash-like landing normally performed onboard aircraft carriers. It was my way of saying thank you to this Lady of the Sky.

We taxied off the runway and maneuvered through the flight line. The control tower operator directed us to the storage area on the southeast side of the base. As we approached, several civilians opened a chain-link fence, and we followed their visual commands to the parking area. I shut down both engines, and they slowly spun to a halt.

This once pride of the Navy was now at rest; it deserved a salute. Instead, civilians, appearing as a cross between gremlins and undertakers, were slowly circling *Dumbo* and making rude comments about its enormous nose.

Glenn and I removed our flight equipment and the large box of aircraft records from the cockpit. After handing the box to the civilian supervisor, we obtained a single sheet of paper signed by him, confirming the official transfer of ownership. After all these years of flying and testing, this single sheet of paper remained our only tangible evidence of years together. We left *Dumbo* to her ultimate fate.

For the next few years, I would occasionally run into some of the Hughes engineers who had flown with me on *Dumbo*. They were sorry the Navy canceled their program and that an aircraft was not available to continue testing the ground radar map technology. They placed great faith in their Hughes design and felt it would eventually find a military customer.

Later the Air Force became interested in SAR for future application on their aircraft and funded several small study contracts. Though the results of our past test flights were classified and the locations we flew secret, the radar ground map technology gradually became top secret. Without me knowing it, the Hughes Aircraft engineers started working on what was later called the AN/APQ-181 radar, designed specially for the Northrop B-2 Spirit stealth bomber. My engineer friends were working in the black world.

Using results of our A3D MMR flight tests, Hughes Aircraft Company designers built a radar system that 16 years later was awarded the 1991 Collier Trophy, widely considered the most prestigious U.S. aviation award. The award was presented to the B-2 industrial team of Northrop and Hughes Aircraft in recognition of the "Design, development, production and flight testing of the B-2 aircraft, which has contributed significantly to America's enduring leadership in aerospace and the country's future national security." Howard Hughes had been awarded the Collier Trophy for his 1938 historic round-the-world flight. By winning the 1991 Collier Trophy, the Hughes tradition of excellence continued.

The AN/APQ-181 radar was in reality two completely redundant radar sets. The radar consisted of five line replaceable units: antenna, transmitter, signal processor, data processor, and receiver/exciter. In the event of a malfunction, the dual components would continue to provide a fully functioning radar system. With two electronically scanned antennas, one on each side of the nose wheel bay, a new feature was added to the radar called Doppler Beam Sharpening (DBS). DBS was a radically new innovation that had been flight tested on a Hughes Aircraft–owned Douglas B-26 from our Culver City airfield in the late 1970s.

The APQ-181 radar operated in Ku-band (12-18 GHZ), which was a higher frequency than the 10 GHz (X-band) used by most fighter radar. Ku-band radar required more time and more power to scan a given volume of the ground. However, it has inherently higher resolution than X-band radar and provides ground mapping with resolutions down to one foot or better at ranges of about 30–40 nautical miles, with positioning accuracy as low as 20 feet.

The B-2 Spirit stealth bomber made its operational debut on March 24, 1999, over the former Republic of Yugoslavia during Operation Allied Force. Two Spirits took off from Whiteman Air Force Base, Missouri, for a 31-hour, nonstop mission and dropped 32 of the global positioning satellites (GPS) directed by Joint Direct Attack Munitions (JDAM). The JDAM is a new form of weapon guided solely by signals from GPS. It is a kit consisting of guidance elements and fins. This allows normal dumb bombs to be turned into smart weapons for less than $25,000 apiece.

Nine B-2s assigned to the 509th Bomb Wing, the combat unit that had deployed the Boeing B-29s that dropped atomic bombs over Hiroshima and Nagasaki in World War II, were on the ramp. Eight of the planes were available for combat missions at any given time, with one reserved for training of new pilots, aircraft test, or mandatory maintenance inspections. The mission capable rate was 75 percent; however, not a single B-2 mission started late. The B-2s operated exclusively at night, sometimes in a two-ship mission, but often alone.

By May 21, when the last mission was flown by a B-2, 652 JDAMs were expended in the bombing campaign. B-2 crews flew more than 45 of the long 30-hour missions. Even though this was less than 1 percent of the total missions, the B-2 accounted for 11 percent of bombs dropped. JDAMs were also used extensively in Afghanistan and most recently in Iraq with superior results. *Dumbo*, our old A3D aircraft, would have been proud of the contribution she made to SAR radar and stealth technology.

CHAPTER 8

Gathering of Eagles and One Turkey

Two of Howard Hughes's accountants were discussing the money problems of the United States.
    "The Internal Revenue Service is its own worst enemy," said one.
    "Not while I'm alive," said Hughes.

Favorite story of Wauhillau La Hay, Syndicated Columnist, Scripps-Howard Newspapers

It was an unusual assembly of Hughes Aircraft employees. In the spring of 1974 the Air Force announced the opening of competition for the air-to-air radar to be installed on their newest fighter, the General Dynamics F-16A Fighting Falcon. In an attempt to come up with the best strategy to beat Westinghouse Electric, Hughes's chief competitor, a meeting of about 25 of the Hughes Radar System Group marketeers was scheduled in a plush hotel in Marina del Rey, only a couple of miles northwest of the Hughes main plant at Culver City.

People who sell goods and services are usually known as salesmen. But defense contractors, who sell military weapons to the U.S. government, hire marketeers to make contact with the military and attempt to influence purchase decisions. Through the years Hughes Aircraft hired a great many retired military officers, who still had personal contacts in their respective services, to perform those services. Most of the officers were either retired Air Force colonels or Navy captains and had worn a metal eagle on their uniform as a sign of their military rank when on active duty. This illustrious "Gathering of Eagles" from Hughes Aircraft offices all over the United States and many foreign countries met for several days to plan the strategy we needed to win the F-16 radar contract.

Usually a test pilot would not be invited to such a meeting. However, I had been the Hughes project test pilot on the team that had beaten Westinghouse four years earlier in a fly-off competition for the air-to-air radar on the F-15A Eagle. My experience was deemed valuable because Hughes would be required to compete for the F-16 radar in another fly-off competition conducted now by General Dynamics (GD) in Fort Worth, Texas, the following year. In addition, I was scheduled to be the project test pilot for our F-16 radar test program.

Our version of the radar would be installed in an Air Force F-4D Phantom, which I would fly on test missions from our Hughes runway at Culver City. Air Force and GD test pilots would fly with me and make recommendations on the selection of the radar contractor. My knowledge of our planned strategy could be critical in influencing these pilots.

In true military fashion, the strategy meeting started at 7 a.m. in the hotel conference room. I recognized many of the marketeers from past test programs I had flown. Robert DeHaven, my boss, the manager of the Flight Test Division, and a reserve Air Force colonel, also attended the meeting.

Retired Air Force Colonel Maurice L. "Marty" Martin, our St. Louis district marketing manager, also attended. Martin flew 350 combat missions in World War II, Korea, and Vietnam. During the D-Day invasion of Europe, he flew four different aircraft and received battle damage on each. Although he was hit by ground fire on every mission, he managed to get back safely to his home base. The only time he was shot down was in 1947 as a truce observer for the United Nations in Palestine. I had worked closely with Martin during the F-15A radar fly-off in St. Louis during the summer of 1970.

Retired Navy Commodore Lewis "Scotty" Lamoreaux looked at the competition from a Navy perspective. Lamoreaux had come in second place in the 1961 Bendix Trophy Race, flying an F4H-1 Phantom from Ontario International Airport, California, to Floyd Bennett Field, New York. I met Lamoreaux three years earlier when he was still on active duty as commander of the Fighter Early Warning Wing, Pacific. At the time I was flying test missions in the F-14A Tomcat from Point Mugu. Lamoreaux flew a test mission in one of our F-14As to evaluate the progress we had made early in the program. I briefed him on our aircraft and acted as a safety chase for him flying a Navy F-4. Later, as a Hughes employee, Lamoreaux kept track of requirements the Navy had for advanced radar and would advise the group on the possibility of selling our radar to the Navy.

Retired Air Force Colonel Emmett "Cyclone" Davis was the marketeer with the best sense of humor. He had flown P-38s during World War II and commanded a fighter test squadron at Eglin Air Force Base, Florida, after the war. He painted the inscription, "Cyclone Davis, the Mormon Meteor, No Guts, No Glory" on his flight helmet and nicknamed his son "Typhoon." Davis had been very instrumental in helping Hughes Aircraft win the F-15 radar program.

Retired Air Force Colonel Barney Turner was one of the finest gentlemen I ever met. Everyone liked Turner; he was handsome, quiet, and pleasant to be around. He had flown P-40s in North Africa during World War II and was a fighter test pilot at Eglin in the early jet era. Turner was the Hughes Aircraft Program Manager for the F-16 radar competition, the perfect person to keep his cool when the competition juices got flowing.

Listening to strategy discussions was new to me because of my flight-test background: Before the meeting, I thought radar programs were won or lost in the air flying test flights. Soon it became evident that more than a long-range radar detection and lock on was needed to win a multi-million-dollar radar contract. In addition to the fly-off, there were many marketing and business strategies that needed to be thought through to put Hughes Aircraft in the best possible position to win. I also heard rumors that a high-stakes poker game was planned for the evening. It was a fitting game, as marketeers were in the bluff-and-bluster business.

During the conference I met William H. "Bill" Bell, a marketeer for Hughes Aircraft who lived in Europe. Bill was about 15 years older than me, and probably 6 feet, 5 inches tall—a massive appearing man. He had a big grin, a wide mustache, and a bone-crushing handshake. Typical of all the marketeers, he was outgoing, always had a joke to tell, and thought Hughes Aircraft could beat any competitor, with any of our products, any place and any time. He was a "rah-rah" kind of guy. I found out that Bell enlisted in the Navy at age 18 and was aboard a minesweeper at Pearl Harbor when the Japanese attacked. He served honorably throughout the war, suffering wounds at Iwo Jima. After the war Bell married, raised two sons and a daughter, and earned a degree in physics from UCLA. In 1950 he went to work for Hughes Aircraft in Culver City.

In the early 1950s, Hughes Aircraft became a major defense contractor and a leading innovator of new electronic technology. Bell became a competent radar system engineer and by the early 1960s managed Hughes projects in the United States. Later, the company reassigned him overseas. By the time of our meeting in 1974, the value of the dollar, vis-È-vis European currencies, declined, and consequently the cost of living in Europe skyrocketed. Bell had always lived beyond his means. It was later learned he had exhausted his savings and his marriage had started to fall apart.

Bill Bell was transferred back to Culver City in March of 1976. At the age of 56, Bell felt shunted aside at Hughes Aircraft in favor of younger men and he judged that his prospects for career advancement were bleak. The Internal Revenue Service (IRS) disallowed large deductions he claimed during his overseas assignment, and four separate IRS offices hounded him for overdue taxes. Overwhelmed by debt, he filed for bankruptcy.

During the fall of 1976, Hughes Aircraft Company received a special request from the Air Force Test Pilot School at Edwards Air Force Base. Because avionics flight test was becoming a greater part of their curriculum, the school asked for a presentation on both the latest Hughes technology and the methods we used to test our products. Bill Bell was selected to talk on technology, and I would explain avionics flight test to the students. I looked forward to speaking to the students because I had graduated from the school 12 years earlier and remembered how much I enjoyed guest speakers during my time.

Bell and I discussed our presentation over the phone. At the time, he was living in the Cross Creek Village apartment complex in Playa del Rey, a couple of miles directly west of the Hughes runway. He told me he planned to drive to Lancaster, a town about 40 miles north of Los Angeles, and rent a motel the night before our talk.

Bell's first marriage ended in divorce and he was now married to a Belgian airline stewardess who was about 25 years younger than him. She had a small son from a previous marriage. Bell asked that I pick him up at his motel and we drive together the last 30 miles to Edwards. This plan would give his wife their car while we were giving our talk.

Bell relayed a tragic story to me while I drove to Edwards. A couple of years earlier his 18-year-old son Kevin and a friend had gone on a camping trip to Mexico. While on the trip a campfire exploded, burning Kevin. The other boy called Bell and explained that Kevin had been burned but was recovering. The following day the boy called again and said that Kevin died. Bell was grief stricken. He and his first wife immediately started arguing over what they could have done to prevent the disaster. The added stress finished off his first marriage. He divorced his wife of nearly 30 years, lost most of his assets, and was obligated to pay alimony of $200 per week. It was obvious to me that Bell was an emotional wreck. In a very short period of time his son died, his marriage failed, and he lost all his money. This was a situation more dreadful than most people can endure.

Bell and I gave our presentation to the test pilot students. He talked about some of Hughes's latest avionics programs in great detail. It seemed to me that parts of his talk might have been classified confidential, but I wasn't sure. If not confidential, then the information would certainly be called "competition sensitive," meaning information we did not want in the hands of our competitors.

All aerospace companies worked with government classified information; Hughes Aircraft was no exception. As employees, we were all given an extensive background check before getting a security clearance. Then we were given careful instructions on the handling of this sensitive material. In addition, Hughes Aircraft was a private company owned by the Howard Hughes Medical Institute in which Howard Hughes was the sole trustee. Hughes himself was a very secretive person. He expected his employees to guard details about his business and personal affairs. Howard Hughes was also very anti-communist.

Hughes Aircraft also had many special designs and plans we called Company Private. Bell was talking about some of them, and I felt uneasy listening to him. At least I knew the students were solid American citizens, remembering the vast background check made on me before I attended the school. Nevertheless, I had great concerns about Bell.

On a fall weekend in 1977, Bell chanced to meet Marion Zacharski, a neighbor in his Playa Del Rey apartment complex. Zacharski introduced himself as the West Coast manager of Polamco, a Chicago company that imported and exported industrial machinery. Although Bell assumed that

Polamco was an American company, the firm was really owned by the Polish government, and Zacharski was a Polish intelligence officer. Handsome, charming, and mannerly, Zacharski was only 26—nearly young enough to be the son Bell had recently lost. Upon learning that Bell specialized in radar systems at Hughes Aircraft, he began behaving toward him as a son and friend. He insisted on playing tennis with him daily and downgraded his superior game so that the matches would be enjoyable for Bell. Explaining that he had a generous expense account for public relations, he stopped by with small yet welcome presents. On the tennis court and over drinks or dinner afterward, he gradually came to fill the void in Bell's life created by the death of his son.

The two friends naturally discussed their work. Zacharski was interested in obtaining work from Hughes Aircraft and requested standard company brochures from Bell. He then asked for a Hughes phone book and organizational charts of radar personnel.

When Zacharski inquired about contacts at Hughes Aircraft who might be interested in buying machinery through Polamco, Bell gave him a few names. Three or four days later, Zacharski unexpectedly appeared in the evening, thanked Bell for the contacts, and, as compensation, handed him $4,000 in cash. Bell was sure that his trivial service had not resulted in sales and did not warrant such a large payment. But as Zacharski knew, Bell needed money.

In the fall of 1978, Zacharski proposed that after retirement from Hughes Aircraft, Bell join Polamco as a consulting engineer. Bell was 58 years old, had worked 28 years with Hughes, and was eligible to retire. Flattered and excited by the offer, Bell saw in the proposal a gratifying new career and an end to financial concerns.

Bell had recently completed a secret study for Hughes, and to impress Zacharski with his qualifications, he showed it to him on the tennis court. Seeing that the document was labeled SECRET, Zacharski asked to take it to his apartment where he could study it safely. Bell knew that was wrong. But after all, he rationalized, it was not uncommon for engineers being interviewed by prospective employers to divulge trade secrets.

The apartment complex at Playa del Rey was being converted to condominiums, and Zacharski asked Bell if he intended to purchase one. Bell replied that he could not possibly afford a down payment. Perhaps,

Zacharski suggested, Polamco could help him because he was likely to become its employee in the future.

Early one evening in January 1979, Bell answered the ring on his doorbell. Smiling, Zacharski silently handed him an envelope filled with 70 $100 bills.

Bell looked at the cash and murmured, "Thank you."

A week or so later, Zacharski came again and, without a word, presented an envelope containing about $5,000. The unexpected funds freed Bell from tormenting financial pressures, enabling him to pay his back taxes and make a down payment on the condominium.

In April 1979 Zacharski gave him another unsolicited present, a Canon camera that had a zoom lens and would photograph documents frame by frame. Then Zacharski asked a favor. His company would like to have some documents from Hughes Aircraft—could Bell photograph them? Grateful to his friend and benefactor, and lured by visions of more money, Bell agreed. He consoled himself with the fiction that he was merely embarking upon industrial espionage. During the next months, he photographed hundreds upon hundreds of pages from documents that he took home with him at night and replaced at Hughes the next morning.

In September 1979 Zacharski announced that Bell must travel to Europe for negotiations. As directed, Bell flew to Switzerland, drove to Innsbruck, and registered at the Grauer Bar Hotel. As he stepped from the hotel lobby in the morning, a man approached. The man introduced himself as Paul.

In nearly faultless English he asked, "Are you a friend of Marion's?"

Paul was Anatoliusz Inowolski, a Polish intelligence officer posing as a trade representative in New York, who had left the United States weeks earlier. Driving away from the hotel with Paul and a younger Polish officer, Bell handed over three cartridges of film, which included information on Hughes's radar systems. At a shopping center, the younger officer left the film with an agent in one of the stores, and they drove to an isolated area in the foothills outside Innsbruck. With his subordinate, Paul led Bell along an empty path and questioned him about his work and access at Hughes Aircraft.

Abruptly, Paul stopped and showed Bell pictures of his young Belgian wife and her small son, taken near their apartment in California.

"You have a lovely family," he said in a tone that chilled Bell.

"Only a very few people know about the operation we're engaged in," he added. "We depend upon each other for our security." Waving the pictures, he warned, "If anybody gets out of line, I personally will take care of them."

The clearly implied threat against his family frightened Bell and stripped away all illusions about what he was doing. When they met again that afternoon near the Olympic ski lift, Paul asked him what he thought his future services would be worth.

"Fifty thousand a year and two or three thousand a month," Bell answered.

Paul gave him $5,000 in $100 bills and $2,000 to compensate for travel costs, together with instructions for their next meeting in Innsbruck on May 7, 1980. Additionally, the Polish intelligence officers gave him a list of specific data to be procured at Hughes Aircraft.

Back at Hughes, Bell dutifully began fulfilling the orders and turned over film to Zacharski, who early in 1980 gave him two payments of $5,000 each. Carrying film revealing the design of numerous advanced radar and missile systems, Bell returned to Innsbruck and drove to the ticket office of a cable car company where Paul's younger partner greeted him. Over the mountains in the cable car, Bell passed the film to him.

As they alighted from the car, Paul stepped forward to shake hands and led Bell away for a walk, leaving his lieutenant to guard against surveillance. The Polish intelligence officers, or rather, the KGB, concluded that what Bell was stealing was worth even more than he had asked.

"A decision has been made to pay you $60,000 and $3,000 a month," Paul informed Bell. "At least at the outset, the payments will be made in gold coins."

Paul insisted that Bell obtain employment at the Defense Advanced Research Projects Agency (DARPA), which sponsored research to achieve major technological breakthroughs in weaponry. Again he threatened reprisals against Bell and his family if there were any security breaches.

While on a business trip to the East Coast in the summer of 1980, Bell did call to see a friend at DARPA. He hoped to gather enough courage to confess to his friend and ask his help in extricating himself from espionage. But the friend was absent. Fearing that he or his family would be harmed, Bell continued to serve his masters. Each month

Zacharski delivered a $5,000 payment, usually in gold coins, though once he dropped cash into Bell's tennis bag near the court.

What Bell did not know was that the CIA had informed the FBI about a leak of classified information at Hughes Aircraft. Jim Easton, who had been the F-15 radar fly-off manager, was the only one brought on board. Easton kept in constant touch with the FBI on Bell's travel and reviewed wire taps of his phone. He also kept Bell off new radar programs, and one time went into his office at night with the combination to his classified safe. Easton surveyed all documents in Bell's possession without disturbing their arrangement.

In midsummer of 1980 Zacharski spoke gravely. He was sure either the FBI or CIA was following him, and Bell also might be under surveillance. They should say nothing incriminating either on the telephone or in their apartments.

Playing tennis on the morning of August 30, Zacharski stopped and nodded toward the nearby parking lot.

"Look! There they are," he said.

Only two cars were on the lot, each occupied by a lone driver.

Bell confronted them, demanding, "Who are you, and what are you doing here?"

They stared at him indifferently and said nothing, so he went to his apartment and from the window photographed the cars. He left his camera on the ledge when he returned to the court. When he came home from tennis, the camera was gone. It was a bad portent, but Bell did not know what to do except go on.

Preparing for his next meeting in Europe, Bell photographed secret and vital documents. On a stormy morning in October 1980, Bill kept his appointment with Paul's partner in Linz, Austria, about an hour's drive from the Czechoslovakian border. They drank coffee in a workers' cafe, whose only other patron was a menacing-looking man dressed as a manual laborer. Paul took the film, disappeared into the kitchen, and upon returning motioned to Bell to accompany him outside. In the gloom, they strode up a narrow path to confer securely in the woods. Above a hedge, the grinning face of the man who had been in the cafe appeared, and Bell thought he was about to be killed. Laughing at his fright, Paul explained that their watcher was guarding him because he was carrying so much cash, including $7,000 for Bell. The officer instructed him about more

documents to be copied and showed him a map of their next meeting site in
Geneva.

Early in 1981 Zacharski moved to Chicago to become president of
Polamco, and Bell worked on his own. As scheduled, on the morning of
April 22, Bell exchanged information with a contact at the Ariana Museum, across the street from the Soviet Mission in Geneva. The film he
had with him contained the most sensitive data yet stolen from Hughes.

Bell followed his contact into the nearby offices of the United Nations
and, on the elevator, passed him the film from his briefcase. The two men
then walked to the edge of Lake Geneva, where the contact gave him
$7,000 and instructions for the next meeting, which was to take place at the
Museum of Anthropology in Mexico City. The contact fairly gloated over
the loot. But Bell left the rendezvous full of foreboding, fearful that he had
been watched everywhere in Geneva.

He was more correct than he could imagine. Alerted by Zacharski
as to what Bell was delivering, the KGB had sent senior officers from
Moscow to monitor the rendezvous and take immediate possession of the
film. The KGB was watching Bell wherever he went in Geneva. In turn,
the CIA was watching both Bell and the KGB officers trailing him.

Agents in the Soviet Bloc friendly to America had intercepted
technology known to exist only at Hughes Aircraft. Their investigation,
conducted with the cooperation of Hughes Aircraft, focused on a number
of suspects, and Bell eventually became one of them. Although still lack-
ing evidence adequate for prosecution, the FBI was sufficiently suspi-
cious to put him under full-time surveillance and ask the CIA to track his
movements in Europe.

When Bell reported to work at Hughes on June 23, 1981, a supervisor
summoned him to a conference room.

"Bell, these gentlemen are from the FBI," he said. "They would like
to speak to you."

Bell slumped into a chair, buried his head in his hands, and, for a while,
said nothing. Then over the next six hours he confessed and ultimately
agreed to help gather additional evidence against Zacharski. On June 28th,
wearing a body microphone, he recorded a clandestine conversation with
Zacharski that further and conclusively proved their guilt.

William Holden Bell stood in a federal court in Los Angeles on
December 14, 1981. Because of his cooperation with the government, he

was given only an eight-year sentence. But for a man of 61, eight years can be a long time.

Zacharski, then 30, was sentenced to life imprisonment, and all his appeals were denied. The Soviet Union did all in its power to extricate him—for its debt to him was great. In June 1985, Zacharski was released in a prisoner exchange among the United States, East Germany, and Poland.

In a damage assessment submitted to the Senate Permanent Subcommittee on Investigations, the CIA revealed that the information in documents Bell passed to the Soviet Bloc put in jeopardy existing weapons and advanced future weapon systems of the United States and its allies. The acquisition of this information saved the Polish and Soviet governments approximately $185 million in research and development efforts by permitting them to implement proven designs developed by the United States and by fielding operational counterpart systems in a five-year shorter time period. It showed how much the Soviet Union valued and desired the research conducted at Hughes Aircraft and the degree they would go to get it.

The arrest of William Bell shocked us at Hughes Aircraft Company. Many had worked with him on radar programs and couldn't believe an employee of 31 years would turn against both his company and his country. Some could not bring themselves to believe the espionage charges against him until he confessed in open court. It was a sad chapter in the history of Hughes Aircraft Company during the Cold War. But it was also a wake-up call to those of us who handled classified information on a daily basis to be extremely vigilant. Most of all, it was a warning that there could always be a turkey in any gathering of eagles.

CHAPTER 9

California Dreamin'

If Howard Hughes ever lies in state, it will be his first public appearance in twenty years.

Favorite quip of Constance Lawn, President, Video News Bureau

It was the spring of 1975. I continued flying from the company's private airfield at Culver City. Previously Hughes Aircraft had won the competition to build the AWG-9 system and AIM-54A Phoenix missile for the Navy's F-14A Tomcat fighter. I had been flight testing the Tomcat for the past three years, firing Phoenix, Sparrow, and Sidewinder missiles at drones over the Pacific Ocean. Hughes had also won the contract to build the radar for the Air Forces top air superiority fighter, the F-15A Eagle. I was the Hughes project test pilot for that program, too, flying a modified B-66 for a couple of years.

In each of these fierce competitions we had won a contract, beating Westinghouse Electric. Now we were in an intense battle again, this time for the F-16A radar. If we could beat them one more time, we might run them out of the fighter radar business.

The Air Force loaned Hughes an F-4D Phantom fighter aircraft to modify with our version of the F-16A radar. We had six months to evaluate and improve this radar at Culver City before another fly-off competition against Westinghouse would be held in September and October of 1975 at the General Dynamics plant in Fort Worth, Texas.

Air Force Captain Joe Bill Dryden was scheduled to be one of six pilots selected to evaluate our radar during the fly-off. Dryden was born and raised in Texas. He was tall and thin, and he wore his flight suit as though it were tailored to him. The zippers on his suit were always closed, and his black flight boots shone to a high luster. He graduated from the Air Force Academy in 1962 and the Fighter Weapons School at Nellis Air Force Base, Nevada, in 1969. He flew combat in Vietnam in the illustrious MiG-killing 555th (Triple Nickel) Fighter Squadron, flying the F-4. Dryden knew the fighter business and would fly test missions with me in the F-4D and our T-33 target aircraft.

By 1975 Captain Dryden was stationed at Edwards Air Force Base. He was part of the military test team that evaluated both the Northrop YF-17 and the General Dynamics YF-16 for the new Air Force Light Weight Fighter (LWF) Program. The YF-16 aircraft had just won the competition; now the Air Force was looking for an air-to-air radar to install in the sleek new fighter. We would be spending a lot of time together; it was important for me to take good care of him.

"Would you like to see the Howard Hughes *Racer*?" I asked Dryden.

My previous offers to military aviators to view the *Racer* had never been turned down before. I was sure Captain Dryden would be interested.

"Howard set a world speed record of 352 mph in 1935," I added.

Bruce Burk held the keys to a World War II–designed Quonset hut where the *Racer* was stored. The hut was located next to our Flight Test Division building. Few Hughes Aircraft employees knew the prized aircraft was stored so nearby. I called Burk, and he agreed to meet Dryden and me at the entrance and unlock the secret building. We could get a peek at the *Racer* if we brought a flashlight.

For the previous 38 years Bruce Burk had been the caretaker of aircraft Howard Hughes had left scattered around the country. Burk came to work for Hughes in January 1937 as an aeronautical engineer. Hughes liked his work and put him in charge of all the aircraft mechanics who took care of Hughes's personal aircraft. His group was called the Rust Watchers.

The Quonset hut was a long metal building without windows. Just a couple of 50-watt bulbs, hanging from a long cord, illuminated the dust-covered collection of old aircraft parts and tools. At one time in the 1940s, half of the building contained special experimental fuels Howard

Hughes was interested in testing. It was hazardous material to store, and it caused a couple of explosions.

Once inside, a chain-link fence formed a center hallway, preventing visitors from touching any of the personal items belonging to Hughes. Items from the XF-11 twin-engine reconnaisance aircraft were stored in huge wooden bins. Molds from the H-4 Hercules were lying against the bins. Parts of the huge XH-17 jet-powered helicopter could be seen gathering dust in a corner.

Behind the locked chain-link fence sat the ghostlike *Racer* covered with a canvas tarp. The vertical tail was exposed, and the double-bladed prop had a blanket wrapped around it. Off to the left leaning against a wall was the *Racer's* second set of wings. Burk used a key to open the lock and politely backed away like a funeral director letting a family have the last viewing.

Pilots have a habit of always looking inside the cockpit of a plane first. Joe Bill Dryden and I lifted the tarp with our hands, stepped under it like a tent, and peeked in at the cockpit. I felt an eerie presence there. I half expected the mysterious billionaire to be sitting in the dusty cockpit pointing out its many innovative design features, far ahead of their time.

The cockpit was as small as that in the F-4 we were flying. How did the long-legged Hughes ever fit into the cramped cockpit? The answer to that question was that both the windscreen and the canopy were a unique design. The canopy was made up of two sections that slid down into the fuselage on each side, like windows of a car. The windscreen could be cranked forward 12 inches so that the seat would move up and forward. This allowed Hughes to see over the nose during takeoff and landing. Because the seat moved both up and forward, Hughes was still able to reach the rudder pedals. He also installed leather pads on both sides of the cockpit sills and the top of the instrument panel to prevent cutting himself on the sharp edges.

The throttle and mixture controls on the *Racer* were very small, each a thin metal rod with a silver ball on the end. The control stick was also very elementary. Our Phantom had a control stick with an electrical trim button, bomb and rocket release buttons, and a nose-wheel steering button. The latest buzzword in the Air Force was Hands-on-the-Throttle-and-Stick (HOTAS). The HOTAS concept called for all controls to operate the aircraft, radar, and weapons to be on the throttle and control stick. In our Phantom, with the modified radar system, we could fly and fight without ever taking our hands off these controls. There were no buttons on the *Racer*'s control stick or throttle. Obviously Hughes had not designed the *Racer* as a fighter, but it was the world's fastest aircraft in its time.

I immediately recognized a turn-and-bank indicator located on the upper right-hand side of the *Racer*'s instrument panel. The same instrument was installed in our Phantom, a plane designed 35 years later. Some features never go out of style. I saw a magnetic compass in the center of the instrument panel and, to the right of it, a three-axis autopilot with directional gyro, horizon, and suction gauge.

Attached to the side of the cockpit was a black leather tool kit. Inside the kit were a screwdriver, crescent wrench, pliers, and an assortment of light bulbs and screws. Joe Bill Dryden and I could not find a map case.

"Except for his record flights," said Burk, "Hughes did not always plot a course or plan his flights very well. Sometimes he just took off and headed in the general direction of his destination."

"Howard had a lot of guts," he added. "He put both his life and his money in this aircraft."

The *Racer* employed features that made it an extremely modern airplane for its era. We could see that the aircraft had a close-fitting bell-shaped engine cowling to reduce airframe drag and improve engine cooling. It had gently curving wing fillets between the wing and the fuselage to help stabilize the airflow, reduce drag, and prevent potentially dangerous eddying and tail buffeting. Even under the tarp I could see that the *Racer* had gracious curves. On the other hand, the Phantom with upturned wing tips and a stabilizer slanted downward, needed brute force to push it through the air.

"Your F-4 looks like someone shut the hangar door on it," said Burk.

A yellow painted handle installed on the right side of the cockpit activated the brakes. This seemed to Dryden and me like a poor design. A pilot would have to take his right hand off the control stick and pull the handle to brake. Normally after landing in a tail-wheel aircraft, the pilot retracted the flaps, applied full aft stick, and placed the aileron into the wind. This procedure would be difficult in the *Racer*. Nevertheless, Captain Joe Bill Dryden and I would have eagerly traded our radar test flights in the Phantom to fly the *Racer*. But that was just California dreamin'.

The General Dynamics F-16A Fighting Falcon is one of the most significant fighters of the latter part of the 20th century. It was originally developed from a concept for an experimental lightweight fighter, and it evolved into an all-weather fighter and precision attack aircraft. As early as 1965, the Air Force began concept formulation studies of a new lightweight Advanced Day Fighter (ADF). The ADF was to be in the 25,000-pound class and have a thrust-to-weight ratio and a wing loading that would be better than the performance of the MiG-21 by at least 25 percent.

Former fighter instructor Major John Boyd and Pierre Sprey, a civilian working in the office of the Assistant Secretary of Defense for Systems Analysis, conceived of the ADF concept. They both disliked the F-15 concept as it then existed and preferred a much simpler design. In the late 1960s, they came up with a design, which was to be a dedicated air superiority fighter with high endurance, minimal electronics, and no long-range missiles.

Deputy Defense Secretary David A. Packard was a strong advocate of returning to the concept of competitive prototyping as a way of containing the ever-increasing costs of new weapons systems. Under the new competitive prototyping philosophy, Air Force officials drew up a set of ground rules in which the initial funding of a new weapons project would be relatively limited, with the initial performance goals and military specifications being kept to a minimum.

The Light-Weight Fighter (LWF) program came into being under Packard's watch, replacing the ADF concept. A request for proposal (RFP) was issued to the industry. The RFP called for an aircraft with a high thrust-to-weight ratio, a gross weight of less than 20,000 pounds, and high maneuverability. No attempt would be made to equal the performance of the MiG-25 Foxbat; the emphasis was being placed instead on the most likely conditions of future air combat—altitudes of 30,000 to 40,000 feet and speeds of Mach 0.6 to Mach 1.6. Emphasis was to be on turn rate, acceleration, and range, rather than on high speed. A small size was stressed, because the small size of the MiG-17 and MiG-21 had made them difficult to detect visually during combat over North Vietnam. The RFP specified three main objectives: The aircraft should fully explore the advantages of emerging technologies, reduce the risk and uncertainties involved in full-scale development and production, and provide a variety of technological options to meet future military hardware needs.

In the meantime, with the selection of McDonnell Douglas to build the F-15 Eagle, General Dynamic's engineers had been concentrating on studies of an aircraft for daytime dogfighting, with only minimal air-to-air electronics being provided. The Source Selection Authority of the LWF program rated the General Dynamics and Northrop proposal ahead of the other competitors, and their design was chosen for further development. Contracts for the two designs were awarded under the designation YF-16 and YF-17, respectively. Rather than the X (experimental) prefix being used, the Y (development) prefix was used in order to indicate that a mixture of off-the-shelf and experimental technologies was being incorporated.

The Air Force ordered two examples of each design. A fly-off of the two designs would be carried out against each other, although there was no assurance that any production of the winning candidate would actually be awarded. At the time, the Air Force was still very much committed to the F-15 fighter, and it visualized the LWF program as more of a technology demonstration project rather than a serious effort for a production aircraft. The contracts covered the design, construction, and testing of two prototypes, plus a year of flight testing.

In February 1974 General Dynamics test pilot Phil Oestricher made the first flight of the YF-16. By then the aircraft had a fly-by-wire control system, and a number of elements were added to aid the pilot in up to 9G combat. These included a side-stick console layout, an ejection seat tilted backwards by 30 degrees, and an all-around vision bubble canopy.

In late fall of that year, the Air Force awarded small contracts to Hughes Aircraft and Westinghouse to develop competitive models of a radar system for the LWF. Air Force officials said the project could eventually produce hundreds of millions of dollars in business for one of the companies. By then the Air Force planned to buy 650 of the fighters and hoped to sell more than 2,000 planes abroad. Hughes Aircraft received a $4 million contract and Westinghouse a $3.9 million award for development, fabrication, and flight-test demonstration of an airborne search-and-track radar.

After the hectic F-15A fly-off competition, Hughes managers decided to change their method of doing business. Even though we had won the F-15 program, it had been a very difficult competition due to aircraft problems and our immature prototype radar. A decision was made to spend enough money to improve our position in every segment of the program. Hughes engineer Jim Easton would again run the flight-test program and this time hand select everyone who participated in the competition.

The air vehicle to be used for the F-16 radar fly-off was an F-4D Phantom, painted in standard green and brown camouflage color. To make certain we knew as much as possible about the individual aircraft that would be loaned to us from the Air Force, I flew it from Kirtland Air Force Base, New Mexico, to Culver City. Because I was not yet checked out in the F-4D, Air Force pilot Major Dick Lawyer flew with me. Lawyer was an old friend of mine from Edwards Air Force Base; he had been in the class ahead of me in the test pilot school.

The modification of our Phantom took three and a half months and was completed in our hangar. Unlike the B-66 used in the F-15A radar program, our F-4D was designed with a complete set of radar controls and displays in both the front and rear seats. A centerline 300-gallon fuel tank was modified to hold a data instrument system. The Phantom's nose and wingtips were painted dayglow orange so that the plane could be easily seen by other aircraft flying in the congested airspace of Los Angeles.

Oops Martin again would service the system with data tapes. Fortunately, the fuel tank was so small Martin couldn't get inside it. However, he was still taking a kidding for mistakenly getting aboard the Westinghouse B-66 in St. Louis four years earlier.

By January of 1975 the Air Force chose the General Dynamics YF-16 for production. Two months later, test pilot Bill Jessup and I traveled to Edwards Air Force Base to check out in the F-4D. This would be the fourth time I went through training in the Phantom. In 1967, as an Air Force test pilot, I flew test programs in the aircraft, evaluating changes to the flight controls. Then when I came to work with Hughes Aircraft in 1969, I again checked out in the plane so I could fly both DynaCords and AGM-65A Maverick missile test missions. Before Jessup and I could in-flight refuel in the F-14A Tomcat, we were required to go through another flight qualification in the F-4J, the Navy version of the

Phantom. With so much flying time in the twin-engine fighter, I looked forward to flying the plane again and another fly-off competition against Westinghouse.

On April 1, Jessup and I made the shakedown flight in the F-4D. Bruce Bromme, who had been the crew chief on the F-4C used on the DynaCords program and the Navy A3D, now had the responsibility of keeping our F-4D Phantom running smoothly.

Compared with the F-15 radar program, we got off to a fast start and were tracking airline targets of opportunity on the second mission. Within a week we were flying radar passes on our T-33 target in the Edwards Air Force Base restricted area. The standard test mission consisted of head-on and tail-on radar passes over a path called Cords Road.

Cords Road was a service road for power lines that ran straight as an arrow for about 50 miles. The west end of the road was just north of the town of Mojave. The east end of the road was Harper Dry Lake.

Harper Dry Lake was the site where Howard Hughes had flown his wooden D-2 prototype bomber aircraft back in 1943. Prior to the start of World War II, Hughes had wanted to design and build a twin-boom, twin-engine aircraft to be used by the Army Air Corps for use in that conflict. He designed a plane with the smoothest finish possible, so he selected Duramold plywood. Duramold was plastic-bonded plywood molded under heat and high pressure.

Hughes taxied the plane at his Culver City airport and then flew it for the first time from Harper Dry Lake. The plane performed poorly and was later lost in a hangar fire. Some evidence of the hangar, which had burned 32 years earlier, could still be seen on the southwest corner of the lakebed.

On the eighth mission of our test program, Captain Joe Bill Dryden piloted his first flight in the Phantom. I flew in the back seat, prepped the radar, and ran the data instrumentation. We made several successful passes on the T-33, which was flying only 500 feet above the ground. This was our first mission against a target flying that low. Over the next months Jessup, Dryden, and I took turns flying the front seat of the F-4D. The radar was performing like dynamite, and we were getting loads of data.

Just when we started to relax, a problem developed. Coming in to land at Culver City, Captain Dryden ingested a bird in the F-4D's left engine. He was able to land safely, but the engine needed to be replaced.

Flying off the Culver City runway continued to be hazardous. Through the years more commercial airline traffic was taking off and landing at nearby Los Angeles International. Also, there were more general aviation aircraft flying around Clover Field at Santa Monica. Using the afterburner for takeoff, we normally got noise complaints from administrators at either Loyola University, sitting up on the Westchester bluff, or residents of Marina del Rey. With all these unsafe conditions we Hughes test pilots thought our days of flying from Culver City were probably numbered.

Crew Chief Bruce Bromme and his mechanics worked around the clock over the weekend to install another J-79 engine. After the engine was installed I couldn't get it to start, so Bromme removed an ignition plug from the old engine. He replaced the plug and I got the engine started, but the generator would not come on-line. With all of these mechanical problems, I wondered if we were returning to the bad luck we had experienced on the F-15A radar program in St. Louis. Finally, we got the F-4D back in commission and continued test missions.

Later, whenever Captain Dryden flew the F-4D and I acted as his target in the T-33, we always saved a little fuel at the end of the last radar pass. As soon as we obtained all the data needed by the Hughes engineers, we started dogfighting (i.e., simulated air-to-air combat). Dryden's F-4D had plenty of power; he could fly faster than my T-33 but couldn't turn as tight. If I kept the T-33 low over the desert and pulled 5Gs, I could keep Dryden in sight and convert every attack he made on me into a head-on pass. We went at it like two old Vietnam War veterans giving their all for an airborne kill.

One time we broke off our air engagement and Dryden flew back to Culver City at high speed. I couldn't keep up with him but could see dark exhaust smoke from his two J-79 engines as he flew south and crossed the town of Palmdale, California. Pushing the T-33 throttle to the forward stop, I tried to keep Dryden in sight as he crossed the mountains north of Los Angeles, but he disappeared from view.

When Dryden and I landed at Culver City we were in trouble—but not because of our air-to-air hassles over the Mojave Desert. Captain Dryden had made a low-level sightseeing trip over Beverly Hills and caused quite a commotion. With the nose and wingtips painted in day-glow orange, our Phantom was very visible to ground observers. No other military aircraft like ours was flying over the Los Angeles basin, so noise complaints came into the Hughes Aircraft switchboard. Influential people lived in Beverly Hills, and a complaint from anyone living there was taken very seriously.

Years earlier Howard Hughes had landed a plane on a Beverly Hills golf course and Noah Dietrich, his business agent, had paid $1,000 to keep the incident quiet. In 1946 Hughes crashed his XF-11 spy plane into two homes in Beverly Hills, nearly killing himself. Dryden had neither landed on a golf course nor crashed; nevertheless, he probably worried the wealthy individuals of Beverly Hills. Some might take action to shut down our airport.

In addition, we heard that the Los Angeles news media had picked up on the story and were coming to the Culver City airport to interview Hughes Aircraft Company public relations officials. I knew the Air Force would get involved with the incident, and there was a chance all flight operations from our airfield could be terminated. Field closure would be terrible news for our F-16A radar program and could possibly affect my employment at Hughes Aircraft if all our test aircraft were returned to the military. We gathered together and planned damage control.

Just as we waited for the news media to gather on our doorstep, a gift from heaven appeared. Another incident occurred that made up for all the bad luck we had experienced in the F-15A radar fly-off in St. Louis and now our current F-16A ills in Culver City. Patty Hearst, who had been kidnapped by the Symbionese Liberation Army in the Bay Area, had been found. The reporters assigned to the Beverly Hills F-4D noise incident were diverted to San Francisco to cover the late-breaking story. We were off the hook, and flight testing returned to normal. The gods were smiling on us—hopefully our luck would continue for the fly-off in September.

Before long the air-to-ground mode of our radar was tested. Just like the air-to-air modes, it operated properly and the system performance was superior. Soon we flew over Catalina Island, Long Beach Harbor, the Channel Islands, and the Naval Air Station at Point Mugu. The ground radar maps were very impressive; a pilot could easily navigate using the images. Five years earlier we had been grossly underprepared to attend a fly-off in the F-15A radar competition, but this time we were ready and raring to go.

Wearing a blue flight suit with red and white vertical stripes, I flew our F-4D to Carswell Air Force Base, Texas, in the latter part of

September to start the fly-off. John H. Richardson, a Hughes Senior Vice President, was there to greet me when I landed. I presented an oil painting of the F-16A to him with much fanfare and celebration. There were neither smoking brakes nor fire department sirens this time as there had been with the B-66 five years earlier in St. Louis.

This celebration was show business at its finest, in the tradition of Howard Hughes. Thirty-two years earlier, during World War II, Hughes had attempted to influence a planeload of Army brass in search of a new reconnaissance aircraft. For several days he hosted a series of parties for the military officers. Hotel bills and meal receipts were all charged to Hughes. Then Hughes personally conducted a tour of his plant in Culver City and airlifted the group to Harper Dry Lake to see his wooden D-2 aircraft. Colonel Elliott Roosevelt—the son of President Franklin D. Roosevelt and a veteran of an African combat tour where he had flown the Lockheed F-5 (the reconnaissance version of the P-38)—headed up the delegation. The president's son enjoyed the parties and attention from some showgirls provided by Hughes. He whispered to Hughes that he thought he had found his plane. Likewise, we hoped to influence the Air Force and General Dynamics and win the F-16A radar contract.

During the fly-off I bought a pair of cowboy boots and a black cowboy hat at K-Mart. Howard Hughes had owned a fedora and had always flown with it because he considered it lucky. Since "bad guys always win," my black hat fit the image we needed for the competition. Oops Martin drew another set of cartoons like he had done on the F-15A radar program. This time he depicted me as the "K-Mart Cowboy."

Dave Kramer, the brilliant electronic engineer who had developed medium pulse repetition frequency for our earlier F-15A radar design, came to Fort Worth to support the competition. He reported that our sophisticated radar system was working as designed.

One night Kramer and I went out to a local bar for a couple of drinks. As we were playing a game of darts, from a distance I thought I saw the chief Westinghouse radar designer. We both took a closer look and confirmed the person we saw dancing was in fact him. We had never met him, as the Hughes and Westinghouse personnel were directed not to have contact with each other. The person I saw dancing was about as fluid and loose as one could be. The designer was definitely a competent dancer, and his gyrations far exceeded anyone else's on the floor. I made a prediction to Kramer: If the Westinghouse dancer designed radar matching his performance on the dance floor, we were doomed.

Even though the fly-off was scheduled to last six weeks, we completed 39 flights in just one month. We flew the required number of valid data passes over the hills and valleys west and north of Fort Worth. The radar worked like a charm, and our official results met General Dynamics and Air Force specifications. Everyone at Hughes thought we were in the winner's circle again. After winning both the Navy F-14A and Air Force F-15A radar programs a few years earlier, we were confident our radar design was unbeatable. We just needed to win the F-16A radar contract; this would be the end of Westinghouse's fighter radar business.

Vice President John Richardson stayed in Fort Worth and spent time during the fly-off talking to both Air Force and General Dynamics' pilots. The pilots praised our radar. Richardson told me that he expected someone in the higher levels of General Dynamics' management to call him. He commented that it was too quiet; he wasn't hearing any rumors. That was a bad sign, he added; all he could do was wait for General Dynamics to make contact with him. They never did.

After the fly-off was completed, General Dynamics announced that Westinghouse Electric had won a $36 million radar contract. The flight-test results were a tie; either radar would do the job for the Air Force. Westinghouse underbid Hughes by 25 percent in price, so they got the nod. The marketeers told me that evidently Westinghouse did not know how much money Hughes Aircraft bid on the contract; they didn't need to underbid us as much as they had.

In marketing talk they said, "Westinghouse left money on the table."

Engineer Bruce Burk was anxious to retire. By 1975, during our F-16 radar program, he had been working directly for Howard Hughes for 38 years. Burk was born in North Dakota and worked on his father's farm until 1935. He grew up during the Great Depression, and he told me that it was the greatest day of his life when he left the dust-bowl conditions of North Dakota.

Burk moved to California to study aircraft engineering at Curtiss-Wright Institute, located at the Grand Central Air Terminal in Glendale.

There he obtained instruction equivalent to a couple of years of college; he got the equivalent of another two years by enrolling in night school. He continued his aviation education by learning to fly before World War II and later obtained his commercial license with instrument and multi-engine ratings.

During Burk's years with Hughes he had modified and restored aircraft located literally all over the world. Those planes were extremely important to Hughes for a while, but then he lost interest in them and they would sit for years. A B-25 Mitchell bomber, modified into an executive transport for Noah Dietrich, sat in the dirt at the western end of our Hughes airfield. The plane had not moved since 1957. A twin-engine Douglas A-20G sat next to it. Even a Convair 240 civilian transport was parked at Clover Field, not flown for years. All were the responsibility of Bruce Burk.

In the summer of 1975 Howard Hughes gave Burk what would turn out to be the last and most important job of his entire career. In preparation for sending the *Racer* to the National Air and Space Museum in Washington, DC, Hughes wanted the plane restored to mint condition. Burk would be responsible for the total undertaking, including truck transportation to Washington. It was vital that the project be completed in record time so that the *Racer* would be available for display when the museum first opened, scheduled for July 1, 1976.

Actually the *Racer* was in good shape; it had been out of the weather and stored in the Quonset hut next to our Flight Test Division building for most of its life. Even though the Quonset hut was not climate controlled and the building was only a couple of miles inland from the ocean, it was rarely opened. The engine was pickled or preserved; the *Racer* could probably be returned to flight status, Burk told me.

Burk pulled the *Racer* out of the Quonset hut and towed it across a road to the Hughes Aircraft flight line. To prevent exposure to the sun, wind, and rain, it was placed in a three-sided wooden enclosure designed to cover reciprocating engines of multi-engine transport aircraft during repair.

Before the *Racer* could be restored, the wing and fuselage needed to be separated. Burk was hampered by the fact that he did not have any drawings or schematics on the plane. Because the *Racer* was never planned to go into production, only layout forms were available, which were not very detailed.

"The *Racer* was never meant to come apart," said Burk. "It would have to be cut up."

His mechanics, which had worked on so many projects for him in the past, took very seriously the restoration of the *Racer* to a pristine condition. Some of the Hughes Aircraft mechanics, who maintained my F-4D and T-33, also assisted Burk's workers.

I watched the restoration progress, stopping to see Burk and the *Racer* every time I walked out to the flight line.

"Are you in contact with Howard Hughes?" I asked.

"Was Hughes concerned about the *Racer*?"

"Would Hughes want to see it after it was restored?"

Burk answered, "Hughes's physical condition is not good—but I keep him aware of the *Racer*'s status."

On a Friday afternoon in late fall of 1975, exactly 40 years after Howard Hughes set the world speed record in it, the *Racer* was ready for its long trip to Washington, DC. The fuselage and wings were each packed in separate large wooden boxes and placed on a flatbed trailer of two trucks. One of Burk's mechanics would accompany the driver of each truck.

It was sad to watch the trucks depart eastbound over the Hughes flight line. A chapter in the history of Hughes Aircraft Company came to an end that day. Part of the mystique of Howard Hughes and glory that made the airport famous was gone. Though I would miss having my special tour package available for visiting Air Force and Navy pilots, I realized that displaying the *Racer* at the Air and Space Museum would allow millions of tourists the opportunity to learn about the historic aviation accomplishments of Howard Hughes.

I was also saddened that we lost the F-16 radar program. Our flight-test organization performed well throughout the competition; it was not our fault Westinghouse beat us this time. Some engineers said it was Westinghouse's time to win; the military didn't want Hughes to win all the radar contracts and have only one contractor left to provide equipment during the Cold War. Regardless of the reason, our F-4D was gone. The Phantom was the last jet fighter to fly from the Culver City runway.

Howard Hughes's Death

By early 1976 I had returned to the Navy base at Point Mugu to fly test missions in the F-14A Tomcat. An announcement was made over the Hughes Aircraft Company public address system on April 5 that Howard Hughes had died. Another chapter in the history of Hughes Aircraft Company was closed. Seven years earlier, when I had gone to work for the company in Culver City, quite a few employees remembered working directly with Hughes. Now there were only a couple of mechanics left that had worked on his planes. He hadn't been seen on our flight line since the late 1950s.

In failing health, a Lear Jet was obtained to fly Hughes back to the United States. He died while airborne from Acapulco, Mexico, to Houston, Texas. The plane departed Mexican air space and was over the Gulf of Mexico at the time of his death. It was fitting that the famous test pilot—who once held the world speed record, two transcontinental speed records, the round-the-world speed record, and all the records at the same time—should die in the air.

Hughes was only 70 when he died of chronic renal disease—kidney failure. Although he had had many successes in the air, he also suffered from eight auto and airplane crashes, which may have contributed to his early death.

An announcement of Howard Hughes's death was printed in the Hughes Aircraft Company weekly newspaper, the *Hughesnews*. It read:

Death of Pioneer Howard Hughes Is a Great Loss to Nation
"America lost one of its great pioneers with the death of Howard Robard Hughes on April 5, 1976," said L. A. Hyland, Vice President and General Manager of Hughes Aircraft Company.

"While most of the world will long remember his aeronautical genius and his contributions to modern aviation, to me his most significant and lasting contributions came in his rather unpublished gifts to mankind through the Howard Hughes Medical Institute," Mr. Hyland said.

"Mr. Hughes' vision and leadership founded and nurtured this company, which contributed so much to the community, the nation, and the world."

"I wish to assure you that the company will carry on in a completely normal manner despite this great loss. The company so well established can now carry on the great vision to itself nurture the Medical Institute established for the benefit of humanity," he concluded.

CHAPTER 10

Hitting the Jackpot in Vegas

It came to pass that a man came upon his friend sobbing bitter tears in the street as he looked at a newspaper.
"What's the matter?" said the man.
"Did you see the rumor, Howard Hughes is dead?"
"So what?" said the first man. "He's not related to you."
"That's it. That's the reason I'm crying," said the friend.

While flying the Grumman F-111B Sea Pig and F-14A Tomcat as a test pilot for Hughes Aircraft, I fired many missiles at unmanned drones. During that time I launched several AIM-9 Sidewinder missiles, a couple of AIM-7 Sparrow missiles, and many, many AIM-54A Phoenix missiles. All of my launches, in the Pacific Missile Test Center outersea test range located 80 miles off shore from Point Mugu, were scored kills. Five missiles actually hit and downed the drones. I considered myself a "test range ace."

The Navy loaned two of the first pre-production F-14A aircraft to Hughes to develop and test the AWG-9 system and AIM-54A Phoenix missile. In 1972 and 1973, our test pilot staff fired a total of 23 Phoenix missiles, scoring 20 hits for an 87 percent success rate, unheard of for a test program. These shots had all been edge-of-the-envelope launches, designed to show the Soviets that the F-14A and AWG-9/Phoenix weapon system could defeat any threat they could launch at a Navy carrier group.

From 1973 to 1975, Navy test pilots also fired Phoenix missiles at drones. Their launches were equally impressive, hitting 59 drones out of 70 shots for a success rate of 84 percent. But though launches against unmanned drones were highly successful, the Tomcat had never flown in actual combat against trained enemy pilots. Next to combat, the best method to determine an aircraft's capability was unauthorized and unscheduled air-to-air hassles by squadron pilots who would then each claim victory. Earlier, Captain Joe Bill Dryden and I had hassled in our F-4D and T-33 aircraft during the F-16A radar program, and we each claimed victory. Military leaders thought that there must be a better and more accurate way to evaluate both new weapons and aircraft, and the pilots who fly them. As it turned out, there was.

One of the most important assemblies of tactical aircraft in the history of air warfare gathered over the barren Nevada desert in 1976 and 1977, during a period of 18 months. The flight competition was called Air Intercept Missile Evaluation/Air Combat Evaluation, or AIMVAL/ACEVAL for short. It was a joint Air Force/Navy project conducted at Nellis Air Force Base, Nevada, 10 miles north of Las Vegas. AIMVAL/ACEVAL brought together for the first time in comparative flying trials, under the most realistic combat conditions possible, the newest and best examples of U.S. advanced fighter technology: the Navy's F-14A Tomcat and the Air Force's F-15A Eagle.

AIMVAL, the first phase of this program, provided data that would be used to define a new short-range (less than 5 miles) air-to-air missile that would be used by both the Air Force and Navy. The second phase, ACEVAL, was concerned with refining aerial combat maneuvers. The F-14A and F-15A were teamed as the friendly Blue Force, with F-5Es taking the part of aggressor Soviet MiG fighters, or Red Force.

The Tomcat's first flight was six years earlier, and it had already spent two years in fleet operation. With maturity and increased use, it had grown steadily better as a total weapon system. Extended use of the aircraft brought about many improvements, which were incorporated in aircraft still coming off the Grumman production line. The Navy chose six of the latest F-14As to take part in the AIMVAL/ACEVAL test. Because the F-14A was further into its development cycle, the Navy scored substantially better in-commission rates (84 percent) than the F-15A (63 percent) and even better than the well-matured F-5E (74 percent).

In terms of air-to-air combat superiority, the F-14A was designed with the capability to make a pilot an ace without his ever having to actually see an enemy aircraft. It did that with our Hughes radar that could detect an enemy fighter at 125 miles and a weapon system that could track 24 targets simultaneously, firing at six aircraft at once—even if they were going different directions at different altitudes—at ranges of 50 to 75 miles. The ultimate test, called the six-on-six shot, was flown at Point Mugu in December of 1973. Six Phoenix missiles were fired at six drones. Four were scored hits, one was a miss, and one was a "no counter" because the drone wandered out of the launch box. In a combat environment where the pilot is cleared to fire on another aircraft beyond visual range, the Phoenix long-range kill was the way to go. Only the Tomcat had this capability at Nellis. It was somewhat like a boxer with a 10-foot arm reach: He can punch his opponent from a distance beyond his ability to hit back.

Most of the Navy aircrew came from the first F-14A squadrons (VF-1 Wolfpack and VF-2 Bounty Hunters) as they were just completing their first deployment to the Western Pacific. The aircrews were transferred to a parent squadron, Air Test and Evaluation Squadron Four (VX-4), located also at Point Mugu. VX-4 had the responsibility for testing and evaluation of all naval aircraft and weapons associated with air superiority missions.

All six of the new Tomcats arrived at Point Mugu in the spring of 1976. Hughes Aircraft had the responsibility to check that our AWG-9 system was operating properly and also install and flight test a visual tracking and search (VTAS) system. I was selected as the Hughes Aircraft AIMVAL/ACEVAL project test pilot and flew my first flight in July 1976.

VTAS was a high-technology electronic system that allowed the pilot and the Naval Flight Officer (NFO) to maneuver both the radar antenna and missile seeker heads with head motion. To accomplish this, we wore specially modified flight helmets with a visor that displayed symbols and an aiming pipper. By depressing a button on the Tomcat's throttle, I could command the radar antenna and missile seeker heads as far as 55 degrees up and down and 65 degrees left and right. By depressing the button on the throttle to the second detent, I could command a lock on. This procedure allowed what was called "off boresight lock."

For close-in maneuvering against an enemy target in a standard F-14-A, the pilot called for the radar to automatically search and lock on to any aircraft that appeared in the head-up-display (HUD) out to 5 miles. This was called the pilot lock on mode. The HUD field of view was much smaller than that of the VTAS, about 10 degrees vertical and 10 degrees wide. The VTAS system greatly expanded the field of view available for missile lock on. After launch, missiles could pull around 30Gs, considerably more than any pilot. This system, if it worked, would greatly improve the lethality of the Tomcat.

The special helmet we wore for all test missions was modified with a helmet-mounted sight (HMS). The helmet was slightly larger and heavier than my standard helmet. In ground tests I wore the helmet, with oxygen mask tightly attached, and measurements were made to calibrate the electronics. Once the system was calibrated, I couldn't scratch my head or face without disrupting the precise optical settings. It was uncomfortable, hot, and sweaty, but we wanted accurate results and the discomfort was a small price to pay for the opportunity to fly advanced weaponry.

A very elaborate set of electronic rules governed the operation of VTAS. Multiple small pink lights would illuminate or blink, indicating status of the radar and missile seeker head in relation to my pipper on the HMS. All the symbols moved and reacted fast; I did not have time to look in the cockpit. My full attention was required to detect the target, maneuver the aircraft, and evaluate the complex sequence of flashing lights. It reminded me of the electronic gaming machines in Las Vegas. Lights were flashing on the display like on the slot machines. Radio transmissions to the target and crew comments on the intercom were continuous, also similar to the "ding, ding, ding" of the slots down on the Strip. It was very fatiguing.

Each test flight involved high G maneuvering against manned Navy targets. The Tomcat was flown over the top, as in a loop, and in extremely high rate aileron rolls. Also, I banked into steep turns in both directions as we recorded data. During these tests, the voice communication inside the cockpit on the intercom and outside the cockpit on the UHF radio was also being monitored for later evaluation.

Years later, when I saw scenes from the 1986 box office hit movie *Top Gun*, it reminded me of the VTAS tests I had flown. The F-14A aircraft played a starring role in *Top Gun*, a major Hollywood film. *Top Gun* told the story of a pilot, a lieutenant named Pete Mitchell, nicknamed

Maverick and played by Tom Cruise. First seen on an aircraft carrier patrolling the Indian Ocean, Maverick is a brash and swaggering loud-mouth. Yet he manages to gain the admiration of his superiors by his cool-ness during a nonshooting encounter with some MiG-28s (actual Northrop F-5s painted black and representing some unfriendly nation that was never identified). As a result, Maverick wins an appointment to the Navy's advanced Fighter Weapons School called Top Gun at Naval Air Station Miramar near San Diego. While attending the school, he falls in love with a female instructor but loses his best friend in a fatal aerial accident. This incident brings about a change in his character, making him a better person and a superior pilot when he returns to the Indian Ocean. *Top Gun* ends with a spectacular climax when Maverick, in his F-14A, takes on an enemy MiG-28. Ironically, 10 years before *Top Gun* was released to the public, I had flown the Tomcat through many of the same combat maneuvers, but it was done in secrecy, without Hollywood in the act.

Newsweek magazine called *Top Gun*, "A young man's macho fantasy about jet fighter pilots, a beautiful blonde flying instructor and MiGs zapped at high altitude. As such, it did more to boost the popularity of the F-14s and naval aviation than anything up until then that ever happened in real life over the Mediterranean Sea." It was unfortunate that Howard Hughes was dead; it was his kind of movie, full of flying, romance, and sex.

After flying five VTAS test missions by early September of 1976, the Navy F-14A program office passed me disturbing news of a Tomcat accident. An F-14A from the VF-32 Swordsmen squadron made headline news when its engines roared up to full power while taxiing across the deck of USS *Kennedy*, and the aircraft plunged into 1,850 feet of water. The plane took along with it a priceless Phoenix missile. Fortunately, the crew ejected safely. At the time of the event, the USS *Kennedy* was operating in international waters and nearby Soviet naval ships had wit-nessed the entire incident.

Fearing the Tomcat and Phoenix missile might fall into Soviet hands, the Navy immediately began a recovery operation. A 10-day sonar search by the first wave of salvage vessels located the Tomcat, but adverse weather suspended the recovery effort. When the operation resumed, the aircraft was relocated, but at a different location. Under the watchful eye of the Soviet ships, the U.S. Navy's nuclear-powered NR-1 research submarine went down to inspect the aircraft. It hooked a cable onto the

Tomcat's undercarriage, and then a British vessel attempted to pull the aircraft to the surface. The cable snapped, so a stronger line was used on a second attempt, but the cable broke again. Clearly a better-equipped salvage ship was needed.

While waiting for the proper recovery vessel to arrive, the NR-1 retrieved the Phoenix missile, which had become separated from the aircraft. When the two West German ships—Taurus and Twyford—arrived on the scene, the operation resumed. They completed a firm attachment to the wreckage, but this time instead of trying to winch it to the surface at once, they lifted it halfway up and then slowly dragged the aircraft to shallow waters, from where it was carefully hauled to the surface. The entire operation lasted almost two months and cost $2.5 million.

One reason for such an expensive and time-consuming endeavor was the need to examine the wreckage and determine the cause of the accident. But it was unquestionably true that the overriding concern was to prevent one of America's most sophisticated weapons, the Hughes AWG-9 system and Phoenix missile, from being compromised to the enemy at a critical time in the Cold War.

My Tomcat test flights were on hold until a Navy investigation was conducted to determine the cause of the accident. Within a few days I was given clearance to continue the tests. As had occurred four years earlier when we were working on our first missile launches and an accident happened, the test program had to go on if humanly possible. I had heard that statement many, many times before during the last few years. We were always under pressure to get flight-test data.

By mid-September I had flown nine VTAS flights and we had completed the installation and checkout of all six of the AIMVAL/ACEVAL Tomcats. Soon VX-4 pilots and NFOs departed for Nellis Air Force Base and the start of formal evaluation. In late September, I flew two flights in the Nellis test range with Marine Captain John Miles acting as my NFO. The Hughes equipment was working fine and the official evaluation was ready to start.

Soon I heard about some of the preliminary results through the military grapevine. Because of its small size, the F-5E was doing better than anticipated. On a head-on pass, the F-5E was extremely difficult to visually acquire beyond about 3 miles. First visual acquisition usually determined the outcome of an engagement.

The number of engagements had been extensive. A 30-mile range was divided into six entry points. Each test required the Blue Force and Red Force to start out at one of those points. The Blue Force aircrews found that to enhance survivability, they needed to enter the range at very high speed. All 12 Blue Force pilots/aircrews had to complete tests using all of the entry points and in engagements involving one-fighter-versus-one, one-versus-two, two-versus-two, two-versus-four, and four-versus-four. Participants never knew the set-up geometry in advance; they had to use both radar and visual observation on head-on passes to find the Red Force.

Both the Air Force and Navy were allowed to pick their aircraft paint configuration. The Navy selected a dark gray on light gray, a scheme used for seagoing operation. The F-5Es, which resembled the MiG-21s in size and speed, were outfitted in camouflage paint and bold red identification numbers exactly like those on Soviet aircraft.

A typical set-up involved a head-on pass in which the Blue Force launched a simulated radar–guided AIM-7 Sparrow missile. Then both Blue Force and Red Force pilots would fire a forward hemisphere AIM-9 infrared guided missile just before the planes merged. Close-in engagements ensued in which the kill weapon became the Gatling gun.

Both the F-14A and F-15A obtained twice as many scored kills on the simulated MiGs as were made on them. These results were not as good as the U.S. military had experienced in World War II, Korea, or Vietnam. It did emphasize the value of the long-range Phoenix missile, a weapon that could strike an enemy aircraft even 100 miles distant.

Lessons learned from previous short-range, air-to-air combat encounters in Korea and Vietnam were still true. They were:

1. Keep your speed up and your head on a swivel (four eyes in the F-14A were better than two in the F-15A).
2. The plane with the most fuel can get another shot off while the pilot low on fuel is thinking about his escape route.
3. Two aircraft can beat one aircraft if they fly and fight as a team.
4. The better-trained force will win regardless of high-technology equipment.

In May of 1977, approximately three-quarters of the way through the evaluation, the Navy requested that I pilot two flights in the Nellis range.

The first mission was completed without incident—some minor problems had been identified in the Hughes electronics and corrected.

The second flight was quite different. After I got airborne and prepared to make my first pass on the F-5E aggressor aircraft, I got a call on the UHF radio from the commander of the Navy AIMVAL/ACEVAL group. He explained that a piece of metal, 18 inches long and 5 inches in diameter, had been found on the Nellis Air Force Base taxiway. His ground crew immediately checked all the F-14s and F-15s on the ramp to see if any of the aircraft were missing part of their structure. The aircraft on the ramp were all in one piece. The Navy commander suggested that we suspend our mission, have the F-5E pilot join me in close formation, and visually check my Tomcat for damage. Before the F-5E pilot could join me, Navy ground crew identified the mysterious metal as definitely coming off an F-14A.

The F-5E pilot joined up and reported that my aircraft looked normal. The Navy commander recommended I extend my landing gear and flaps and have the F-5E pilot recheck the Tomcat. This time the F-5E pilot found a problem: A large section of my left landing gear wheel rim was missing. He could not tell if the tire was still inflated, but the remaining tire rim was very rough and jagged.

My mission in the test range was canceled; discussions followed on the best course of action to safely get my Tomcat back on the ground. The Air Force had already lost one of their F-15As during the AIMVAL/ACEVAL program in a mid-air collision with an F-5E. The Navy did not want to lose an aircraft; prestige and honor were at stake. From the tone of voice of the Navy commander, I believed he was very uncomfortable that a former Air Force pilot, and now a civilian, was flying his precious Tomcat. But, nothing could be done now to change that reality.

According to the Navy commander, another F-14A pilot in the fleet had also experienced loss of a part of a tire rim. When the Tomcat pilot landed, the tire blew, causing the aircraft to swerve and run off the runway. The landing gear collapsed in soft ground, causing extensive damage. The commander suggested I consider an approach-end engagement.

Though it was true that I had been trained by the Air Force and never landed on a carrier, I had made an arrested landing in the F-111B at Point

Mugu eight years earlier. That event had been the closest I had come to being killed in 11 years of flying. At the time of my F-14A wheel emergency I had been flying Air Force and Navy jets for 19 years. It seemed the gods of Las Vegas and the spirit of Howard Hughes were testing me.

While I orbited the test range at 10,000 feet altitude, other jets flying missions were recalled to land at Nellis. The Air Force wanted to get all their aircraft on the ground in case I crashed and blocked the runway, preventing other planes from landing. I still had a lot of fuel, giving me time to plan the best course of action. It also gave me time to worry. The odds were not good on the gaming tables in Las Vegas; I wondered what my odds were of making a safe engagement. It would be like rolling the dice down on the Strip.

Extensive planning was also going on in the Navy operations office. Several admirals, who were visiting Nellis to get a briefing on the progress of the AIMVAL/ACEVAL program, were listening to the status of my airborne emergency. The admirals and every F-14A pilot had advice or suggestions they gave the Navy commander to pass on to me.

I started dumping fuel to reduce the Tomcat's weight and enable me to fly a lower landing speed. My NFO locked his shoulder harness, and I did likewise. The F-5E chase aircraft broke off formation and entered the Nellis landing pattern. Everyone had helped me, as much as was possible; now it was time for me to perform a little magic by pulling a rabbit out of the hat. I contacted Nellis tower and declared an emergency.

While on final approach to a straight-in landing, the Navy commander continued giving me advice. He recommended that I be prepared to use full afterburner power if the hook skipped the arresting cable.

"Just push in full power if you get in trouble," he said. "Then get the Tomcat back into the air."

The Navy commander was several years younger than I and probably had less flying time and experience. But as commander of the Navy unit, he was ultimately responsible for the safety of his Tomcats. However, it was my butt on the line.

From several miles out on final approach, I spotted the arresting gear. It was standard equipment installed at all military bases and could be used for a landing arrestment or for aborted takeoffs. The gear was located 1,500 feet down the runway. My plan was to land about 50 feet directly in front of the arresting gear, allowing the Tomcat's nose to drop on the runway. That way, if the tire were flat, it wouldn't have time to cause the plane to swerve before the tail hook engaged.

On final, I slowed the Tomcat to approach speed. The aircraft angle of attack indication on the instrument panel was proper for my weight, and the indexer (angle of attack) light showed a green donut. My glide path angle was correct, with no wind gusts to bounce me around as I'd experienced eight years earlier in my F-111B mishap.

The F-14A touched down smoothly, just as I had planned. The nose dropped, and immediately I felt deceleration from the tail hook catching the wire. The NFO and I came to a complete stop, exactly on the center line of the runway with our wings level. The tire had not been flat after all and didn't blow out because of my smooth landing.

The Nellis fire trucks rapidly approached, along with several Navy pickup trucks. A new problem developed. Now the rescue crews were afraid that the weight of the Tomcat pressing against the jagged rim would puncture the tire. If it did, the rim might blow off the tire and injure Navy ground crew or damage the F-14A.

I watched for several minutes as the Navy ground crew, looking like the Keystone Cops from old 1920s movies, ran multiple circles around the Tomcat, accomplishing nothing. There was a lot of arm waving and shouting. Finally a Navy chief restored sanity to this three-ring circus. He gave me the "cut engines" hand signal and brought out a giant wooden board. The board had over a hundred nails driven through it, all sticking up. A tow bar was hooked up to my Tomcat and the tire was pulled across the board. The tire slowly deflated; my emergency was finally over.

Like Howard Hughes, I had been lucky in Las Vegas. Although Hughes had died a year earlier, he had spent four of his later years in Las Vegas. There he purchased many casinos, the North Las Vegas airport, an aircraft charter business, and thousands of acres of raw land for a proposed new airport. Though he never personally enjoyed his properties, his estate was greatly enriched by the luck of his fortuitous purchases. It was time to see if my luck would hold on the gaming tables on the Strip.

CHAPTER 11

A Hornet with Two Stings

While Hughes was in Las Vegas, his overworked accountant was asked what should be done about a gambling bill that was passed by the Nevada Legislature. Snapped the accountant, "If Howard Hughes owes the bill, he'll pay it."

After Hughes Aircraft lost the F-16A radar program in 1975, our remaining flight-test organization at Culver City was moved to the Navy base at Point Mugu. We even moved our leased Air Force T-33 there, and it sat on the ramp surrounded by Navy aircraft. However, the following year we heard rumors we might once again be in competition for a fighter radar. This time the customer was the U.S. Navy.

Competition for the Navy's new F-18 radar was another head-to-head contest between Hughes Aircraft and Westinghouse. McDonnell Douglas was the aircraft prime contractor, and would choose which company would be its subcontractor to design and manufacture the radar. This time, in contrast to the F-15 and F-16 programs, there was no fly-off to determine the technology winner. Each company made extensive written proposals and showed laboratory test results of new devices. The choice was complex, involving innovative designs, previous development and production successes, schedule and price credibility, as well as the competitors' understanding of the Navy's needs and desires. In a very close decision, even though Hughes Aircraft's price was higher, they were selected. Hughes had now won three of the four battles for fighter radars.

The F/A-18 Hornet aircraft is a fighter strong enough and fast enough to meet and master the best an enemy can send aloft. It is also an attack aircraft that can pinpoint and pulverize ground targets. It is indeed a Hornet with two stings. Years ago these disparate missions would have required two specialized airplanes. Today, one aircraft—equipped with a unique Hughes radar set that performs both the fighter and attack functions—can execute both missions with equal efficiency.

The Hornet is a proud name in naval history. Navy ships have been named *Hornet* for more than 200 years. Tradition, an intangible factor in war, is often reflected in names like Hornet to remind those present today of yesterday's heroes. The steadfast resolve of those who went before us stands as a reminder of the cost of freedom. Hornet is a fine example of this tradition. Since the American Revolution, eight vessels named *Hornet* have served our nation. *Hornets* bombarded Tripoli and the Barbary Pirates, engaged Spanish gunboats and shore batteries off Manzanillo, launched the Doolittle Raid, won the Battle of Midway and the Marianas Turkey Shoot, and recovered the first men to walk on the moon. The latest Hornet is a U.S. Navy and Marine Corps twin-engine, multimission jet fighter and attack aircraft that can operate from either aircraft carriers or land bases.

The origin of the F/A-18 Hornet is one of the strangest stories in aircraft procurement history. On January 13, 1975, Air Force Secretary John McLucas announced that the General Dynamics YF-16 had been selected as the winner of the Air Force Air Combat Fighter (ACF) contest over the Northrop YF-17. The reasons given for this decision were the facts that the YF-16 was a little faster than the YF-17, and that its Pratt & Whitney F100 engine was in use in other warplanes that were already in service. The F-16 went on to become successful beyond anyone's wildest imagination; over 3,500 have been built, with production still continuing.

It would appear, then, that the YF-17 would be consigned to oblivion, to be remembered today only as an obscure footnote in aviation history. The loss of the Air Force ACF contract to the General Dynamics YF-16 might ordinarily have been the end of the line for the Northrop design, were it not for the Navy's desire for a new fighter. All throughout the early 1970s, some Navy officers had been expressing interest in a low-cost alternative to the F-14 Tomcat, which was at that time experiencing severe teething troubles and suffering from a series of cost overruns. This alternative program came to be known as VFAX.

VFAX was envisaged as a multirole aircraft that would replace the F-4 Phantom, the A-4 Skyhawk, and the A-7 Corsair II in Navy and Marine Corps service. To meet the VFAX requirement, a stripped version of the Tomcat (named F-14X) had been proposed by Grumman, but it had been summarily rejected by the Deputy Defense Secretary. In May of 1974 the House Armed Services Committee announced that it was not going to have anything to do with a stripped-down Tomcat either, and dictated that the VFAX would have to be a wholly new aircraft.

Apparently having forgotten the sorry experience with the F-111A and F-111B, the Committee wanted the Air Force and Navy to purchase basically the same plane. However, the Navy (unlike the Air Force) wanted the VFAX to be capable of filling both air-to-air and ground-attack roles. In August of 1974 Congress decided that the budget simply could not afford another major aircraft development project at that time and informed the Navy that the VFAX project would have to be canceled.

Congress took money intended for VFAX and diverted it to a new program known as Navy Air Combat Fighter (NACF) and directed the Navy take a close look at the Air Force's Light Weight Fighter/Air Combat Fighter (LWF/ACF) contenders as possible candidates for the NACF requirement. The Navy's NACF would be basically a navalized LWF/ACF. Most Navy officers were still solidly committed to the F-14 and wanted nothing to do with either the VFAX or the NACF. Undeterred by the pro-Tomcat faction, in September of 1974 the Navy pressed forward with the NACF project and formal requirements were issued.

Once the formal requirements had been issued, the Navy announced that it would select a single contractor to begin engineering development of the NACF. Northrop thought that they had a potential candidate for the NACF in the YF-17, because the Navy tended to prefer the added safety offered by a twin-engine aircraft and the design seemed to have greater potential for growth into a radar-equipped multirole aircraft. However, the Northrop Company had no experience with carrier-based aircraft, so they accepted an offer from McDonnell Douglas to collaborate on a naval adaptation of the YF-17 for the NACF contest. Under the terms of the agreement worked out between the two corporations, McDonnell would market the aircraft to the Navy, and Northrop would be the prime subcontractor. In addition, Northrop was to be given the rights to market a land-based version of the design to various foreign air forces.

In 1975 the Navy announced that they had opted for the Northrop/ McDonnell Douglas proposal. The Navy liked the twin-engine format of their submission, which they felt would be better suited to operations at sea. In addition, the Navy felt that the YF-17 development possessed greater potential for a multimission capability.

According to the original plan, the Northrop/McDonnell Douglas aircraft was intended to be procured in three closely related models: the single-seat F-18, which would replace the F-4 Phantom in the fighter role; the single-seat A-18, which would replace the A-4 Skyhawk and A-7 Corsair II in the attack role; and the two-seat TF-18A, which would be a combat trainer. The F-18 and the A-18 were to share the same basic airframe and engine arrangement, but they were to differ in stores attachments and in the avionics. The two-seat TF-18A was to retain the full mission capability and armament suite of the F-18A, but it was to have slightly reduced fuel capacity. Eventually careful redesign made it possible to merge the two single-seat fighter and attack versions into a single aircraft, which was initially referred to as F/A-18A in Defense Department press releases. This rather awkward designation did not actually become official until 1984.

The F-18 program went ahead with the award of letter contracts to General Electric for the development of the F404 turbofans and to McDonnell for nine single-seat and two two-seat full-scale development aircraft. First flight was to take place in July of 1978.

As part of the agreement between McDonnell Douglas and Northrop, it was decided that fabrication of the baseline F-18 would be split roughly 60/40 between McDonnell and Northrop, respectively. If orders were received for the F-18L land-based version, these proportions would be reversed. Northrop was to build the center and aft fuselage sections of the F-18, as well as both vertical fins. McDonnell's contribution would consist of the wings, the horizontal tail, and the forward fuselage, including the cockpit. The major subassemblies were to be shipped to McDonnell at St. Louis, where final assembly would take place.

In anticipation of the appearance of the F-18, the second YF-17 was turned over to the Navy for test duties with the Pacific Missile Test Center at Point Mugu, California; the Naval Air Test Center at Patuxent River, Maryland; and the Naval Weapons Center at China Lake, California.

Under contract to McDonnell Douglas to conduct flight test of the F-18 radar, the Navy loaned a twin-engine North American T-39D Sabreliner, Bureau Number 150987, to Hughes Aircraft. The Sabreliner was designed as an eight-passenger transport aircraft able to fly at 35,000 feet with its jet fighter brothers. It was powered by two Pratt & Whitney 2,400-pound, J60-P-3 axial turbojets and could cruise at 540 mph for a range of 1,100 nautical miles. The aircraft arrived at Culver City in September 1977 for the start of a five-month modification process to convert it into a "flying test laboratory."

Hughes engineers designed a 4-foot extension to the existing Sabreliner nose to hold radar electronic units. Then an F-18 radome was attached to this nose extension. With all the added weight in the nose, the aircraft was balanced at its forward center of gravity (cg) limit. Flights in this condition required very heavy yoke pressure to lift the nose for takeoff and full aft trim for landing.

Thirty-five years earlier Howard Hughes had ended up with a twin-engine aircraft loaded forward of its center of gravity limit. In 1937 Hughes purchased a Sikorsky S-43 seaplane, planning to use it to set a round-the-world record. After modifying the plane with four large fuel tanks, Hughes found that the S-43 was too slow and used too much fuel for its intended purpose. He parked the plane at the Union Air Terminal in Burbank, California, and forgot about it. In 1943 the U.S. Army Corps of Engineers laid claim to Hughes's prized amphibian to shuttle engineers back and forth between outposts from Nova Scotia to Iceland during World War II. By then Hughes had replaced the original Pratt & Whitney engines installed at the Sikorsky factory with two more powerful Wright R-1820 engines. This change greatly improved the aircraft's performance—especially in lakes at high elevation, such as Lake Tahoe in the California Sierras. But it also moved the aircraft's cg forward, requiring ballast to be installed in the tail just as we had done in our Navy T-39D.

Because so many changes had been made to the S-43, the Corps of Engineers asked the Civil Aeronautics Administration (CAA) to fly and certify the airplane. Howard Hughes, two of his employees, and two officials of the CAA flew the final test mission on Lake Mead in May of 1943. As they came in for their first landing, Hughes began a smooth descent. The Army had removed ballast in the tail, because they planned to install radio equipment in its place and a radioman to operate it.

However, this equipment had not yet been installed. Hughes had failed to evaluate the seaplane's cg and did not know the aircraft had exceeded its forward limit for safe operation.

Just after a normal landing, the aircraft made a very violent and uncontrollable turn to the right. Hughes lost control of the seaplane. The 10-ton Sikorsky S-43 crashed, killing two crew members and critically injuring Hughes. Flying any aircraft outside of its approved center of gravity limits is very dangerous; I planned to calculate the cg very carefully on every T-39D test mission.

Larger DC generators were installed on both engines of our T-39D because of the need for a substantial increase of electrical power for the radar. Then 24 transformer-rectifier units were added to the tail section to convert the DC generator power to AC power. Because of this added weight in both the nose and tail, the plane resembled a dumbbell from a structural standpoint. Hughes's structural engineers thought this design was a dangerous configuration.

Through the years the Navy bought 42 of the T-39Ds. They were used as a training aircraft for Naval Flight Officers (NFOs). Typically an instructor could train three students in the operation of Navy radar. Unfortunately, five months before we received our aircraft, a Navy T-39D crashed near San Diego, California. The aircraft was on a low-level cross-country flight and experienced heavy turbulence. The horizontal tail ripped off the plane, and it nosed into the ground. Without ejection seats or parachutes, all five crew members were killed.

Taking into account the Navy accident, Hughes engineers beefed up all the racks holding our electronic equipment in both the nose and aft cabin. In addition, they designed an electronic sensor system to alert the pilot to unsafe conditions. If external vibration or turbulence reached a dangerous limit, the system would activate an amber light in the pilot's cockpit. If flight conditions worsened, a red light would illuminate.

The standard test crew consisted of a pilot, a Hughes engineer who acted as a radar operator and sat in the copilot's seat, and two engineers in the aft cabin. For added safety, all four crew members wore parachutes. In reality, if either the horizontal or vertical tail departed the aircraft, no crew member would be able to overcome the resultant Gs and tumbling to exit the plane. Our best course of action was to overdesign the structure and avoid turbulence as much as possible.

Ever since the loss of the F-16 radar program, Bill Jessup and I had been spending full time at Point Mugu, flying the F-14A and TA-3B. Our offices in the Flight Test Division building at Culver City were closed and given to other organizations. With the F-18 radar program on the horizon, we would be spending part-time back in Culver City. A desk was moved into the hangar for us to share. It was a far cry from the time eight years earlier when we had had four pilots flying eight aircraft on six different test programs.

In preparation for the first flight, Jessup and I flew a commercial airline flight to Naval Air Station Pennscola, Florida, to attend a five-day ground school on the T-39D. After completing the training, we returned to California and checked out in a T-39D located at Point Mugu. A Navy instructor pilot flew copilot with each of us so that we could accumulate five hours of flying time and make five landings. We were then qualified and current by Navy standards.

On February 1, 1978, Jessup and I made the first flight in our T-39D. After many months of modification, we simply flew a shakedown flight to verify that the engines, flight controls, and systems were still operational. All the metal racks and wiring were installed but no radar black boxes.

Because our T-39D was flying 10 months before the first flight of the F-18 in St. Louis, we used the call sign Hornet One. Our flight was the first part of the program to get airborne; we were off to a good start. As a company, we were proud we had completed the aircraft modification and first flight on time and were ahead of the Navy and McDonnell's contract schedule.

Because of winter weather over the Los Angeles basin, Jessup and I flew the first flight of the T-39D to the clear air of the Mojave Desert. After confirming that the Sabreliner was flying satisfactorily, we set up to make a couple of landings on the Edwards Air Force base runway. Being a former Marine pilot, Jessup didn't have experience in the Edwards flight pattern and by mistake set up to land on the Edwards South Base runway. South Base was the original post–World War II runway, but in 1978 it was used only by the civilian Aero Club and for arresting gear tests. Fortunately, I directed him to the correct runway before the Edwards control tower operator detected his error. It would have been an embarrassment to land on the wrong runway.

After a couple of landings we flew back to Culver City. Awaiting us there was a huge group of Hughes employees who had worked on the aircraft. In addition, the Hughes marketing organization had arranged a celebration to include a military band and a cake-cutting ceremony. Senior Navy and McDonnell program personnel were also in attendance.

Jessup made a smooth landing in front of the crowd and braked to a stop near the end of the runway. Up to that point our mission had gone well, and we began to relax. Being relaxed was a big mistake.

Both of us had flown numerous military aircraft from the Culver City runway for the past nine years, so I assumed Jessup was aware that the runway was only 85 feet wide with no taxiway. This meant a pilot had to make a 180-degree turn on the runway to be able to turn back toward the ramp. In several of the aircraft I had flown, like the F-111B and B-66, their nose wheel steering system was not sharp enough to easily make the 180-degree turn on a narrow runway. The maneuver required a pilot to taxi to the extreme right side of the runway before starting a left turn. Then he needed to apply full left rudder, tap the left brake, and turn the aircraft at a spot on the runway where the nose wheel would cross over a small patch of asphalt where a road intersected the runway. Jessup had been flying both the F-4 and A-3D aircraft, which had a very sharp turning capability due to their design for carrier operations.

Jessup started his 180-degree turn before I could warn him about this unusual feature. As a result, before he could complete the 180-degree turn, the T-39D nose wheel went off the runway. The nose wheel quickly sunk into the mud, because it was February and the winter rains had softened the ground. Thankfully we were beyond view of the assembly of people waiting to celebrate the first flight of the F-18 radar program.

Jessup shut down both engines and called the control tower operator to request mechanics meet us at the plane. The band waited to play *Anchors Aweigh*, and the celebration cake started to dry out. After much delay, a tow bar was hooked to the nose gear and a tug pulled us out of the mud. We were then towed back to the ramp in view of hundreds of well wishers. Eight years earlier I had been embarrassed in front of the McDonnell F-15A and Air Force program personnel when the brakes of the B-66 overheated in St. Louis. Now we made another inglorious arrival, being towed behind a tug with mud on the nose wheel tire.

Also similar to the F-15A radar development flights in the B-66, we got off to a slow start in the F-18 radar missions. During the first three months we had limited success and were unable to get a medium PRF detection on the T-33 target until mission number 14. Because of radar problems, Jessup and I waited a long time between T-39D test flights. Fortunately, we continued to fly the F-14A and TA-3B at Point Mugu.

By the summer of 1978 Hughes electronic engineers had developed a preliminary capability in the ground map radar. We made radar maps of Point Mugu, the Channel Islands, and the coastal city of Santa Barbara. The Navy program office encouraged us to obtain data over naval installations because these maps would be recognizable by the senior Navy officers.

Finally, by the end of the summer we were able to get the radar to track an airborne target. It was opportune that we were achieving some measure of success because a Navy Preliminary Evaluation was planned for October. Several Navy pilots and NFOs spent two weeks at Culver City getting briefings on the status of the radar development and flights in the T-39D. We flew 10 flights for them, with marginal air-to-air performance. However, the air-to-ground capability came on strong, with very good maps of the Naval Weapons Center at China Lake. This base was a Navy test facility located on the eastern slope of the Sierra Nevada range, about 100 miles north of Los Angeles. The base specialized in air-to-ground weapon delivery.

On November 17, 1978, McDonnell test pilot Jack Krings made the first flight of the F-18A Hornet in St. Louis. Krings was an old friend of mine. We had first met 11 years earlier, when I was an Air Force pilot testing the F-4C at Edwards. My test results had shown some major deficiencies in the Phantom during maneuvering flight. I had briefed these results to senior Air Force test managers, but Krings objected and defended the aircraft. Though Krings and I had had differences of opinion on the flying qualities of the F-4C, we were on the same team with the F-18A Hornet. By the time Krings made the first flight in the F-18A, we had flown 65 radar test missions and the radar was officially designated the APG-65.

Wayne Wight, a McDonnell radar operator, came out to fly with us again. Previously, he had flown in the B-66 at Culver City and during the F-15A fly-off in St. Louis. During November and December we obtained good data, and the program seemed to be solid. Overall, we had fewer maintenance problems with the T-39D than we had had earlier with the B-66. A fuel control went out and caused the engine to surge, but the problem was cured by our mechanics in a short time. Unlike the heavy-weight B-66, the T-39D could be flown with a full fuel load, allowing us two hours of test time in the Edwards restricted area.

Though operating the T-39D at Culver City was less hazardous than operating the B-66, flying in the Los Angeles International Airport area had become much more dangerous. One morning I was sitting at my desk in the hangar when a mechanic yelled to me that there had been a mid-air collision over our Culver City runway. I rushed outside to see smoke rising from a parking lot about two miles northwest of the field. A plane had crashed with several fatalities. Thankfully, no Hughes Aircraft Company planes were involved.

A similar accident occurred two and one-half years earlier, the same month Howard Hughes died. Besides our Experimental Test Flight Department, there was a Corporate Flight Department within the Flight Test Division. About eight corporate pilots flew a DH-125 twin-engine executive jet, two Aero Commanders, a Convair 240, and a Bell 206 jet helicopter. These planes were used to transport company executives around the country.

In the spring of 1976, corporate pilot Don Bolt dropped off several Hughes employees at the company plant in Santa Barbara. He then flew solo back to Culver City in one of the twin-engine, high wing Aero Commanders. While he was flying a right downwind entry to Culver City Runway 23, a light civilian aircraft flying northbound over Los Angeles International descended toward Clover Field at Santa Monica. The pilot in the civilian aircraft did not see the Aero Commander under his aircraft's nose, and Bolt did not see the other light aircraft approaching him. The small plane was obscured by Bolt's right wing. The two aircraft collided just north of our airfield, and Bolt's Aero Commander crashed into a police station on Washington Boulevard. Don Bolt did not survive the accident.

With the second midair collision over the field in such a short time, it became painfully obvious that flight operations around the Culver City runway were more hazardous than ever. When Howard Hughes died two years earlier, his assets were placed in an estate that would soon be divided. Eventually the real estate that included the runway and Hughes Aircraft buildings would be sold. Our days flying from the Culver City airport were numbered.

By the end of 1978 we had flown 75 flights in the T-39D. Our part of the radar test program was planned to end two months later and the plane then scheduled to be transferred to McDonnell in St. Louis. There, McDonnell would install and flight test the other F-18A avionics just as had occurred with the B-66 on the F-15A radar program eight years earlier. For the remaining months, our effort focused on improved ground maps at different naval facilities and classified work in the Nellis Air Force Base range.

Early in January 1979, I flew the T-39D to the Naval Weapons Center near China Lake to obtain improved radar images. During winter, strong winds cross the Sierra Nevada range and create mountain waves on the leeward side. While flying a test mission about 4,000 feet above the ground, we encountered the greatest amount of clear air turbulence I had ever experienced. My crew members and I bounced around like corks in a bathtub, unable to get the radar data we had planned to obtain. In addition, I could feel high-frequency vibration in the horizontal tail through the flight control yoke. I immediately slowed the plane and turned east to exit the turbulence. Neither the amber nor the red warning light illuminated on the instrument panel. The fact that the lights didn't illuminate was not comforting because I believed we were very near complete destruction or, at the very least, aircraft damage. I aborted our mission and carefully flew the T-39D back to Culver City.

After landing I asked the mechanics and engineers to search through the aircraft structure for any damage. Nothing was found, but from that time on I never trusted the warning system.

As we came to the end of our flight-test program, we had one final classified mission to perform. The Navy program office wanted to collect air-to-ground data on a Surface to Air Missile (SAM) site in Restricted Area 4807, located in the Nellis range. The plan was to ferry the T-39D to Nellis and land, then depart from the base with a full load of fuel. Up until this mission we had always landed the plane at either Culver City or Point Mugu. At both of these locations Hughes mechanics serviced our plane.

Operating from Nellis, I relied on Air Force mechanics to refuel the plane and assist me in starting the engines. A small blue and white plastic credit card was carried in all military aircraft and used to account for government assistance. Since our T-39D was under contract to Hughes

Aircraft, we did not have a military credit card. Hughes financial personnel prepared an old-style IBM punch card that gave our contract number for government assistance. These Hughes personnel promised me the IBM card would be accepted by Air Force units at Nellis.

A precise range time was scheduled for our tests on the SAM site. I met with an Air Force intelligence officer at Base Operations at Nellis, and he gave me very exacting information on where to fly in the test range—and more important, where not to fly.

After the briefing I found that the Air Force refueling officer would not accept my IBM card.

"There is no possible way you can get fuel without a government credit card," he said.

Without fuel, I wouldn't be able to complete the planned test mission or even return to Culver City. No matter how I pleaded and asked him to understand our unique situation, it was futile. No government credit card, no fuel. The time for our scheduled range mission was drawing near, and it looked like our whole effort was a bust. Then the Air Force refueling officer made a statement that was music to my ears.

"Since you don't have a credit card," he said, "I'll make one for you."

Within a couple of minutes, he copied the long list of contract numbers from the IBM card and transferred them to a new blue and white plastic credit card. He ran his reader over my new card, and I was authorized to receive fuel.

Soon my crew members and I were airborne and made our passes on the SAM site. Just as with most events in the test program, this was another cliffhanger. We wished we could have gotten more and better data, but it was good enough to finish the test plan.

When we arrived home at Culver City, we debriefed Hughes management and engineers on the status of our passes on the SAM site. Our financial and contract people were surprised the Air Force did not accept their carefully prepared IBM card. For whatever reason the IBM card was not accepted, I told them I was the one left holding the bag. I was the one who had to solve the problem on the spot or risk failure of the mission. They asked for my precious blue and white military credit card, but I did not give it to them. If I ever needed fuel or other services in any other military aircraft I flew for Hughes Aircraft, I planned to whip out the card and present it to the officials. Our financial managers could then sort out the details after the fact, a luxury a pilot didn't have in the heat of battle. Twenty-six years later, I still have the magic credit card.

With the APG-65 radar flight tests complete, the Flight Test Division's last work on the F-18 program was to prepare the T-39D aircraft for a flight to St. Louis. On March 8, 1979, I took off from Culver City with crew chief Bob Snarr sitting in the copilot seat. The APG-65 radar tests were completed. This was the last military program to be flown out of the Culver City airport and my last takeoff from the airport.

During the life of the F-18 program, the U.S. Navy and Marine Corps and foreign countries like Australia, Canada, Finland, Kuwait, Malaysia, Spain, and Switzerland purchased 1,479 Hornets. Total sales for Hughes Aircraft Company were around $6 billion; the F-18 radar was the company's most profitable program on record.

With Hughes dead, his world speed record *Racer* moved to the National Air and Space Museum in Washington, DC, and the runway scheduled to be closed, the final chapter had been written in the history of Howard Hughes and Hughes Aircraft Company. The mystique and glory of the golden years of flying from the secret runway had finally come to an end after 40 years.

CHAPTER 12

The Dream

*Howard Hughes had a dream that he was on his deathbed and
wanted to confess his sins. So he confessed that he had merged
companies, fired loyal workers, donated a lot of money to
politicians (giving money to both sides of a campaign), and left
sobbing girls at the altar.*

*An angel came to him and said, "Are you prepared to renounce
the devil?"*

*"I'd like to, I really would," said Hughes, "but I don't think
this is the time to make anybody mad I may be seeing soon."*

Favorite story of John Metelsky, Public Affairs Officer, AID

After the F-18 Hornet flight-test program was completed, I continued to
fly the F-14A and TA-3B at Point Mugu for several more years. When
the Hughes runway at Culver City was closed in 1980, the Corporate
Flight Department moved their civilian transport aircraft to a facility at
an airport in Van Nuys, California. The operation continues there to this
time. By 1982 flight test on the Hughes AWG-9 system and AIM-54
missile also came to an end. The F-14s were given back to the Navy and
the TA-3B placed in long-time storage at Van Nuys.

By then Howard Hughes had been dead for six years and his land
in Culver City had slowly moved into its third great transition. The first
transition occurred when the barren land was used for farming. The second transition occurred when the agricultural land was purchased by
Howard Hughes in the early 1940s to form a business complex to build
war materiel for World War II.

The third transition started after Howard Hughes's death in 1976. At the
time of his death, his principal assets and properties were held and being
managed by Summa Corporation, his wholly owned holding company.
Because Hughes had apparently died without a will, William R. Lummis,

a first cousin, became the principal court-appointed administrator of his estate and subsequently also became a court-appointed trustee of the Howard Hughes Medical Institute, the owner of Hughes Aircraft Company. Summa developed a $1 billion plan in January 1978 for a large mixed-use development called Playa Vista, which won approval from the city of Los Angeles in September 1984. The Summa Plan, as it became known, proposed hotels, a regional mall, high-rise office buildings, and homes, as well as a golf course in the Ballona Wetlands. The Los Angeles County, City, and Coastal Commission approved the plan in 1984.

Public concern about the project's impacts resulted in growing community opposition. The Coastal Commission's approval of the Summa Plan was legally challenged by the Friends of Ballona Wetlands. In 1989 Maguire Thomas Partners became the managing partner of Playa Vista. They brought together urban design professionals with neighborhood and government representatives, developing a new Playa Vista Master Plan. The City of Los Angeles approved the first phase in late 1993. Meanwhile, in 1992, McDonnell Douglas acquired Hughes Helicopters and moved it to Mesa, Arizona. Some Hughes Aircraft Company engineering offices remained on the site.

With its massive hangars perfectly suited for movie sets, Playa Vista attracted film companies scrambling for production space following the 1994 Northridge earthquake. As a result, Playa Vista's first-phase plans were redesigned to incorporate a state-of-the-art entertainment, media, and technology district, known as The Campus. The Los Angeles City Council approved the modified plan in December 1995. In 1997, a new ownership team purchased the project and established a separate company, Playa Capital Company, LLC, to manage the project. First-phase construction began shortly thereafter, in 1998.

The first-phase project, approved back in 1993 and including 3,246 residential units, is almost two-thirds complete and occupied. The first office buildings at Playa Vista are complete and occupied by Electronic Arts, a video game manufacturer. In September 2004, the City Council approved the Village at Playa Vista. The Village represents the balance of development at Playa Vista. When complete, the Village will bring 2,600 homes and a mixed-use neighborhood retail center with a grocery store, restaurants, and shops, to provide the heart of the Playa Vista community. Of the 1,087 acres owned by Summa, 483 were purchased by the State of California from the developer for $139 million in late 2003. Another 64 acres were already being held in trust by the state.

The Ballona Freshwater Marsh, which was developed by Playa Capital, was a key component of the settlement agreement resolving the lawsuit filed by the Friends of the Ballona Wetlands, and it includes 23 acres of restored wetlands and another 28 acres under development. This marshland was gifted to the State of California.

Late in 2004 the planning for the restoration of the Ballona Wetlands was initiated under the direction of the State Coastal Conservancy, the California Department of Fish and Game, and the State Lands Commission. The project site covers approximately 600 acres now owned by the State of California. The commissions are proposing the Ballona Wetlands be designated as an ecological reserve. Based on experience with other wetlands restoration projects, the restoration of the saltwater marsh may take 10 years. The design, technical studies, environmental impact reports, permitting, and construction are all lengthy processes.

The third great transition of Hughes's property remains incomplete over 25 years after it was initiated due to lawsuits and controversy over its use. Howard Hughes was always involved with lawsuits; it was fitting his land would experience the same situation.

The first transition, farming, had begun in the early 1900s. Richard Chikami explained to me that his grandfather, Yoshitaro Chikami, came to the United States at that time. As a Japanese immigrant, his grandfather could not become an American citizen and thus he could not own land. So he became a sharecropper in the area between Ballona Creek and the Westchester bluff. The land, which Howard Hughes would buy 40 years later, was a cross between a swamp and a dry riverbed—what is presently called wetlands. Only a small number of people lived near the land, and there were few roads. What roads there were serviced the Venice oilfields dug into the sands on the beach of the Pacific Ocean.

Richard Chikami told me the land his grandfather worked was not considered good farming land. But keeping saltwater and freshwater apart was something he knew about from his Japanese ancestry. After his grandfather cleared the swampy areas, he decided to grow celery and lettuce. Soon he started to produce bumper crops.

As a Japanese farmer, the only place he could sell his produce was the Central Market in downtown Los Angeles, which paid farmers very poorly. His grandfather thought people were taking advantage of him at the Central Market, so he secretly started to offer produce to restaurants in the Hollywood area before selling the rest at the Central Market. Managers of the restaurants were glad to get fresh produce at prices they considered a bargain. A few lug boxes of celery and lettuce sold to the restaurants sometimes equaled a whole truckload to the Central Market. Eventually the word got out that his grandfather was doing so well that the owner took back the land.

Ninety-five-year-old John "Angel" Jamar, of Basque descent, was born on a portion of the Howard Hughes property in 1909. Later he lived on the central coast of California and we met after my book *Howard Hughes: Aviator* was published. I was able to interview him for this book before he died in late 2005.

Jamar's father leased the land and grew alfalfa. When Jamar was young, he remembers his father was mowing alfalfa when his favorite dog got caught in a scythe. The scythe cut off one of the dog's feet, but it lived and continued to hobble on just three legs. Later when his father retired, Jamar worked the land.

In 1940 Hughes bought over 1,200 acres of land from Joseph Mesner, an old-timer who owned a lot of land in the Westchester and Culver City area. John Jamar contacted Howard Hall, one of Hughes's attorneys, and asked to lease a portion of the property. Jamar knew Hughes bought a lot of land and wouldn't use it all. He signed a five-year lease for 300 acres of land and planned to grow lima beans. Previously, the Japanese farmer had irrigated the celery and lettuce from shallow water wells on the property. Howard Hughes wouldn't allow Jamar to use irrigation. Hughes feared that open areas of water next to his grass strip would be a danger if one of his planes skidded into the ditch. Jamar told me he became a "dry farmer" and still produced a good harvest. He planted beans in May and June and harvested them in September and October.

Whenever he tilled the soil, worms could be seen on top of the ground. The worms attracted birds, which were a hazard to planes on takeoff and landing. Seagulls from the nearby ocean and flocks of starlings fed on the easy pickings.

Jamar watched Howard Hughes take off in his XF-11 spy plane on Sunday afternoon, July 6, 1946. He had men working near the runway.

Jamar didn't know Hughes had crashed until he read about it in the newspaper the following day.

Gale J. Moore, a helicopter test pilot for Hughes Aircraft, flew the giant XH-17 helicopter from the strip. He completed about 30 flights in 10 hours of flying in the 130-foot diameter rotor blade monster powered by two jet engines. Moore told me the whirling blades made a mess of the lima beans; Jamar agreed.

Jamar bought several old sheds from the Japanese farmer. The sheds were near several eucalyptus trees on the north side of the strip near Jefferson Boulevard. He used the sheds to store his equipment and tractors. Howard Hughes used one of the sheds to store an old Chevy he used to drive around the plant at night.

Hughes also parked his airplanes near the trees, far away from the main plant, and had a guard stand by for security. Jamar said he "got into Dutch" one time when one of his men cut weeds under the wing of Hughes's airplane. Hughes felt the worker was too close to his plane and could have damaged it.

There was a gate on Jefferson Boulevard where Hollywood actresses could enter and exit the property. Company pilots assigned to fly these starlets called their operation the Shady Tree Air Service. The worst encounter Jamar had with Howard Hughes concerned this gate on Jefferson. Jamar told me it was "quittin' time," and he drove his pickup truck over to the field to get his hired hand.

"Hughes was madder than a hoot owl!" Jamar said of Hughes when he found the gate locked.

Hughes was expecting a young lady to arrive and obtain flying lessons. Hughes did not have a key to the gate, so Jamar opened it for him. With the gate opened, Hughes took the young lady for a flight.

Jamar retired from farming in the late 1960s and a friend of his took over the operation. After farming the land for 30 years, Jamar told me, "I felt the land was mine."

All of us who worked for Hughes Aircraft Company, from the pilots to the engineers, mechanics, and thousands of other employees through the years, thought part of the land was ours as well. Certainly we didn't own the land in reality, but at least symbolically we felt we had earned a piece of its history.

At the senate investigating committee hearings in 1947, Hughes stated, "I put the sweat of my life into this thing [the H-4 Hercules Flying Boat]. I have my reputation rolled up in it, and I have stated several times that if it was a failure I probably will leave this country and never come back, and I mean it."

Likewise, as Hughes employees, we had the sweat of our life wrapped up in the weapons we built and tested for the company. We had our reputation on the line for a dream—the dream to defend our great country during the Cold War. When the Berlin Wall came down in November 1989, the war was over and the dream fulfilled.

The new dream is to expand freedom and opportunity throughout the world. Hughes Aircraft Company designed weapons that have been successfully used by the U.S. military in all the recent conflicts in the Middle East. A burst of momentum enveloped that area in recent years, with encouraging elections in Afghanistan, Iraq, and the Palestine territories. Tentative reforms in Egypt, Qatar, and Saudi Arabia, and an uprising in Lebanon that expelled an unpopular occupier, have reinforced the democratic prospects for these troubled lands.

The dream lives on.

Epilogue

Hughes Aircraft test pilot **Ollie Deal**, who scared the pants off the flight-test engineers flying the YB-58, died while riding a bicycle on the beach of the Pacific Ocean near Santa Monica, California. Deal lost traction in soft sand and fell off the bike, with his head hitting a concrete curb. Ironically, after his extreme concern for safety, he had lost his life going just a few miles per hour, not supersonic in a four-engine bomber.

Jim Eastham, the test pilot who replaced Ollie Deal flying the YB-58, went on to pilot the first flight in the Lockheed YF-12 Blackbird, was inducted into the Kansas Aviation Hall of Fame, and was selected for the test pilot Walk of Fame in Lancaster, California. Eastham had an illustrious test pilot career. His YB-58 Hustler finished its career as a target on the Edwards Air Force Base bombing range.

Bill Bush, the Naval Flight Officer (NFO) who had flown with me when I crash landed the F-111B at Point Mugu and had also flown with me in the F-14A Tomcat when we launched an AIM-54A Phoenix missile at a Foxbat drone, died of a heart condition in the early 1980s. Bill didn't live long enough to see the photo of our Tomcat in the National Air and Space Museum in Washington, DC, and learn of the aviation history we made that day over the Pacific Ocean.

Bill Bell, the Hughes Aircraft engineer who had passed classified information to the Polish Communists, was given a relatively light sentence of eight years at the U.S. Penitentiary in Terminal Island, California, because of his full cooperation with investigative authorities. He remained there until released after serving about five years.

After four years of confinement, Bell sent a letter to his former supervisor at Hughes Aircraft. He commented that prison wasn't so bad, but he would rather be sailing. He had friends there, none that he would associate with on the street. He had a room to himself with his own key, a desk, bookshelf, and radio. "What else does one need?" he wrote. "One thing for sure, I'm well 'dried out,'" he added.

Marion Zacharski, the Polish spy, was sentenced to life imprisonment, but he only served about three years when he was exchanged for U. S. agents who had been picked up by the Russians.

Robert DeHaven, the former World War II Pacific theater ace and early Hughes Aircraft test pilot, took over as manager of the Flight Test Division in 1962. DeHaven wanted a World War II warbird for his personal use. After the war the U.S. government sold surplus Vultee BT-13 trainer aircraft on the civilian market. Glenn Odekirk, Howard Hughes's first mechanic, bought two of them for Hughes Aircraft Company for around $2,000. Only one aircraft was licensed to fly, and it was used for general transportation in the Los Angeles basin. Like all the aircraft Howard Hughes had purchased, both were transferred to caretaker Bruce Burk.

Over time, the once flight-worthy aircraft deteriorated and needed corrosion repair, new fuel tanks, and refurbished fabric flight controls. DeHaven managed to sweet-talk Nadine Henley, Hughes's longtime secretary and administrative assistant (who had the power to dispose of Hughes property) into selling the BT-13 to him for a nominal sum. Some said he "stole" it from the company because Henley didn't realize its value. DeHaven was cautioned about using Hughes Aircraft mechanics on company time to renovate his plane. Throughout his 38-year career at Hughes Aircraft, DeHaven had taken advantage of his managerial position by having employees under him work on his personal projects. This time he got caught, and work stopped on the BT-13.

In 1985 DeHaven retired from Hughes Aircraft and moved the plane to a repair facility at Santa Barbara Airport. He contracted with a company to restore the plane. Like Howard Hughes had done so many times, DeHaven traveled to witness the progress of work on his plane. He was pleased with the results. Unknown to DeHaven, the contractor was using parts from his plane to restore another BT-13. One day DeHaven drove to Santa Barbara, only to find both his plane and the fly-by-night contractor gone. The plane he had stolen from Hughes Aircraft Company was stolen from him. It was a fitting end to his career with the company; what goes around comes around.

Test pilot **Charles "Al" McDaniel** retired from Hughes Aircraft Company in 1986 after 36 years of service with the company. Six years earlier he had become the manager of the Flight Test Division when DeHaven was removed from that position. The Hughes runway was closed after Hughes died, and McDaniel moved both the military and corporate flight operations to the Van Nuys Airport in the San Fernando Valley, where it remains to this day.

Throughout his years at Hughes Aircraft McDaniel invested in many homes and even a 56-acre plot of land overlooking the Camarillo Airport. He was always able to sell at a profit, enabling him to pay alimony and child support to former wives. At age 85 he is now remodeling a million-dollar house in exclusive Carmel, California.

Because McDaniel had flown the F-106 for Hughes Aircraft, General Dynamics gave him a Mach 2 tie tack that displayed M2. McDaniel joked and said it stood for "married twice." In fact, he was married more than twice, and some suggested that he obtain an SR-71 pin that displayed M3 +.

Test pilot **Chris Smith** also retired from Hughes Aircraft in 1986, after 35 years with the company. When he left he told me he had three goals in the remaining years of his life: to learn to play a musical instrument, to improve his stamp collection, and to write a memoir for his three daughters. I talked with him from time to time, and he told me that while looking for stamps at a garage sale, he had found an autographed copy of

Charles Lindbergh's book *We*. He never did learn to play a musical instrument, but he did write his memoirs in longhand on legal paper.

Chris was married to his beloved wife Jeri for 50 years. She died in 2001; he died six months later of a broken heart.

Eighty-eight-year-old **Bruce Burk** still has a wonderful memory. He was always able to answer my questions about Howard Hughes and his aircraft. As the caretaker of all the aircraft Hughes had purchased and stored around the world, his group was called Rust Watchers.

Bruce maintained Hughes's flight logbook in the early days of his flying career. Although he never made a copy of it, he still remembers many of the entries and how accurately Hughes kept it in his early flying years.

Bruce also kept his own personal diary, in which he logged all the instructions and counter-instructions Hughes gave to him. Hughes changed his mind so often that Bruce needed a permanent record to keep track of his orders. In the 1950s he lent his diary to Hughes so that he could use it in a lawsuit and never got it back.

After 39 years of service, Bruce retired in 1976. He moved to the Sacramento area of central California and published several books with his drawings of wildlife.

Test pilot **Bill Jessup** retired from Hughes Aircraft Company in 1989. He told me had had his fill of airplanes and aviation. Bill moved to Hawaii to spend time in the sun trying to perfect his near-par golf game. Golf was also a favorite sport of Howard Hughes back in the 1920s; he gave up the game when he couldn't improve his handicap of two.

While employed at Hughes Aircraft, Bill developed 80 acres of land into an avocado orchard in Ventura County. In Hawaii, he tried his hand at growing strawberry papayas. Just before his first harvest in 1992, Hurricane Iniki hit the island of Kauai with devastating force and destroyed his entire crop as well as the orchard. It also blew the roof off his house. Then his third marriage came to an end—but his golf clubs never failed him.

Test pilot **Hal Farley**, the one who had checked me out in the F-14A, soon left Grumman and joined the Lockheed Skunk Works. He made the first flight of the F-117A Nighthawk stealth fighter on June 18, 1981. Farley retired, and he now lives on a boat in the state of Washington. **Pete Purvis**, the other Grumman test pilot at Point Mugu, shot himself down in the F-14A. He launched a Sparrow missile during a minus-3G maneuver and it struck the underside of his Tomcat, damaging a main fuel line. The F-14A caught fire and Purvis and his NFO ejected very near where Bill Bush and I had had our flight control emergency in the F-111B. Both Purvis and his NFO were rescued in the Pacific Ocean, unhurt.

Eugene "Oops" Martin, the instrumentation technician who had installed data tapes in both the B-66 on the F-15A radar program and the F-4D on the F-16A radar program, drew humorous cartoons for both radar fly-offs. He retired in 1983. He continues as a freelance cartoonist and has been published in the *Saturday Evening Post, National Enquirer,* and *The New Yorker.*

Air Force test pilot Lieutenant Colonel **Joe Bill Dryden** retired from the Air Force in 1981. Joe Bill and I had flown together in both the F-4D Phantom and the T-33 during the F-16A radar competition. I tried to hire Dryden as a test pilot for Hughes Aircraft, but he chose employment with General Dynamics (GD). Joe Bill moved to Fort Worth, Texas, and flew test missions in advanced versions of the F-16, wrote safety articles for the company *Code One* magazine, and worked with the GD customer relations department in educating foreign pilots.

In May of 1994 he flew a new F-16 fresh off the factory floor on its first post-production flight. Another GD test pilot flew a second F-16, also on its first flight. After the pilots completed their system checks, they set up to run head-on radar passes against each other, a maneuver called "bumping heads." After completion of each pass, they continued on the same heading and separated several miles in preparation for another pass. Joe Bill started to reverse course by attempting a split-S at 2,100 feet above the ground, an extremely low altitude. He ejected at 640 feet because the F-16 was in a 40-degree dive angle. The F-16 crashed; Joe Bill's parachute did not have time to fully deploy. Tragically, he did not survive the accident. Dryden is one of 32 test pilot friends I lost during my 25 years as a military and civilian test pilot.

After I retired and moved to a small town about 200 miles north of Los Angeles, I lost track of most of my Hughes Aircraft friends. Some years later my wife, Jan, saw **Bruce Bromme**'s name in our local newspaper. Sadly, it was his obituary. Jan remembered that I had talked about a person by the name of Bruce Bromme who had been a crew chief on the F-4C DynaCords program, the A3D on the Synthetic Aperture Radar program, and the F-4D on the F-16A radar program. I told her the Bruce Bromme I knew lived near Long Beach, California. Then she read further in the obituary that this Bruce Bromme had also worked for Hughes Aircraft Company. I knew then that the person listed in the newspaper had to be the mechanic with whom I'd worked for so many years at Hughes Aircraft. I found his wife's name in our phone book and called her. A couple of years earlier she and Bruce had moved to my area to be near their son, who had taken over the family's sprint car racing business.

A memorial service was held a few days later, and I flew my World War II 1945 Stinson L-5E tail-wheeled, propeller aircraft in formation with another antique warbird over the son's ranch. We passed low over the assembled crowd, who only knew Bruce and his son due to their participation in auto racing. I felt I alone represented Hughes Aircraft Company at the service and saluted Bruce for his 28 years of service. The pilots who flew test aircraft were the benefactors of his precision aircraft handiwork. The flyover was my way of saying thanks to Bruce and all the other mechanics who had maintained the test aircraft I had had the opportunity and pleasure to fly.

In October 1989 I, **George Marrett**, retired from Hughes Aircraft Company. After spending 31 years employed in the military service and aerospace industry, I soon witnessed the end of the Cold War when the Berlin Wall came down in Germany the following month. It was a tremendous feeling to have played a part in the defense of freedom against what President Ronald Reagan called "the Evil Empire." The Cold War had lasted a grueling 45 years, but in the end we won the showdown with the Soviet Union without a head-to-head military confrontation.

Retired Air Force Colonel John P. Stapp told me he believed the Cold War was won over the skies of Southern California by aerospace companies that stayed well ahead of the Soviet Union in aircraft and weapon design and the civilian and military test pilots who risked their lives daily to test this equipment. These test pilots often ended as unheralded casualties, the "testing deaths," of the Cold War.

In addition Stapp felt that leaders of the Soviet Union closely followed the Israeli and Egyptian war of 1973 and the Iranian and Iraqi conflict of 1980–1988. In both cases U.S.-supplied weapons were far superior to ones provided by the Soviet Union. For their country to prevail in an engagement with the United States, the Soviets would need to develop and field a totally new generation of advanced weapons at great financial expense. The cost was too great a burden; they simply threw in the towel.

In my opinion the Cold War can be divided into three phases. In the first phase (1945–1970) the United States and its allies came to recognize that the Soviet Union had replaced Nazi Germany as their principal adversary, and devised a strategy—containment—to deal with it. President Harry S. Truman deserves credit for saving Western Europe from Soviet domination. Creation of the Marshall Plan, the Berlin Airlift, and NATO, and the aligning of Western Germany with the free world, all halted the spread of communism in Europe.

In the second phase (1970–1980), containment was discredited by the war in Vietnam, and the United States cast about for a new strategy. While serving as a pilot in the U.S. Air Force, I was involved with the theory of containment and spent a year flying combat in Vietnam as an A-1 Skyraider rescue pilot. It was a very difficult year for me because 12 of my squadron mates were killed, 2 were burned so badly they were sent home, and another was injured so severely on ejection he was medically retired. Our squadron also lost 26 aircraft during that horrific year in our country's history. A book about my experiences in combat titled *Cheating Death: Combat Air Rescues in Vietnam and Laos* was published by the Smithsonian Institution Press in 2003.

Alexander Solzhenitsyn's great contribution to America's victory came during the second phase of the struggle. It was largely thanks to him that American anti-communists on both the left (the AFL-CIO) and the right (the Ronald Reagan Republicans)—all of whom were demoralized by America's defeat in Vietnam and the subsequent policy of détente—returned to their earlier conviction that the Cold War was a titanic moral struggle between good and evil, freedom and tyranny. At the time former Secretary of State Henry Kissinger was dismayed by this approach, but in retrospect it is clear that for the United States to summon the energy to prevail, the Cold War had to be viewed morally.

The two great figures of the third phase (1980–1989) of the struggle were Pope John Paul II and President Ronald Reagan. Neither would have succeeded without the other. The Pope is one of the architects of victory because it is impossible to conceive of what occurred in 1989 without the rise of Solidarity in Poland in 1981, and it is impossible to imagine the rise of Solidarity absent the Pope. Though it called itself a free trade union, Solidarity was really a nonviolent revolutionary movement aimed at toppling Soviet tyranny in Poland, and the Polish Pope was its principal inspirer, advocate, and protector. Acting through their Polish surrogate, General Wojciech Jaruzelski, the Soviets managed to suppress Solidarity, but again thanks to the Pope it was never destroyed. And when, under Mikhail Gorbachev, the Soviet Union released its grip on Poland, Solidarity was able to step into the power vacuum and to inspire other anti-Soviet movements in Eastern and Central Europe, and finally in the Soviet Union itself. In other words, the rise and success of Solidarity finally vindicated the much-criticized domino theory, only in reverse.

But why was Gorbachev's Soviet Union willing to release its grip on Poland in the first place? Here we come to Ronald Reagan's great contribution. When he took office, Reagan believed that the Soviet Union, for all of its outward signs of vigor, was faced with insoluble economic and social problems at home. If the United States exploited these problems, it could bring about internal reforms leading to what the key foreign policy document of the Reagan era, National Security Decision Directive 75 (NSDD 75), called "a more pluralistic political and economic system in which the power of the privileged ruling elite is greatly reduced." Following the detailed game plan laid out in NSDD 75, Reagan pounded the Soviet Union. Soviet leaders indignantly accused him of trying to reverse the gains of détente, and they were absolutely right. The Reagan Doctrine, the Strategic Defense Initiative, the Democracy Initiative, the military buildup, the covert assistance to Solidarity, and the various economic sanctions against Moscow, all were meant to force an already shaky system to embark on a course of radical reform. And when a Soviet reformer named Mikhail Gorbachev came along halfway through Reagan's presidency, the veteran Hollywood actor embraced him with all his warmth and charm—but never once let up on the pressure. This forced Gorbachev to adopt ever more far-reaching reforms, until the system over which he presided, and which he had sought to save, finally collapsed, just as Ronald Reagan hoped it would. Thanks to this strategy, the West won the Cold War as decisively as any conflict has ever been won. Our adversary, the Soviet Union, no longer exists; the communist ideology in whose name it waged war is totally discredited; and our democratic capitalist way of life has prevailed.

In 1991 I watched on TV as the U.S. military, under President George H. W. Bush, took on Saddam Hussein in Iraq during Operation Desert Storm. I was gratified to see the military develop a massive armada of weapons, including many of the "smart weapons" I had helped test for Hughes Aircraft Company, and use them to finish off the enemy in just a few days. Unlike the war of attrition we had fought in Vietnam, our military went in with overwhelming force, went in to win, and quickly defeated the enemy.

The Hughes AGM-65 Maverick played a major part in the quick destruction of Iraqi armor and in the U.S.'s victory. The Air Force sent 144 A-10s to the theater. While flying only 30 percent of the Air Force's total sorties, these aircraft achieved more than half of the confirmed Iraqi equipment losses and fired 90 percent of the precision-guided Maverick missiles launched during Desert Storm. A count of 5,296 missiles were fired with a hit rate around 85 percent. Before Desert Storm, Iraq had more tanks than Great Britain and Germany combined. With the precision capability of American aircraft, one $100,000 Maverick equated to the loss of a $1.5 million T-72 tank. That was a $15-to-$1 advantage for the U.S. forces. By the turn of the century over 65,000 Maverick missiles had been built in six varieties, with 14,000 launched, including 800 in Operation Allied Force (the three-month bombing campaign in Yugoslavia). During these conflicts Maverick achieved a 93 percent success rate.

Two versions of the F-15 Eagle, each with a Hughes radar, were flown in combat in Desert Storm. One hundred twenty of the air-superiority F-15C/Ds were deployed to the Persian Gulf and flew more than 5,900 sorties. The F-15C achieved 33 of the 38 air-to-air kills, and no Eagles were lost.

From day one of the air war, F-15E Strike Eagles were used in an attack role against Iraqi ground positions. Forty-eight of the aircraft, using sophisticated night-fighting equipment called LANTIRN (Low Altitude Navigation and Target Infra-Red Night), flew more than 2,200 sorties destroying Iraqi enemy airfields and communication systems with spectacular results. They were also used to hunt Scud missiles and launchers at night. Only two F-15Es were lost.

On the first day of Desert Storm, U.S. Navy pilots Lieutenant Nick Mongillio and Lieutenant Commander Mark Fox flying an F-18 Hornet, with a Hughes radar, became the first pilots to register air-to-air kills while still completing their original air-to-ground mission. While going out from USS *Saratoga* in the Red Sea to bomb an airfield in southwestern Iraq, an E-2 Hawkeye warned them of approaching Iraqi F-7As (Chinese-built MiG-21) aircraft. The Hornets shot down the two MiGs with AIM-9 Sidewinders and resumed their bombing run before returning to the *Saratoga.*

During the Gulf War of 1991, 190 Navy and Marine Corps F-18 Hornets were used in the action—106 on aircraft carriers and 84 with land-based Marine Corps units. One was lost in combat, and two were lost in noncombat accidents. Three more F/A-18s were hit by infrared-homing surface-to-air missiles, but they were able to make it back to their launch points where they were repaired and used again, demonstrating the essential robustness of the airframe and weapon system.

The F-14 Tomcat has been regarded as a top-of-the-line interceptor for its designed role of providing air defense for carrier battle groups. The only regret for the Tomcat in the fleet-defense role is that it has never been seriously tested in combat in that scenario. There were many test firings of the AIM-54 Phoenix missile that have demonstrated a high kill ratio, including a test performed with a Tomcat ripple—firing six Phoenix missiles to destroy six targets. This exercise was described by Navy pilot Commander John "Smoke" Wilson as financially equivalent to "setting fire to a 10-story car park filled with brand-new Cadillacs."

This is by no means saying that the Tomcat has never fired a shot in anger. Although Tomcats performed top cover flights during the evacuation of Vietnam in 1975, they saw no combat in that exercise. The F-14A saw its first combat in 1981, during confrontations between the United States and Libya. The U.S. government under President Ronald Reagan had "fingered" Colonel Muammar Gaddafi, the eccentric Libyan dictator, as a sponsor for international terrorism and wanted to show him who was the boss. Colonel Gaddafi had declared the Gulf of Sidra, bounded by Libya's coast in the Mediterranean, as Libyan waters. In the summer of 1981, and in defiance, Reagan ordered the Navy to steam into the gulf and dare Gaddafi to do something about it.

There was a confrontation between Navy Tomcats and Libyan fighters on August 18th, but nobody made any wrong moves and nobody opened fire. The next day the Libyans got more aggressive, and fighting broke out. Two Libyan Sukhoi Su-22 ground-attack fighters, built by the Soviet Union, confronted two F-14As, piloted by Commander Henry Kleeman and Lieutenant Larry Muczynski from the carrier USS *Nimitz*. The Su-22s approached head-on, with the first firing an air-to-air missile that failed to track. Both Tomcats focused on the lead Su-22 because it was the most immediate threat, but when Muczynski reported that he had a target lock on the bandit, Kleeman turned to get on the tail of the second Su-22, which was passing them. Both F-14As fired AIM-9L Sidewinders and scored hits. The Libyan pilots ejected, though only one parachute was seen to open. It hadn't been much of a contest, with Muczynski saying their opponents were "a couple of bush-leaguers who couldn't even make the second-string team." However, it was an early and classic example of Ronald Reagan's grasp of political theater, which as a professional actor he understood instinctively, and it went over very well in the American news media and with the public.

Tomcats flew air patrols again during the 1988–1989 Persian Gulf convoy operations, occasionally firing missiles at Iranian F-4 Phantoms but not scoring any kills. F-14s also flew during Desert Storm, performing air patrols to protect Navy ships, which as it turned out were never presented with any real threat. The only kill scored by F-14As during the conflict was of a Soviet-built Mil Mi-8 Hip helicopter, shot down by two Tomcats on February 6, 1991. Tomcats armed with photo pods did get more into the thick of things, with one being shot down by ground fire, on January 21, 1991. Both aircrew ejected safely. Lieutenant Devon Jones, the pilot, was rescued by a combat search-and-rescue team, but his NFO, Lieutenant Lawrence Slade, was captured and remained a prisoner for the rest of the brief war. This was the only combat loss of a Tomcat. During the rest of the year, the final act of the end of the U.S.S. R. played itself out, and by the end of 1991 the Soviet Union was history and so was the Cold War. It was the Tomcat's fortune (or misfortune) to go into service in the role of defending the carrier fleet at a time when threats to U.S. ships at sea were on the decline. So during that era the Tomcat didn't really see a great deal of shooting action.

Relative to its numbers and length of service, the F-14 Tomcat's combat history has been relatively modest, but it has had an interesting movie career. The best-known movie involving the Tomcat is *Top Gun*, starring Tom Cruise. Although popular, it is arguably less entertaining to an aircraft enthusiast than *The Final Countdown*, which puts the Tomcat almost in a starring role with Kirk Douglas and Martin Sheen in support. Filming the Tomcat for movies has a certain justice, considering its role in Reagan-era political theater.

In 2003 I watched on TV as President George W. Bush took on Saddam Hussein. Weapons developed by Hughes Aircraft were used again. Saddam's two sons were killed by Hughes tube-launched, optically tracked, wire-guided missiles that had been developed and tested at the Culver City airport for the U.S. Army.

Unquestionably, one of the greatest successes in combat operations between 1990 and 2004 has been the loss of no U.S. military aircraft to enemy aircraft. Technological superiority of our fighters over their opponents in Yugoslavia, Afghanistan, and Iraq in the late 1990s and early 2000s, coupled with superior pilot training, contributed to the ability of U.S. aircrews to shoot down 48 enemy aircraft in aerial dogfights while losing none. If there were any Taliban fighters mission-capable in Afghanistan, they did not even get into the air. Attacks on Iraqi airfields and aircraft on the ground prevented enemy fighters from even taking off. This action was the ultimate in air superiority. The Air Force has been so successful in eliminating enemy aircraft from engaging in air-to-air combat that top graduating pilots from flight school now choose aircraft that fly air-to-ground missions.

In 2004 the Naval Institute Press published my book titled *Howard Hughes: Aviator*. While employed with Hughes Aircraft Company for 20 years, several of the mechanics and engineers that worked on the military planes I flew also worked on Hughes's personal aircraft. Similarly, several of the older test pilots, who had been with the company since the end of World War II, had flown with Hughes as a passenger or with Hughes as the pilot. For that book I reconnected with 17 people to interview them about their unique flying experiences with Howard Hughes. Additionally,

I interviewed another 12 persons who were either wives, sons, or daughters of men who had flown with Hughes. Others were people who had left writings and transcripts of their rich and colorful time with the mysterious aviator. All that I interviewed were pleased that a nonfiction account of Hughes's aviation achievements was being documented for future generations. Since many were quite elderly, my book is likely to be the last account of Howard Hughes, the pilot, that can be written from personal interviews.

Two of Howard Hughes's most spectacular aircraft, the *Racer* and the H-4 Hercules Flying Boat, are now on public display. The *Racer* is in the National Air and Space Museum in Washington, DC, and the H-4 Hercules is in the Evergreen Aviation Museum in McMinnville, Oregon. Hughes did not live to see either of the planes on display, but I'm sure he would be pleased they are preserved for future generations to view. Bruce Burk, the caretaker of his aircraft, can take a well-deserved rest.

Two of the planes I had flown for Hughes Aircraft Company are also on public display. The number nine built F-14A Tomcat, the one I flew for the Foxbat shot, is the gate guard at Naval Air Station (NAS) Oceana, Virginia. Of all the fighters I flew, the Tomcat was my favorite, a superb flying machine.

The Navy T-39D Sabreliner I used to test the F-18A radar is now in the Patuxent River Naval Air Museum near Lexington, Maryland. I ferried the plane to McDonnell Douglas in St. Louis, Missouri, in early 1979, and it was flown there for a couple of years, developing F-18 avionics. Later it was transferred to the U.S. Navy Test Pilot School, also at Patuxent River, and used to teach avionics testing to students before becoming a museum piece. The Navy certainly got its money's worth out of the old Sabreliner.

The Douglas TA-3B bomber, which Hughes Aircraft had received from the U.S. Navy in 1969, is still flying at the airport in Van Nuys, California. I flew the TA-3B for nearly 10 years at Point Mugu, testing the Hughes Aircraft AWG-9 system and AIM-54A Phoenix missile. Raytheon Corporation purchased the radar and missile business from Hughes Aircraft in 1994. Raytheon now owns all the remaining Navy A-3 aircraft and they use them for a variety of government flight-test programs involving national defense.

Soon after retiring, I helped found the Estrella Warbird Museum at the Paso Robles, California, airport. While searching for military aircraft to put on static display, I encountered the number seven built Grumman F-111B. It was in the disposal area at NAS China Lake, California. The plane was the last F-111B built, the best of the lot and the one I had used to fire many AIM-54A Phoenix missiles at drones over the Pacific Ocean. Now it is simply a 70,000-pound hunk of metal slowly aging on the windswept high desert of California. My hope is that some aviation museum will claim this historic plane and give it a proper resting place.

Recently our museum acquired an F-14 Tomcat from the Navy to put on static display. Tomcats are being removed from active service to be replaced by an advanced version of the F-18—the F-18E/F Super Hornet. This plane, with an improved Hughes Aircraft Company radar, will serve the Navy well into the 21st century. I witnessed the F-14 fly into our airport on its last flight. While our museum members cheered I shed a tear, realizing I had seen my last Tomcat in the sky.

Several years ago the Estrella Warbird Museum did locate and restore a former NASA Lockheed F-104G Starfighter that had spent time at Edwards Air Force Base. I had flown the Starfighter to Mach 2.15 and zoomed to 80,000 feet while a student in the Air Force Test Pilot School. The F-104 was one of the most streamlined aircraft ever built, the Hughes *Racer* equivalent of the 1950–1970 jet age. This aircraft is symbolic of all the aircraft designed and flown during the Cold War era. The Starfighter is now the gate guard at our museum, and my name is proudly displayed just below the canopy.

Flying and the defense of freedom have been my life and passion—it's been an unforgettable ride.

Bibliography

Allen, Thomas B., Clifton F. Berry, and Norman Polmar. *CNN: War in the Gulf.* Atlanta, GA: Turner Publishing, 1991.

Allward, Maurice. *F-86 Sabre.* New York: Charles Scribner's Sons, 1978.

Barron, John. *KGB Today: The Hidden Hand.* New York: Reader's Digest Press, 1983.

Barron, John. *MiG Pilot.* New York: McGraw-Hill, 1980.

Blesse, Major General Frederick C. "Boots." "The Changing World of Air Combat." *AIR FORCE Magazine*, October 1977.

Boyne, Walter J. "Nickel Grass." *Air Force: Journal of the Air Force Association*, December 1998.

Brenner, Eliot, and William Harwood. *Desert Storm: The Weapons of War.* New York: Orion Books, 1991.

"Cavalier Offers Turboprop P-51 to TAC." *Aviation Week & Space Technology*, October 21, 1968.

"Clasped Hands." *Hughesnews*, December 20, 1974.

Cooper, Tom, and Farzad Bishop. *Iranian F-14 Tomcat Units in Combat.* Oxford: Osprey Publishing, 2004.

Crickmore, Paul F. *Lockheed SR-71.* Oxford: Osprey Publishing, 1993.

"Death of Pioneer Howard Hughes As a Great Loss to Nation." *Hughesnews*, April 16, 1976.

Ethell, Jeff. *F-15 Eagle*. London: Ian Allan Ltd., 1981.

"Grumman F-14 Launches Hughes Phoenix Missile." *Aviation Week & Space Technology*, October 16, 1972.

Gunston, Bill. *F-16 Fighting Falcon*. London: Ian Allan Ltd., 1983.

————. *F/A-18 Hornet*. London: Ian Allan Ltd., 1985.

————. *F-111*. New York: Charles Scribner's Sons, 1978.

"Interim Operational Helmet Mounted Display (IOHMD)." Hughes Aircraft Company Technical Proposal, April 1973.

Kolcum, Edward H. "Configurations of F-111A, B Unveiled." *Aviation Week & Space Technology*, June 1, 1964.

Leighton, Frances Spatz, and Jim Gordon Atkins. *The Encyclopedia of Howard Hughes Jokes*. Washington, DC: Acropolis Books, 1972.

Marrett, George J. *Cheating Death: Combat Air Rescues in Vietnam and Laos*. Washington, DC: Smithsonian Institution Press, 2003.

————. *Howard Hughes: Aviator*. Annapolis, MD: Naval Institute Press, 2004.

————. "Mach Buster." *Sabre Jet Classics*, Fall 2000.

————. "Sore Feet." *The Hook: Journal of Carrier Aviation*, Fall 1999.

Miller, Jay. *Lockheed SR-71 (A-12/YF-12/D-21)*. Austin, TX: Midland Counties Publications, 1983.

O'Leary, Michael. "Return of the Enforcer." *Air Classics*, April 1982.

Reed, Arthur. *F-14 Tomcat*. New York: Charles Scribner's Sons, 1978.

"Rocket Sled Rides in '50s at New Mexico Base Saved More Than 250,000 Lives." *Albuquerque Journal*, December 12, 2004.

Schelden, Bruce. "Hughes Culver City Site." Hughes Aircraft Retirees Association Flyer, March 2005.

Smallwood, William L. *WARTHOG: Flying the A-10 in the Gulf War*. Washington, DC: Brassey's, 1993.

"Test Pilot Finds Himself in Hughes History." *Hughesnews*, June 3, 1983.

Thomason, Tommy. *Grumman F-111B Swing Wing*. Simi Valley, CA: Ginter Books, 1998.

Thornborough, Anthony M. *Airborne Weapons of the West*. Osceola, FL: Motorbooks International, 1992.

Wagner, Ray. *The North American Sabre*. New York: Doubleday & Company, 1963.

Index

About the Author

GEORGE J. MARRETT served in the U.S. Air Force and flew the F-86L SabreJet, the F-101B Voodoo, and the Douglas A-1 Skyraider, this last as a Sandy rescue pilot in the 602nd Fighter Squadron (Commando) in Thailand, completing 188 combat missions in Southeast Asia during the Vietnam War. Currently, he flies his 1945 Stinson L-5E Sentinel for air shows. Marrett was inducted into the Nebraska Aviation Hall of Fame in January 2006. He is the author of *Cheating Death: Combat Air Rescues in Vietnam and Laos* and of *Howard Hughes: Aviator.*